Microsoft® Office 2010 Illustrated Projects™

D1540907

Carol M. Cram

Capilano University, North Vancouver, B.C.

COURSE TECHNOLOGY
CENGAGE Learning™

Australia • Brazil • Japan • Korea • Mexico • Singapore • Spain • United Kingdom • United States

Microsoft® Office 2010—Illustrated Projects™
Carol M. Cram

Vice President, Publisher: Nicole Jones Pinard

Executive Editor: Marjorie Hunt

Associate Acquisitions Editor: Amanda Lyons

Senior Product Manager: Christina Kling Garrett

Associate Product Manager: Kimberly Klasner

Director of Marketing: Cheryl Costantini

Senior Marketing Manager: Ryan DeGrote

Marketing Coordinator: Kristen Panciocco

Developmental Editor: Pamela Conrad

Content Project Manager: Heather Hopkins

Copy Editor: Goodin Everything, Inc.

Proofreader: Harold Johnson

Indexer: Rich Carlson

QA Manuscript Reviewers: John Freitas, Susan Pedicini

Print Buyer: Fola Orekoya

Cover Design: GEX Publishing Services

Text Designer: Black Fish Design

Cover Artist: Mark Hunt

Composition: GEX Publishing Services

For product information and technology assistance, contact us at
Cengage Learning Customer & Sales Support, 1-800-354-9706

For permission to use material from this text or product, submit all requests online at **cengage.com/permissions**
Further permissions questions can be emailed to
permissionrequest@cengage.com

ISBN-13: 978-0-538-74848-3

ISBN-10: 0-538-74848-6

Course Technology
20 Channel Center Street
Boston, Massachusetts 02210
USA

Cengage Learning is a leading provider of customized learning solutions with office locations around the globe, including Singapore, the United Kingdom, Australia, Mexico, Brazil, and Japan. Locate your local office at:
international.cengage.com/region

Cengage Learning products are represented in Canada by Nelson Education, Ltd.

For your lifelong learning solutions, visit **course.cengage.com**

Purchase any of our products at your local college store or at our preferred online store **www.cengagebrain.com**

Microsoft and the Office logo are either registered trademarks or trademarks of Microsoft Corporation in the United States and/or other countries. Course Technology is an independent entity from Microsoft Corporation, and not affiliated with Microsoft in any manner. Microsoft product screen shots reprinted with permission from Microsoft Corporation.

Printed in the United States of America
2 3 4 5 6 7 17 16 15 14 13 12 11

A Note from the Author

As instructors, I believe our goal is to teach our students to become independent learners who have the confidence to tackle and solve problems. My greatest satisfaction in the classroom comes when my students learn the information, skills, and techniques they need to function effectively in the workplace and to accomplish tasks related to their own needs and interests. Students need to learn what to do with a software application. They need to "see the forest" and not just the trees.

To address this need, I developed a philosophy of teaching software applications that has evolved into the Illustrated Projects series. Each text in this series provides students with step-by-step instructions to create documents or perform tasks appropriate to the software package they are learning. As students complete the projects, they learn how a variety of functions combine together to produce a tangible product.

But the Illustrated Projects approach to teaching software doesn't stop with the projects. In my classroom, the significant learning occurs when students are given the opportunity to create their own version of a project document. That's when I feel a kind of magic creeping into my classroom. Students take the structure offered by a project and then, in the Independent Challenges, adapt this structure to explore practical business applications and to express their own interests. Suddenly, my students are willing to take risks, to solve problems, and to experiment with new features as they work toward the creation of a document that belongs to them. Pride of ownership inspires learning!

In Illustrated Office 2010 Projects, you will find new projects such as creating a term paper in the MLA and APA styles and revised projects that incorporate the new features of Office 2010.

This book owes everything to the talent and dedication of the Course Technology Illustrated team. I particularly wish to thank Pam Conrad, the Developmental Editor of this book, for her encouragement, patience, and support and her amazing attention to detail. This book is dedicated to all the wonderful students I have taught over the years at Capilano University.

Carol M. Cram, January 2011

Contents

UNIT F: Access Projects

UNIT G: Integration Projects II

UNIT H: PowerPoint Projects

UNIT I: Integration Projects III

Index

Preface

Welcome to *Microsoft Office 2010—Illustrated Projects*. This highly visual book offers a wide array of interesting and challenging projects designed to apply the skills learned in any Office 2010 book. The Illustrated Projects book is for people who want more opportunities to practice important software skills.

Organization and Coverage

This text contains a total of nine units. Six units contain projects for the individual programs: Word (two units), Excel (two units), Access (one unit), and PowerPoint (one unit). Three other units contain projects that take advantage of the powerful integration capabilities of the Office suite. Each unit contains three projects followed by four Independent Challenges and a Visual Workshop. Students will also gain practice gathering and using information available on the Internet in a variety of the projects and independent challenges.

About this Approach

What makes the Illustrated Projects approach so effective at reinforcing software skills? It's quite simple. Each activity in a project is presented on two facing pages, with the step-by-step instructions on the left page and large screen illustrations on the right. Students can focus on a single activity without having to turn the page. This unique design makes information extremely accessible and easy to absorb. Students can complete the projects on their own, and because of the modular structure of the book, can also cover the units in any order.

The two-page spread for each activity contains some or all of the elements shown below.

Road map—It is always clear which project and activity you are working on.

Introduction—Concise text that introduces the activity and summarizes new procedures. Steps are easier to complete when they fit into a meaningful framework.

Troubles and Hints—Troubleshooting advice to fix common problems that might occur and tips for using Microsoft Office 2010 more effectively. These appear right next to the step where students need help.

Numbered steps—Clear step-by-step directions explain how to complete the specific activity. These steps get less specific as students progress to the third project in a unit.

Additional Practice—Provides information on which end-of-unit exercises allow students to practice the same set of skills.

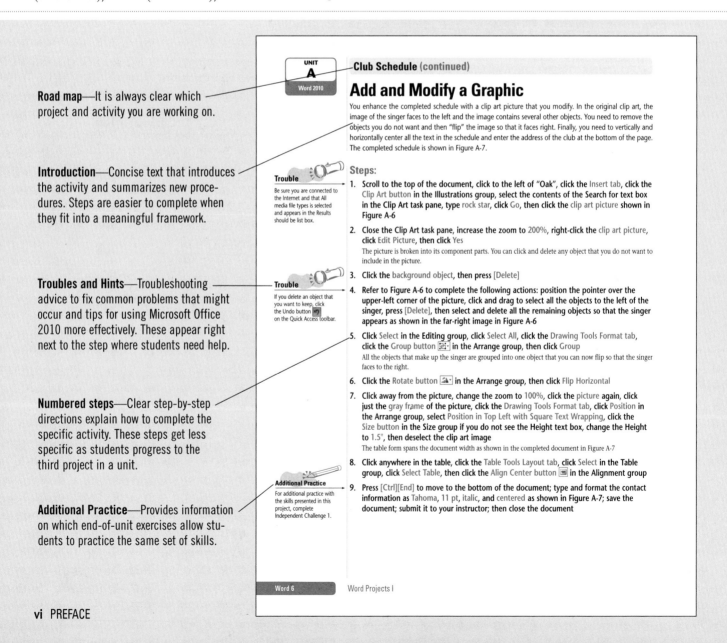

The Projects

The two-page activity format featured in this book provides students with a powerful learning experience. Additionally, this book contains the following features:

▶ **Meaningful Examples**—This book features projects that students will be excited to create including a personal resume, a term paper in MLA style, a budget, an integrated report, and a sales presentation. By producing relevant documents that will enhance their own lives, students will more readily master skills.

▶ **Start from Scratch**—To truly test if a student understands the software and can use it to reach specific goals, the student should start from the beginning. In this book, students create projects from scratch, just like they would in the real world. In selected cases, supplemental data files are provided.

▶ **Outstanding Assessment and Reinforcement**—Each unit concludes with four independent challenges and a Visual Workshop.

Independent Challenges 1 to 3 relate directly to Projects 1 to 3 and provide students with instructions to create their own version of the project document. Independent Challenge 4 and the Visual Workshop are new projects that test students' ability to apply the skills they have learned. In the Visual Workshop, students see a completed document, worksheet, database, or presentation, and must recreate it on their own.

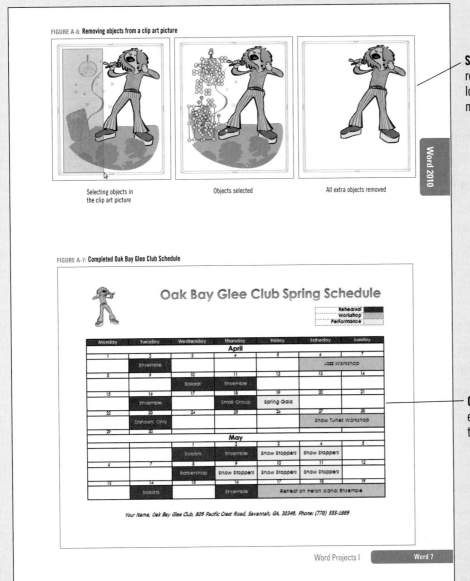

FIGURE A-6: Removing objects from a clip art picture

Selecting objects in the clip art picture

Objects selected

All extra objects removed

Word 2010

Screen shots—Every activity features representations of what the screen should look like as students complete the numbered steps.

FIGURE A-7: Completed Oak Bay Glee Club Schedule

Oak Bay Glee Club Spring Schedule

Rehearsal
Workshop
Performance

Monday	Tuesday	Wednesday	Thursday	Friday	Saturday	Sunday
			April			
1	2	3	4	5	6	7
	Ensemble				Jazz Workshop	
8	9	10	11	12	13	14
		Ballad	Ensemble			
15	16	17	18	19	20	21
	Ensemble		Small Group	Spring Gala		
22	23	24	25	26	27	28
	Dancers Only				Show Tunes Workshop	
29	30					
			May			
		1	2	3	4	5
		Soloists	Ensemble	Show Stoppers	Show Stoppers	
6	7	8	9	10	11	12
		Barbershop	Show Stoppers	Show Stoppers	Show Stoppers	
13	14	15	16	17	18	19
	Soloists		Ensemble	Retreat on Heron Island: Ensemble		

Your Name, Oak Bay Glee Club, 609 Pacific Crest Road, Savannah, GA, 30349, Phone: (770) 555-1889

Completed document—At the end of every project, there is a picture of how the document will look when printed.

Word Projects I   Word 7

Summary of Skills Covered in Projects

In each unit, students can practice the skills covered in the first project in Independent Challenge 1, the skills covered in the second project in Independent Challenge 2, and the skills covered in the third project in Independent Challenge 3.

Unit A Word Projects I

Project	Page	Skills
Schedule for Oak Bay Glee Club	2	Table setup, table formatting, themes, text effects, remove objects from clip art
Term Paper in MLA Style	8	Headers and footers, MLA guidelines for formatting term papers, find and replace text with formatting, add and edit citations, manage sources, Works Cited list
Business Cards for Pierre Lefèvre	14	Labels, symbols, paragraph formatting, WordArt, clip art: rotation and cropping
Term Paper in APA Style	22	Headers and footers, APA guidelines for formatting term papers, citations, bibliography
High Seas Adventure Letterhead	24	Clip art edits, WordArt, paragraph formatting

Unit B Word Projects II

Project	Page	Skills
Five-Page Proposal for Lakeview College	26	Headers and footers, style sets, styles (modify, update, create), footnotes, paragraph formatting (line spacing, paragraph spacing, indenting), Reveal Formatting, shapes (rounded rectangle), SmartArt graphics, table of contents, section breaks, cover page
Six-Panel Brochure for French Country Tours	36	Shapes (lines), margins, page orientation, clip art in footers, columns, drop caps, styles, background removal, artistic effects, picture wrapping, borders, WordArt, picture position
One-Page Resume for Ian Robinson	42	Style sets, modify styles, table properties, resume setup
Six-Panel Brochure for San Diego School of Drama	48	Color scheme, new paragraph style, WordArt, columns
Rosemary Designs SmartArt	50	SmartArt graphic, style set, color scheme, styles

Unit C Excel Projects I

Project	Page	Skills
Projected Budget for Camp Orca	52	Worksheet setup and formatting, sheet tabs, themes, copying formulas, AutoFill, absolute and relative values, "what-if" questions, sparklines, printing setup
Travel Expense Report for Bright Lights Learning	60	AutoSum, enter formulas, format values, border lines, problem solving, sheet references in formulas, conditional formatting, row height, custom width, custom margins
Planning Budget for a European Vacation	66	Themes, cell styles, text orientation, what-if analysis,
Vacation Budget with Dynamic Content	72	Worksheet setup and formatting, Web queries, data refresh
Six-Month Budget	74	Formulas, AutoFill, format values, absolute and relative values, "what-if" questions

Unit D Excel Projects II

Project	Page	Skills
Sales Forecast for Central Green Consulting	76	Workbook setup, Scenario Manager (current, best case, worst case), column chart, maximum Y-axis value, custom header
Course Grades Analysis for Psychology 200	84	Absolute values in formulas, lookup table, Lookup function, Subtotals function, Sort & Filter, pie chart, Find and Replace, table format
Sales Report for Home Organics	90	PivotTables, field settings, summarize values, filter results, column chart, slicers, refresh data
Forecasts for Aqua Marine Sailing	96	Scenario Manager, bar chart, maximum X-axis value, custom header
Survey Results	98	Sort, Subtotals function, pie chart

Unit E Integration Projects I

Project	Page	Skills
Job Performance Reviews	100	Word: styles, table properties, Developer tab, form content controls, Paste Special, paste link, Edit Links to Files, edits to link sources Excel: column chart, maximum x-axis, edits to chart data, change chart source
Sales Report for Paradise Resorts	108	Word: Paste Special, paste links, format pasted objects, callout shapes: draw, format, copy Excel: formulas, Scenario Manager, Goal Seek, column chart built from data in two worksheets, format maximum axis, decimal format
Marketing Update for Endless Sun Tours	114	Word: Research task pane, screenshots, wrap text, Paste Special, Excel: Copy charts to Word as links, update links
Sales Summary for Time Goes By Books	121	Word: styles and themes, update links Excel: copy links to Word, Goal Seek
Game Movers Sales Report	124	Word: Paste Special, update links Excel: cone chart, copy and paste links

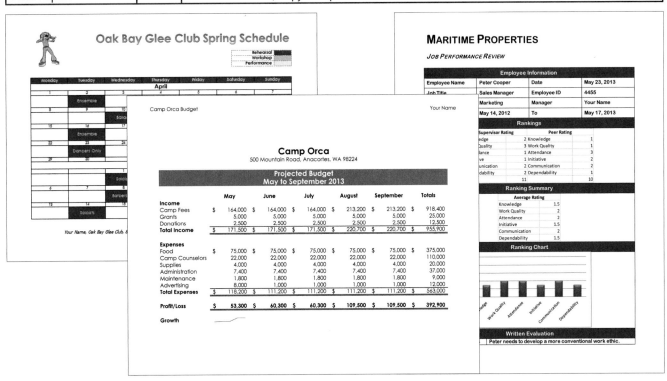

Unit F Access Projects

Project	Page	Skills
Inventory for Global Artisan	126	Data types (Text, Hyperlink, and Number, Lookup wizard), relationships, referential integrity, forms, logo added to a form and a report, form and report properties, Query Wizard, Expression Builder, Report Wizard, adjustments to report layout
Author Database for Eaglecliff Books	134	Lookup Wizard, relationships, format Number field, Query Wizard, Expression Builder, reports (theme, layout, Group & Sort, Sum, properties)
Tour Database for Winding Road Tours	140	Data types: (Memo and Date/Time), field formatting, attachments, import table from another database, queries, sort fields in reports
Database of Study Abroad Programs	147	Database setup, find data online and enter into a database, create and modify the report (orientation, theme, column widths)
Employee Travel Expenses	148	Create and relate two tables, formulas in queries, report (add group, apply theme, show subtotals)

Unit G Integration Projects II

Project	Page	Skills
Job Search Package for Marlene Daly	150	Access: default values in tables, Yes/No data type, Lookup Wizard, create a form on a blank grid, merge with Word, copy data to Excel Word: Merge a letter with an Access database, Match Fields Excel: Analyze data from Access, column chart
Proposal for Natura Beauty Products	158	Access: Import an Excel workbook and append records to a table Excel: Prepare a workbook to export to Access Word: Rotate WordArt in a header, set tabs, Insert Text from File, copy data from Excel: Paste Special, copy a report from Access and reformat
Art Collection Catalogue for Horizons Art Gallery	164	Access: Merge to labels in Word, export data to Excel Word: Merge data from Access to create a sheet of labels, field codes Excel: sort data, Subtotal function, doughnut chart
Sales Report for Game Time, Inc.	170	Report in Word contains a table created in Access and then exported to Word, and a chart created from data exported from Access to Excel and then analyzed (sort, subtotal)
Analysis of Garden Wizard Products	172	Table created in Word and copied to Access, data modified in Access and then exported to Excel for analysis and presentation

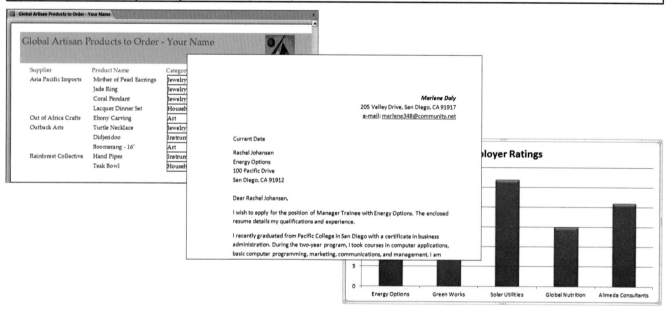

Unit H PowerPoint Projects

Project	Page	Skills
Training Presentation on Oral Presentation Skills	174	Outline tab, customizing a theme, background styles, Slide Master, Edit Shapes, rotation (text box), Clip Art, SmartArt graphic, modifying one element in a SmartArt graphic, animate a SmartArt graphic, animation scheme
Poster for Seymour Nature Preserve	182	Blank slide layout, drawing and aligning shapes and text boxes, create and modify table, create new theme colors, text effects, background removal, Lock Aspect ratio, rotate (Flip Horizontal), create PDF
Lecture Presentation on Project Management	188	Portrait orientation, organization chart, modify clip art (remove objects), shapes (block arrow), align and distribute objects, print as handouts
Home-Based Business Presentation	194	Change color scheme, modify objects in the slide master, Pyramid SmartArt graphic, artistic and color effects
Saving the Rainforest Slides	196	Slide Master, blank slide layout, Picture SmartArt graphic

Unit I Integration Projects III

Project	Page	Skills
Status Report for Mount Grant Health Clinic	198	Word report contains three slides copied from PowerPoint, a table and a report copied from Access, data copied from Excel, and a table of contents
Inventory Orientation for Otter Bay Estates	206	PowerPoint presentation contains a table copied from Word, a chart copied from Excel that contains data originally entered in Access. Links from Access to Excel to PowerPoint are created, updated, and then broken.
Class Party Presentation	214	A form is created in Access that contains a picture formatted and saved from PowerPoint, data is entered in Excel and a chart created in PowerPoint based on the Excel data, text is entered in a Word document and copied to PowerPoint, the Set Transparent Option is applied to a picture in PowerPoint
Volunteer Orientation	221	An outline is created in Word and inserted in PowerPoint, a chart is created in Excel and copied to PowerPoint, a report is created in Access, then pasted into PowerPoint as a screenshot
Cultural Tours Presentation	224	Data from Access and Excel is linked to PowerPoint, a screen clipping is created in Word, all links between applications are broken

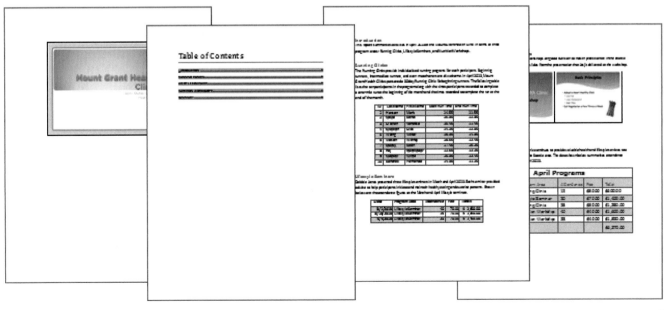

Instructor Resources

The Instructor Resources CD is Course Technology's way of putting the resources and information needed to teach and learn effectively into your hands. With an integrated array of teaching and learning tools that offer you and your students a broad range of technology-based instructional options, we believe this CD represents the highest quality and most cutting edge resources available to instructors today. The resources available with this book are:

Instructor's Manual

Available as an electronic file, the Instructor's Manual includes detailed lecture topics with teaching tips for each unit.

Solution Sample Syllabus

Prepare and customize your course easily using this sample course outline.

Figure Files

The figures in the text are provided on the Instructor Resources CD to help you illustrate key topics or concepts. You can create traditional overhead transparencies by printing the figure files. Or you can create electronic slide shows by using the figures in a presentation program such as PowerPoint.

Solutions to Exercises

Solutions to Exercises contains every file students are asked to create or modify in the lessons and end-of-unit material.

Data Files for Students

Data Files contain every file students need to create the projects and end-of-unit material. You can post the Data Files on a file server for students to copy.

Students' Frequently Asked Questions

What are Data Files?

A Data File is a partially completed file that is used to complete the steps in the units and exercises to create the final document that is submited to your instructor.

Where are the Data Files?

Your instructor will provide the Data Files a location on a network drive from which they can be downloaded.

What software was used to write and test this book?

This book was written and tested using a typical installation of Microsoft Office 2010 installed on a computer with a typical installation of Microsoft Windows 7 Ultimate. The browser used for any steps that require a browser is Internet Explorer 8.

Do I need to be connected to the Internet to complete the steps and exercises in this book?

Some of the exercises in this book assume that your computer is connected to the Internet. If you are not connected to the Internet, see your instructor for information on how to complete the exercises.

What do I do if my screen is different from the figures shown in this book?

This book was written and tested on computers with monitors set at a resolution of 1024 × 768. If your screen shows more or less information than the figures in the book, your monitor is probably set at a higher or lower resolution. If you don't see something on your screen, you might have to scroll down or up to see the object identified in the figures.

The Ribbon (the blue area at the top of the screen) in Microsoft Office 2010 adapts to different resolutions. If your monitor is set at a lower resolution than 1024 × 768, you might not see all of the buttons shown in the figures. The groups of buttons will always appear, but the entire group might be condensed into a single button that you need to click to access the buttons described in the instructions.

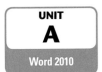

Word Projects I

Files You Will Need:

PR A-1.docx
PR A-2.docx

You can use Microsoft Office Word to produce many different kinds of documents, ranging from attractively formatted schedules and lists to a multiple-page term paper complete with citations and a bibliography to a sheet of business cards. Your challenge when using Word is to take the skills you know and apply them to create useful and interesting documents. For example, you can use the versatile table feature to create forms, questionnaires, schedules, inventory lists, or just about any document that presents information in a grid format with multiple rows and columns. In this unit, you will apply your Microsoft Word skills to create and format a schedule; insert and modify clip art pictures and photographs; create WordArt objects; insert footnotes, citations, and a bibliography; and modify a sheet of labels to create business cards.

In This Unit You Will Create the Following:

Club Schedule

Term Paper in MLA Style

Business Cards

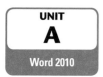

Schedule for Oak Bay Glee Club

The Oak Bay Glee Club in Savannah, Georgia provides its members with a schedule of events in three categories: Rehearsals, Workshops, and Performances. As the office manager for the glee club, you need to create the Spring schedule that covers dates in April and May. You will **Create Tables**, **Format Tables**, and **Add and Modify a Graphic**. The completed schedule appears in Figure A-7 on page 7.

Create Tables

You need to set up the document in landscape format so that the completed schedule is 9" wide. Then you need to create a small table to contain the legend and a large table to contain the schedule.

Steps:

1. Open a new blank document in Word, click the Page Layout tab, click the Orientation button in the Page Setup group, click Landscape, click Margins in the Page Setup group, then click Custom Margins

2. Type the margin settings shown in Figure A-1, click OK, then save the document as PR A-Oak Bay Glee Club Schedule to the location where you save the files for this book

3. Click Themes in the Themes group, click Austin, click the View tab, click the Page Width button in the Zoom group, type Oak Bay Glee Club Spring Schedule, select the text, click the Home tab, then increase the font size to 28 pt

4. Verify that the text is still selected, click the Bold button **B** in the Font group, click the Text Effects button 🅰 in the Font group, click Gradient Fill – Orange, Accent 6, Inner Shadow (fourth row, second column), then click the Align Text Right button ▤ in the Paragraph group

5. Press [Enter] once, click the Clear Formatting button 🧹 in the Font group, click the Insert tab, click the Table button in the Tables group, drag to create a table that is 2 columns wide and 3 rows high, then enter text as shown in Figure A-2

Hint
You use the Table Properties dialog box to make changes to all components of the table including rows, columns, cells, and the table itself.

6. Click cell 1 (contains "Rehearsal"), click the Table Tools Layout tab, click Properties in the Table group, click the Column tab, select the contents of the Preferred width text box, type 1.5, click Next Column, select the contents of the Preferred width text box for column 2, then type .6

7. Click the Table tab in the Table Properties dialog box, click the Right button in the Alignment section, click OK, click Select in the Table group, click Select Table, click the Table Tools Design tab, click the Bottom Border list arrow ▦ in the Table Styles group, click No Border, then press [↓] once

   With the table borders removed, you can see faint lines, called gridlines, that indicate the location of rows and columns. If you cannot see gridlines after removing the table borders, click anywhere in the table, click the Table Tools Layout tab, then click View Gridlines in the Table group.

8. Press [Enter] once, click the Insert tab, click the Table button in the Tables group, click Insert Table, type 7, press [Tab], type 18, then click OK

9. Enter the text for the first three rows as shown in Figure A-3, then save the document

FIGURE A-1: **Page Setup dialog box**

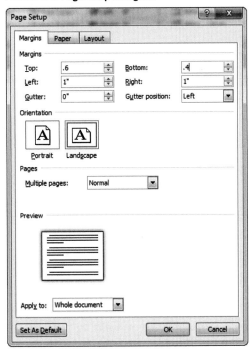

FIGURE A-2: **Text for the legend**

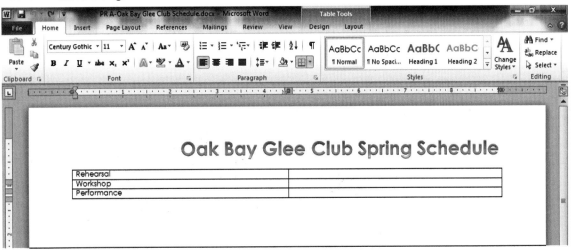

FIGURE A-3: **Text for rows 1 to 3**

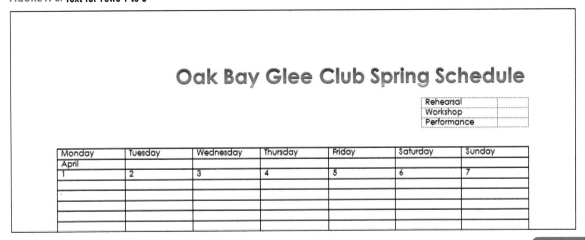

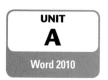
Format Tables

In the completed schedule, some cells are merged to create larger cells, the dates are formatted in a small font size and different levels of shading indicate the different schedule categories. You need to enter text into the table and format the schedule.

Hint

Clicking to the left of a table row selects the entire row.

Steps:

1. Click to the left of April to select all the cells in row 2, click the Table Tools Layout tab, click Merge Cells in the Merge group to merge the seven cells into one cell, click the Home tab, click the Grow Font button A⁺ in the Font group two times, click the Bold button B in the Font group, then click the Center button ≡ in the Paragraph group

2. Click the cell below 2, type Ensemble, press [Tab] four times, type Jazz Workshop for Saturday, select the two cells under 6 and 7, then merge them into one cell
   You've entered the two events being held during the first week in April.

3. Refer to Figure A-4 to enter the remaining text, merge cells where needed and use the Format Painter to match the formatting of "May" with the formatting of "April"

4. Click to the left of row 1 (contains the days of the week), click the Table Tools Design tab, click the Shading list arrow ⬛⁻ in the Table Styles group, click Green, Accent 1, Darker 50%, right-click the selected cells, click the Font Color list arrow A⁻ on the Mini toolbar, click the White, Background 1 box, then apply bold and centering

5. Click the cell to the right of the Rehearsal cell in the legend table, click the Shading button ⬛ in the Table Styles group to fill the cell with Green, Accent 1, Darker 50%, refer to Figure A-5 to fill the remaining legend table cells, then format the text in column 1 of the legend table with bold and right alignment

Hint

You use the [Ctrl] key to quickly select nonadjacent rows.

6. Click to the left of the row containing the dates for the first week of April (1, 2, 3, etc.), press and hold [Ctrl], click to the left of each of the rows containing dates so that only the eight rows containing dates are selected, click the Home tab, click the Font Size list arrow, then click 9

Trouble

If you change the height of the wrong row, click the Undo button ↺ on the Quick Access toolbar, select a row and apply the row height, then use the [F4] key for the remaining rows.

7. Select the row containing the two events for the first week of April (row 4), click the Table Tools Layout tab, select the contents of the Height text box in the Cell Size group, type .4, press [Enter], click in the row containing the events for the second week of April ("Ballads," "Ensemble"), press [F4], press [▼] two times, press [F4], then continue to use [▼] and [F4] to set the height of only the rows containing events
   The [F4] key is the repeat command on most computers. You can use the [F4] key to repeat the last command you performed, which in this case is changing the height of a table row. If the [F4] key does not work as expected on your computer, use the Repeat key ↻ on the Quick Access toolbar.

8. Move the pointer over the left side of the cell containing "Ensemble" in row 4 until the pointer changes to ➤, click once to select the cell, press and hold [Ctrl], select all the cells filled with Dark Green as shown in Figure A-5, click the Table Tools Design tab, click the Shading list arrow ⬛⁻, click Green, Accent 1, Darker 50%, right-click any selected cell, then click the Font Color button A on the Mini toolbar

Hint

Remember you can save time by using the [Ctrl] key to select multiple cells at once.

9. Refer to Figure A-5 to fill all the cells containing workshops with Green, Accent 1, Lighter 40% and all the cells containing performances with Green, Accent 1, Lighter 80%, then save the document

Monday	Tuesday	Wednesday	Thursday	Friday	Saturday	Sunday
April						
1	2	3	4	5	6	7
	Ensemble				Jazz Workshop	
8	9	10	11	12	13	14
		Ballads	Ensemble			
15	16	17	18	19	20	21
	Ensemble		Small Group	Spring Gala		
22	23	24	25	26	27	28
	Dancers Only				Show Tunes Workshop	
29	30					
May						
		1	2	3	4	5
		Soloists	Ensemble	Show Stoppers	Show Stoppers	
6	7	8	9	10	11	12
		Barbershop	Show Stoppers	Show Stoppers	Show Stoppers	
13	14	15	16	17	18	19
	Soloists		Ensemble	Retreat on Heron Island: Ensemble		

FIGURE A-5: Shading for Oak Bay Glee Club schedule

Fill with Green, Accent 1, Lighter 80%

Fill with Green, Accent 1, Lighter 40%

Rehearsal	
Workshop	
Performance	

Monday	Tuesday	Wednesday	Thursday	Friday	Saturday	Sunday
April						
1	2	3	4	5	6	7
	Ensemble				Jazz Workshop	
8	9	10	11	12	13	14
		Ballads	Ensemble			
15	16	17	18	19	20	21
	Ensemble		Small Group	Spring Gala		
22	23	24	25	26	27	28
	Dancers Only				Show Tunes Workshop	
29	30					
May						
		1	2	3	4	5
		Soloists	Ensemble	Show Stoppers	Show Stoppers	
6	7	8	9	10	11	12
		Barbershop	Show Stoppers	Show Stoppers	Show Stoppers	
13	14	15	16	17	18	19
	Soloists		Ensemble	Retreat on Heron Island: Ensemble		

Fill all cells shaded this color with Green, Accent 1, Darker 50%

Fill all cells shaded this color with Green, Accent 1, Lighter 40%

Fill all cells shaded this color with Green, Accent 1, Lighter 80%

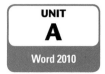
Club Schedule (continued)

Add and Modify a Graphic

You enhance the completed schedule with a clip art picture that you modify. In the original clip art, the image of the singer faces to the left and the image contains several other objects. You need to remove the objects you do not want and then "flip" the image so that it faces right. Finally, you need to vertically and horizontally center all the text in the schedule and enter the address of the club at the bottom of the page. The completed schedule is shown in Figure A-7.

Steps:

1. Scroll to the top of the document, click to the left of "Oak", click the Insert tab, click the Clip Art button in the Illustrations group, select the contents of the Search for text box in the Clip Art task pane, type rock star, click Go, then click the clip art picture shown in Figure A-6

2. Close the Clip Art task pane, increase the zoom to 200%, right-click the clip art picture, click Edit Picture, then click Yes

   The picture is broken into its component parts. You can click and delete any object that you do not want to include in the picture.

3. Click the background object, then press [Delete]

4. Refer to Figure A-6 to complete the following actions: position the pointer over the upper-left corner of the picture, click and drag to select all the objects to the left of the singer, press [Delete], then select and delete all the remaining objects so that the singer appears as shown in the far-right image in Figure A-6

5. Click Select in the Editing group, click Select All, click the Drawing Tools Format tab, click the Group button 📐▾ in the Arrange group, then click Group

   All the objects that make up the singer are grouped into one object that you can now flip so that the singer faces to the right.

6. Click the Rotate button 📐▾ in the Arrange group, then click Flip Horizontal

7. Click away from the picture, change the zoom to 100%, click the picture again, click just the gray frame of the picture, click the Drawing Tools Format tab, click Position in the Arrange group, select Position in Top Left with Square Text Wrapping, click the Size button in the Size group if you do not see the Height text box, change the Height to 1.5", then deselect the clip art image

   The table form spans the document width as shown in the completed document in Figure A-7

8. Click anywhere in the table, click the Table Tools Layout tab, click Select in the Table group, click Select Table, then click the Align Center button ▣ in the Alignment group

9. Press [Ctrl][End] to move to the bottom of the document; type and format the contact information as Tahoma, 11 pt, italic, and centered as shown in Figure A-7; save the document; submit it to your instructor; then close the document

FIGURE A-6: Removing objects from a clip art picture

Selecting objects in
the clip art picture

Objects selected

All extra objects removed

FIGURE A-7: Completed Oak Bay Glee Club Schedule

Oak Bay Glee Club Spring Schedule

Rehearsal	
Workshop	
Performance	

Monday	Tuesday	Wednesday	Thursday	Friday	Saturday	Sunday
April						
1	2	3	4	5	6	7
	Ensemble				Jazz Workshop	
8	9	10	11	12	13	14
		Ballads	Ensemble			
15	16	17	18	19	20	21
	Ensemble		Small Group	Spring Gala		
22	23	24	25	26	27	28
	Dancers Only				Show Tunes Workshop	
29	30					
May						
		1	2	3	4	5
		Soloists	Ensemble	Show Stoppers	Show Stoppers	
6	7	8	9	10	11	12
		Barbershop	Show Stoppers	Show Stoppers	Show Stoppers	
13	14	15	16	17	18	19
	Soloists		Ensemble	Retreat on Heron Island: Ensemble		

Your Name, Oak Bay Glee Club, 809 Pacific Crest Road, Savannah, GA, 30349, Phone: (770) 555-1889

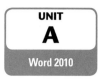

Term Paper in MLA Style

A well-written term paper presents an argument, supports the argument with logical points, and presents a clear conclusion. In addition, term papers include references to the sources used to write the paper, as well as a bibliography or a works cited list. Most term papers are formatted according to one of the three common styles: MLA, APA, and Chicago. To format the term paper according to MLA guidelines, you need to **Format the Text in MLA Style**, **Add and Format References**, and **Add a Works Cited List**. Selected pages from the formatted term paper appear in Figure A-14 on page 13.

Format the Text in MLA Style

Hint
You can find more detailed information about formatting term papers in the *MLA Handbook for Writers of Research Papers*.

You open a document containing the text of a term paper written for an English Literature course and then you format the title page and text according to the MLA style. Table A-1 lists the general requirements for formatting a paper in MLA style.

Steps:

1. **Start Word, open the file** PR A-1.docx **from the drive and folder where you store your Data Files, save it as** PR A-Literature Term Paper **to the location where you save the files for this book, click the** Page Layout tab, **click the** Margins button **in the Page Setup group, then click** Normal

2. **Click the** Home tab, **click** Select **in the Editing group, click** Select All, **click the** Line and Paragraph Spacing button ⬚ **in the Paragraph group, then click** 2.0

3. **Verify that all the text is still selected, click the** Font list arrow, **type** ti **to move quickly to Times New Roman, click** Times New Roman, **click the** Font Size list arrow, **then click** 12

4. **Click at the beginning of the paper, press** [Tab] **once to indent the first line, then increase the zoom to** 140%
   No action is required on the remaining paragraphs in the paper because they are already indented.

Hint
The MLA format specifies that a separate title page is not necessary for a term paper. Instead, information about the course is entered in the upper-left corner of page 1 of the paper.

5. **Click the** Insert tab, **click** Header **in the Header & Footer group, click** Edit Header, **verify that the Different First Page check box in the Options group is not checked, press** [Tab] **two times to move to the right margin, type your last name, press** [Spacebar], **click the** Page Number button **in the Header & Footer group, point to** Current Position, **select the** Plain Number **style as shown in Figure A-8, then click the** Close Header and Footer button **in the Close group**

6. **Press** [◄] **once, press** [Enter], **press** [▲] **to position the insertion point at the left margin, type your full name, press** [Enter], **type the name of your instructor or professor, press** [Enter], **type** English 326, **then press** [Enter]

7. **Click the** Insert tab, **click** Date & Time **in the Text group, verify the Update automatically check box is not selected, click the date format corresponding to** 20 April 2013, **then click** OK

8. **Press** [Enter], **click the** Home tab, **click the** Center button ▤ **in the Paragraph group, type the title of the essay as shown in Figure A-9, making sure to format** *Pride and Prejudice* **in italics, return the zoom to** 100%, **then save the document**

FIGURE A-8: Inserting a page number at the current position

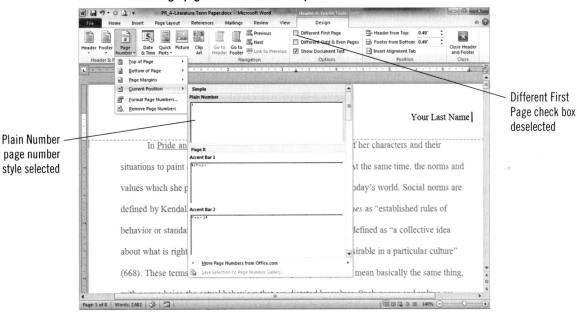

Plain Number page number style selected

Different First Page check box deselected

FIGURE A-9: Term paper header, course information, and title

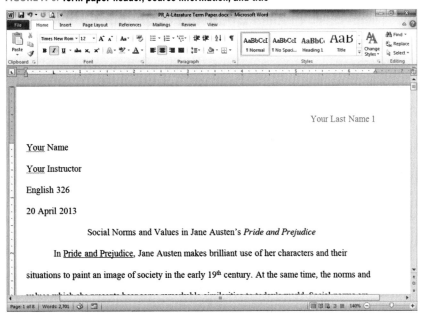

TABLE A-1: Summary of general MLA guidelines for formatting a term paper*

guideline	description
Paper and margins	Print the term paper on standard, white, 8.5" × 11" paper and set all four margins to 1".
Spacing	Double-space all content including quotations and the bibliography.
Font and font size	Use a legible font and font size such as Times New Roman and 12 pt.
Sentence spacing	Leave only one space after a period and before the start of the next sentence.
Paragraphs	Use the [Tab] key to indent the first line of each paragraph one-half inch from the left margin.
Header	Include a header with your last name and a page number in the upper-right corner of each page.
First page	Include each of the following on its own line in the upper-left corner of page 1 of the paper: your name, the professor's name, the course name and number, and the current date written in day, month, year format.
	On a new line after the course information, center the title of the essay; italicize book titles such as *Pride and Prejudice*, but do not underline or otherwise change the formatting.

*Check the most recent MLA version for possible changes.

Add and Format References

Most term papers include references to the books, articles, and Web sites that the writer consulted while writing the paper. A paper formatted in the MLA style includes source information in the body of the term paper at the location where the source is cited. In the MLA style, source information is included in parenthesis and follows the author-page format. For example, a quotation from page 460 of a work by James Watson would be cited as (Watson 460). Some exceptions occur. If you provide the name of the author in the sentence preceding the citation, you include only the page number in the parenthesis. If the citation references a quotation from the literary work that is the subject of the paper (for example, *Pride and Prejudice*), then only the page number is included. You also need to italicize the title of any book included in the text of a term paper. First, you use the Find and Replace function to find every instance of <u>Pride and Prejudice</u> and replace it with *Pride and Prejudice,* and then you insert a citation to a new source that you create and a citation to a source already associated with the term paper.

Steps:

1. **Click** Replace **in the Editing group, type** Pride and Prejudice **in the Find what text box, click** More **if necessary to expand the dialog box, click** Format, **click** Font, **click the** Underline style list arrow, **click the underlining style shown in Figure A-10, then click** OK
   You have established that Word should search for every instance of <u>Pride and Prejudice</u> formatted with underlining.

2. **Click in the** Replace with text box, **type** Pride and Prejudice, **click** Format, **click** Font, **click** Italic **in the Font style list, click the** Underline style list arrow, **click** (none), **then click** OK
   Figure A-11 shows the Find and Replace dialog box with these settings.

Trouble
Click Yes if a warning box opens.

3. **Click** Replace All, **click** OK, **then click** Close **to close the Find and Replace dialog box**
   All underlined instances of <u>Pride and Prejudice</u> are replaced with italicized instances of *Pride and Prejudice.*

4. **Click** Find **in the Editing group to open the Navigation pane, type** history and geography **in the Find text box, then click in the document after the quotation mark following "geography" and before the period**
   You've set the location where you need to insert a citation to provide a source for the quotation. You also need to ensure that the current citation style is set to MLA.

5. **Click the** References tab, **click the** Style list arrow, **then click** MLA Sixth Edition **to select it**

6. **Click** Insert Citation **in the Citations & Bibliography group, click** Add New Source, **verify that Book is selected as the Type of Source, enter the information for the source as shown in Figure A-12, then click** OK
   The name of the author (Faye) appears in parenthesis. MLA style specifies that the page number where the quotation is located should also appear in a citation.

7. **Click the** citation, **click the** Citation Options list arrow, **click** Edit Citation, **type** 87-88 **in the Pages text box, click** OK, **then click away from the citation to deselect it**
   The name of the author and the page numbers indicating where the quotation can be found are entered as a citation in the document.

8. **Search for** deportment, **click after the ending quotation mark and before the period, click** Insert Citation, **click** Faye, Diedre Le, **then edit the citation and enter the page number** 90

9. **Search for** late teens, **insert a citation to** Diedre Le Faye's book, **then save the document**
   The citation (Faye) appears. You will modify this citation by changing the name to Le Faye and inserting a page number in the next lesson.

FIGURE A-10: **Selecting the Underline style**

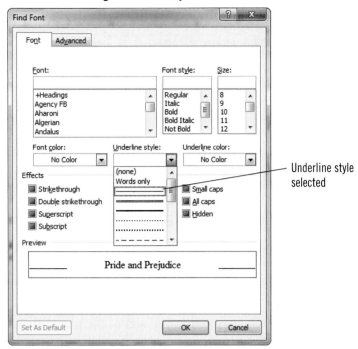

FIGURE A-11: **Selecting the Underline style**

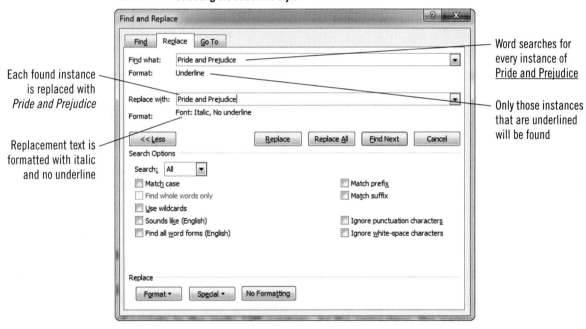

Each found instance is replaced with *Pride and Prejudice*

Replacement text is formatted with italic and no underline

Word searches for every instance of <u>Pride and Prejudice</u>

Only those instances that are underlined will be found

Underline style selected

FIGURE A-12: **Source information**

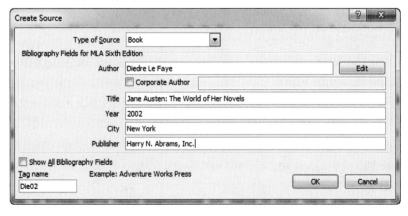

Word 2010

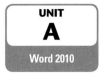

Term Paper (continued)

Add a Works Cited List

On a new page following the last page of your term paper, you can insert a bibliography or a works cited list. A bibliography lists all the sources you consulted when writing the term paper, even if you did not quote them in the paper. A works cited list includes only the sources you quoted. You edit some citations, view the citations in the Manage Sources dialog box so you can edit the sources, and then generate and update a works cited list.

Steps:

1. **Click** (Faye), **click the** Citation Options list arrow, **click** Edit Citation, **enter** 113 in the Pages text box, **click** all three check boxes **in the Suppress area as shown in Figure A-13 to select them, then click** OK

   Only the page number appears. You do not need to include the name of the author because the author name appears at the beginning of the sentence that includes the citation.

2. **Press** [Ctrl][End] **to move to the end of the paper, then press** [Ctrl][Enter] **to insert a page break**

3. **Click** Bibliography **in the Citations and Bibliography group, click** Works Cited, **then scroll up to view the list of works cited**

   The list of works cited in the term paper appears. Two of the entries are incorrect. The entry for "Faye" should be listed as "Le Faye" and "Jane Austen" should be listed as "Austen, Jane."

4. **Click** Manage Sources **in the Citations & Bibliography group, note the list of citations on the right side of the Source Manager dialog box, click the entry for** Faye, **then click** Edit

5. **Select the contents of the** Author text box, **type** Le Faye, Diedre, **click** OK, **then click** Yes

   Because "Le" is part of the author's last name, you need to enter the name exactly as you want it to appear in the Works Cited list.

6. **Click the entry for** Jane Austen, **click** Edit, **change Jane Austen to** Austen, Jane, **click** OK, **then click** Yes **if prompted**

   Normally, you can enter the first name and last name in the Author text box in the Create Source dialog box and Word will insert the source in the last name, first name format in the works cited list or bibliography. In a source that includes more than one author, however, the name of the first author should be listed in last name, first name order, and the names of the other authors should be listed in first name, last name order.

7. **Click** Close, **click** Works Cited, **then click** Update Citations and Bibliography

   The entries for Diedre Le Faye and Jane Austen are now correct.

8. **Scroll up and click in the document, search for** history and geography, **then verify that the citation now reads** "(Le Faye 87-88)"

   The Works Cited list should be double-spaced.

9. **Close the Navigation pane, scroll to the Works Cited list, select the text in the Works Cited list from "Works Cited" to the end of the source for James Thompson, right-click the selected text, click** Paragraph, **click the** Line spacing list arrow, **click** Double, **then click** OK

10. **Save the document, submit a copy to your instructor, then close the document**

    Four pages from the term paper appear as shown in Figure A-14.

Hint

You need to carefully check the MLA Guidelines and your entries to ensure your citations follow standard MLA citation formatting, and you should not rely solely on the software for correct formatting.

Additional Practice

For additional practice with the skills presented in this project, complete Independent Challenge 2.

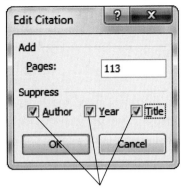

Select all three check boxes to suppress the associated information from being included in the citation

FIGURE A-14: **Pages 1, 4, 6, and 9 of the completed term paper**

Your Last Name 1

Your Name

Your Instructor

English 326

26 July 2013

Social Norms and Values in Jane Austen's *Pride and Prejudice*

In *Pride and Prejudice*, Jane Austen makes brilliant use of her characters and their situations to paint an image of society in the early 19th century. At the same time, the norms and values which she presents bear some remarkable similarities to today's world. Social norms are defined by Kendall, Murray, and Linden in *Sociology in Our Times* as "established rules of behavior or standards of conduct" (664), while a social value is defined as "a collective idea about what is right or wrong, good or bad, and desirable or undesirable in a particular culture" (668). These terms can be used fairly interchangeably; they both mean basically the same thing, with norms being the actual behaviors that are dictated by values. Such norms and values are shown in a multitude of ways throughout *Pride and Prejudice*. There are norms associated with most every aspect of society, including the norms for class, money, gender, and marriage most commonly explored in Austen's novels. Austen shows society's values both through satire and through presenting what she considers to be the better alternative. The society of Austen's time no doubt differs from today in [...]

closely examined, it becomes [...]

Money and class had a [...]

19th century. The higher one's [...]

in society. Darcy, with his £10[...]

the Bennets, who make only £[...]

Your Last Name 4

gentleman is a harsh shock, and he realizes that he must change his behavior. Later in the book, Darcy's true nature as a gentleman is revealed when Elizabeth goes to Pemberley. His housekeeper, Mrs. Reynolds, describes him as "the best landlord, and the best master" (213), and she has nothing but praise for him. When Darcy arrives at Pemberley, he proves himself to be courteous and well-mannered, and Elizabeth is amazed at "his behavior, so strikingly altered" (216).

In Austen's world, merely being born an aristocrat does not make someone a lady or a gentleman. Lady Catherine de Bourgh is a prime example of the ill-breeding that can be found in people of high class and wealth. She is a very rich, upper-class widow who owns a great deal of land and who has a great deal of power over her tenants. Her behavior, however, is not at all befitting of a lady. She is rude and inconsiderate, as she proves when Elizabeth visits her and later when she tries to force Elizabeth not to marry Darcy. When Elizabeth visits Rosings, Lady Catherine talks constantly and "in so decisive a manner as proved that she was not used to having her judgment controverted" (145). She exerts firm control over her tenants, and she spends a great deal of time telling them how to run their households, as can be seen when she "enquired into Charlotte's domestic concerns familiarly and minutely, and gave her a great deal of advice, as to the management of them all" (145). Austen satirizes Lady Catherine by [...]pleasantness in a near-comical manner. Mr. Collins, too, is certainly not a [...]he attempts to act in a courteous manner, he evidently has very little grasp on [...]society, as can be seen when he introduces himself to Mr. Darcy and is ridiculed [...]the rest of the party. He is a figure of constant mockery, and the other characters [...]down upon hi[...] when he prov[...]

Your Last Name 6

reads a passage from the book in volume 1, chapter 14. Here, again, we see conflicting values. As the Longman Cultural Edition of *Pride and Prejudice* states, "[the sermons] lessons are pointedly and disastrously ignored by the one character who needs to listen" (385). This person is, of course, Lydia Bennet, who could in fact do with a few lessons in propriety. On the other hand, as the book continues to state, "Austen, like many writers of her day, was clearly skeptical about the authoritativeness of conduct-book stands of femininity" (385). Education for young women at the time was usually minimal. They were taught "needlework, both for necessity and for pleasure; simple arithmetic; fine hand writing, which was considered a very elegant accomplishment; enough music to be able to sing and play…; a little drawing…; and some very scrappy ideas of history and geography" (Le Faye 87-88). For women educated at private seminaries, "the prime object was to instill Decorum, Manners, and Deportment" (Le Faye 90). The emphasis on proper manners in *Pride and Prejudice* is evident, and can be seen at the Netherfield Ball when Elizabeth is embarrassed by her mother's and younger sisters' improper behavior: "To Elizabeth it appeared, that had her family made an agreement to expose themselves as much as they could during the evening, it would have been impossible for them to play their parts with more spirit, or finer success" (95). Certainly, Lydia's disgraceful behavior shows the norms and values of the time. In running off with a dishonorable man such as Wickham, she brings shame to her entire family. Sexual relations out of wedlock were taboo at the time; Fordyce, in his *Sermons*, speaks of the suffering parents feel "when a daughter…turns out unruly, foolish, wanton; when she disobeys her parents…; when she throws herself away on a man unworthy of her…". Mr. Collins' reaction, as stated earlier, would not have been uncommon at the time, especially among clergymen.

Your Last Name 9

Works Cited

Austen, Jane, Claudia L. Johnson, Susan J. Wolfson. Pride and Prejudice, A Longman Cultural Edition. New York: Longman, 2003.

Kendall, Diane, Jane Lothian Murray, Rick Linden. Sociology in Our Times. Scarborough, Ontario: Thomson Canada Limited, 2004.

Le Faye, Deidre. Jane Austen: The World of Her Novels. New York: Harry N. Adams, Inc., 2002.

Litz, A. Walton. "Into the Nineteenth Century: Pride and Prejudice." Interpretations of Pride and Prejudice. Ed. Rubinstein. E. Englewood Cliffs: Prentice-Hall, Inc., 1969. 59-69.

Thompson, James. Between Self and World: The Novels of Jane Austen. University Park and London: The Pennsylvania State University Press, 1988.

Business Cards for Pierre Lefèvre

Pierre Lefèvre works from his apartment in Los Angeles as a composer of film scores. Pierre has asked you to create a sheet of business cards for him. He wants you to combine text and graphics to make his business cards eye-catching. To create Pierre's business cards, you need to **Create Labels and Enter Text**, **Add a WordArt Logo**, and **Add a Graphic**. The completed sheet of business cards is shown in Figure A-22 on page 19.

Create Labels and Enter Text

You use a business label sheet that you select in the Labels Options dialog box as the basis for Pierre's business cards. You enter text in one label and use the Symbol dialog box to insert the "è" in Pierre's last name (Lefèvre). Finally, you format the text on the business card to emphasize Pierre's name and position.

Steps:

1. **Start Word, click the** Mailings tab, **then click** Labels **in the Create group**
   On the Labels tab of the Envelopes and Labels dialog box, you can select the size and type of label you need to create a sheet of business cards.

2. **Click** Options, **click the** Label vendors list arrow, **then scroll to and click** Avery US Letter

3. **Scroll down the** Product number list box, **click** 5371 Business Cards, **click** Details, **verify that the Label height is** 2" **and the Label width is** 3.5", **click** OK, **then click** OK

4. **Verify that the** Full page of the same label option button **is selected in the Print section, then click** New Document
   You click New Document because you want to show the label sheet as a table in which you can include both the text and a WordArt object for the business card.

5. **Change the zoom to** 130%, **then type** Pierre Lef **in the upper-left table cell**
   You'll add the "è" next.

6. **Click the** Insert tab, **click** Symbol **in the Symbols group, click** More Symbols, **select** (normal text) **as the Font type if necessary, select the contents of the Character code box, type** 00E8 **to select the** è **as shown in Figure A-15, click** Insert, **then click** Close

7. **Type** vre **so the full name is Pierre Lefèvre, save the document as** PR A-Business Cards for Pierre Lefevre **to the location where you save the files for this book, press [Enter] once, then type the remaining text for the business card as shown in Figure A-16**

8. **Click the first line of text, click the** Page Layout tab, **select the contents of the** Before text box **in the Spacing area of the Paragraph group, type** 36, **press [Enter], select the six lines of text, click the** Home tab, **click the** Align Text Right button **in the Paragraph group, enhance** Pierre Lefèvre **with** Bold **and a font size of** 14 point, **change the font size of the remaining text to** 10 point, **then enhance** Film Score Composer **with** Italic

9. **Select all six lines of text, click the** Page Layout tab, **select the contents of the** Right text box **in the Indent section of the Paragraph group, type** 0.4, **press [Enter], deselect the text, then save the document**
   The formatted text for the business card is shown in Figure A-17.

FIGURE A-15: Symbol dialog box

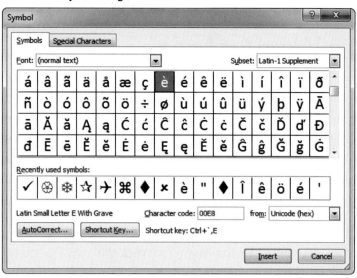

FIGURE A-16: Text for business card

Pierre Lefèvre
Film Score Composer
Suite 300 – 1200 Buena Vista Place
Los Angeles, CA 90231
e-mail: pierrel@composerman.com
Phone: (323) 555-8910

FIGURE A-17: Business card text formatted

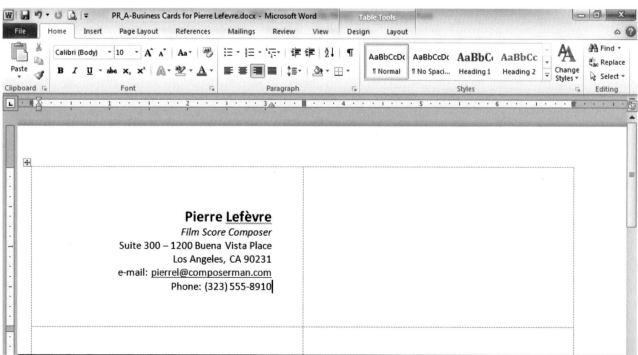

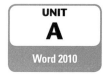

Business Cards (continued)

Add a WordArt Logo

You need to add a WordArt object to the business card and then modify it.

Steps:

1. **Click to the left of "Pierre", click the** Insert tab, **then click the** WordArt button **in the Text group**

   The WordArt Gallery opens.

2. **Click** Gradient Fill - Purple, Accent 4, Reflection **(fourth row, fifth column) as shown in Figure A-18**

3. **Type** PL, **select** PL, **click the** Home tab, **click the** Font list arrow, **type** MV, **then select the** MV Boli **font**

   White sizing handles appear around the WordArt object to indicate it is selected.

4. **Click the** Line and Paragraph Spacing button ⬚ **in the Paragraph group, then click** Remove Space Before Paragraph

   The WordArt object now fits neatly in the upper-left corner of the table cell as shown in Figure A-19.

Trouble

The WordArt object must be selected to access the Drawing Tools Format tab.

5. **Click the** Drawing Tools Format Tab, **click the** Text Effects button ⬚ **in the WordArt Styles group, point to** Reflection, **then click** No Reflection

   You can modify a WordArt object in many ways by selecting different options from the list of enhancements that appear when you click the Text Effects button in the WordArt Styles group. You can add a shadow, a reflection, a glow, or a bevel, apply a 3-D rotation effect, and use the Transform option to change the shape of the WordArt object.

6. **Click the** Text Effects button ⬚ **again, point to** Shadow, **click** Offset Diagonal Bottom Left **(top row, third column in the Outer section), click** ⬚ **once more, point to** Bevel, **then click** Cool Slant **(first row, fourth column in the Bevel section)**

7. **Click the** Rotate button ⬚ **in the Arrange group, click** More Rotation Options, **select the contents of the Rotation text box, type** 340, **then click** OK

   You can rotate an object either by dragging the green rotation handle that appears at the top of the selected object or by entering a specific rotation setting on the Size tab of the Layout dialog box.

8. **Click away from the WordArt object, save the document, then compare the business card to Figure A-20**

FIGURE A-18: Selecting a WordArt style

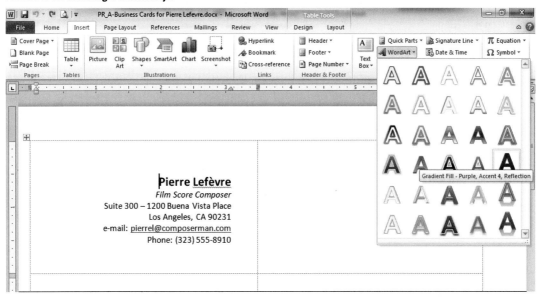

FIGURE A-19: WordArt logo positioned

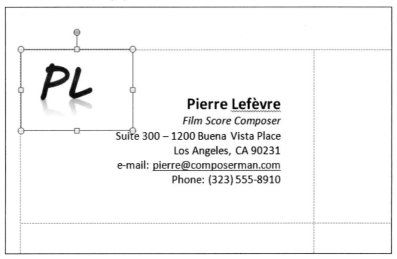

FIGURE A-20: Completed WordArt object

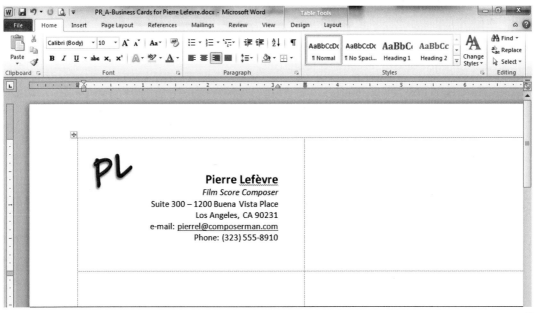

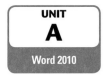
Business Cards (continued)

Add a Graphic

You need to add a clip art picture and then modify it so that only part of the picture remains, and then you need to change the theme applied to the document so that different fonts and fill colors are used. The completed label sheet is shown in Figure A-22.

Trouble

Don't worry if the picture displaces the WordArt object and the text. You will position the clip art image after you modify its size.

Hint

You can press the up, down, left, and right arrow keys to position the image precisely.

Additional Practice

For additional practice with the skills presented in this project, complete Independent Challenge 3.

Steps:

1. **Click to the left of "Pierre", click the** Insert tab, **click** ClipArt **in the Illustrations group, delete the contents in the Search for text box in the Clip Art task pane, type** musical notes border, **click** Go, **then click the clip art picture that includes the keyboard image shown in Figure A-21**

    You can use the Crop function to select just a portion of a clip art picture.

2. **Close the ClipArt task pane, click the** Crop button **in the Size group, click** Crop **if the Crop command is not active, drag the lower-middle crop handle up as shown in Figure A-21, then release the mouse button to set the crop**

3. **Click away from the image to deselect it, click the** image **again, click the** Picture Tools Format tab, **click the** Wrap Text button **in the Arrange group, then click** Square

4. **Click the** launcher ⬜ **in the Size group, click the** Lock aspect ratio check box to **deselect it, enter** .25 **in the Height Absolute text box, enter** 2.8 **in the Width Absolute text box, then click** OK

5. **Drag the keyboard image to the bottom of the business card, then release the mouse button so the keyboard image appears as shown in Figure A-22**

6. **Click anywhere in the text of the business card, click the** Table Tools Layout tab, **click** Select **in the Table group, click** Select Cell, **click the** Home tab, **click the** Copy button 🖹 **in the Clipboard group, click in the upper-right table cell, then click the** Paste button **in the Clipboard group**

7. **Click away from the table cell to deselect it, click the** Page Layout tab, **click** Themes **in the Themes group, move the pointer over each of the themes to view how the fill color of the WordArt object and the font applied to text changes, then click** Black Tie

8. **Click the** View tab, **click** One Page **in the Zoom group, click the** Home tab, **then click each blank table cell and use the** Paste button **to paste the contents of the business card in each of the remaining table cells**

9. **Select the** telephone number **in the lower-right card, type your name, save the document, submit a copy to your instructor, then close all open documents**

    A complete sheet of cards is shown in Figure A-22. If Pierre were printing his business cards, he would insert several sheets of the perforated cards he purchased into his printer before he clicked the Print button.

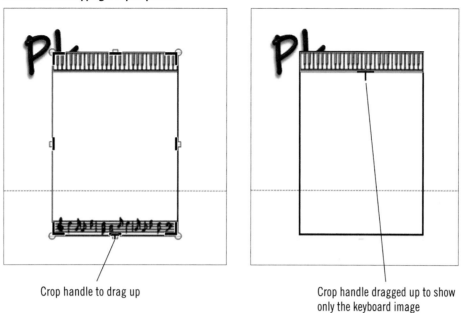

Crop handle to drag up

Crop handle dragged up to show only the keyboard image

FIGURE A-22: Completed sheet of business cards

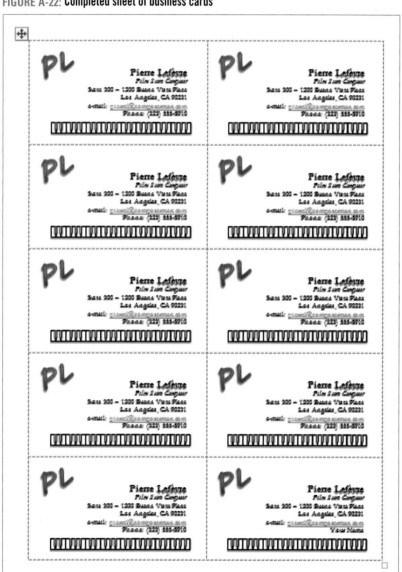

Word 2010

Independent Challenge 1

Use the Table feature in Word to create a schedule for a series of activities, such as a weekly course schedule or a monthly calendar of events. For example, you could create a schedule that displays all the concerts or plays offered over a six-month period at a local theater, or you could create your personal weekly schedule that includes all your work, school, and leisure activities. To help you determine the information required for your schedule, follow the directions provided below.

1. Determine the purpose of your schedule. Do you want to keep track of your courses each week, or create your personal fitness schedule, or perhaps create a calendar of events for a local community group? Enter the purpose of your schedule in the box below.

Schedule Purpose: _____

2. Determine the column and row labels required for your schedule. If you are creating a weekly schedule, your column labels will be the days of the week; if you are creating a monthly schedule, your column labels will be the months of the year. List the column and row labels required for your schedule in the box below.

Column Labels: _____

Row Labels: _____

3. Calculate the total number of rows and columns required to complete your schedule. For example, if you are creating a weekly schedule, you will need to create a table consisting of eight columns. Column 1 will contain the time increments (e.g., 8:00 to 9:00) and columns 2 to 8 will contain the days of the week.

4. Open a new blank document, then set up your document so that it prints in landscape orientation. Change the margins, if you wish.

5. Save the document as **PR A-My Schedule** to the location where you are save the files for this book.

6. Create an attractive heading for your schedule, using text that describes the content of the schedule (such as "My Fitness Schedule" or "Monthly Events Calendar"). Apply, and then modify a text effect to the schedule heading.

7. Create the table based on the number of columns and rows you calculated in Step 3. Note that you can add new rows to the table by clicking in the last cell of the last row, then pressing [Tab]. You can add columns to the table by selecting a column, clicking the Table Tools Layout tab, then selecting the appropriate option in the Rows & Columns group.

8. Enter the information required for your schedule. Use the Copy and Paste features to minimize repetitive typing.

9. Shade selected cells. Use varying shades of the same Accent color. Remember that you can use the [Ctrl] key to select and then fill nonadjacent cells with the same shading color.

10. Include a clip art picture that you have modified in some way. For example, you could remove some of the objects that make up the picture, group the remaining objects into one object, and then flip the picture horizontally.

11. Size and position the clip art picture in an attractive location (use a text-wrapping option).

12. Enter your name at the bottom of the document, check the spelling and grammar, save the document and submit it to your instructor, then close it.

Independent Challenge 2

Format a term paper in the MLA style. If possible, choose a paper that you wrote for a course you have taken or are taking in an area of the humanities, such as literature or history. To help you format the paper correctly, refer to Table A-1 in Unit A Project 2 and the guidelines provided below. You can also consult recent resources on the Internet. The MLA style has changed over the years so make sure you refer to at least three Web sites that have been updated within the last two years. You can also refer to the MLA Web site at www.mla.org for useful summaries. In addition, you can consult the two reference books published by MLA: the *MLA Handbook for Writers of Research Papers* and the *MLA Style Manual and Guide to Scholarly Publishing*.

1. Select a term paper that is 5 to 10 pages in length, then save it as **PR A-My Term Paper** to the location where you save the files for this book.
2. Set all four margins to 1", then double-space all the text in the document.
3. Format all the text in the Times New Roman font and 12 pt, and make sure that the first line of each paragraph is indented one tab stop (which should be set to one-half inch).
4. Insert a header in the upper-right corner of every page (make sure you click the Different First Page check box to deselect it). The header should include your last name and the page number.
5. At the left margin, enter your full name, the name of your instructor or professor, and the course name and number on three separate lines.
6. On the next line, insert the date using the day, month, year format.
7. Center the title of the term paper.
8. Ensure that any reference to a published book is formatted in italics. (*Hint*: Use Find and Replace.)
9. Ensure that your term paper includes at least three citations to credit sources you quote in the paper. Use the MLA format for the citation, which is (author last name then page number). If the name of the author is cited in the same sentence where the citation is placed, include only the page number from which the quotation was taken.
10. On a new page at the end of the term paper, generate either a works cited list or a bibliography, depending on the sources you used to write the paper. If you cited all the sources in your paper, generate a works cited list. If you used sources for research but did not cite all of them in the term paper, generate a bibliography.
11. After you generate the works cited list or bibliography, work in the Source Manager dialog box to make changes where necessary. For example, you may discover that a source is missing or that a source contains a misspelling.
12. Update the works cited list or bibliography, then double space it.
13. Save the document, submit a copy to your instructor, then close the document.

Independent Challenge 3

Use a business card label product, such as the Avery 5371 label, available in the Envelopes and Labels dialog box, to create a sheet of business cards for yourself. Follow the directions to create your business cards.

1. Draw a business-card sized rectangle (generally 2" × 3.5") on a piece of paper, and then spend some time experimenting with different designs for your business card. For example, you could right-align your name and address and include a WordArt logo of your initials in the upper-left corner of the business card, or you could center your name and address on only two lines along the bottom of the business card, then insert a logo centered in the middle of the business card. Draw several versions of your business card until you find the one that meets your needs.

Independent Challenge 3 (continued)

2. Open a new blank document, open the Envelopes and Labels dialog box from the Mailings tab, select one of the Business Card products from the list of available label products in the Label Options dialog box, click OK, verify that the labels will print on a full sheet, then click New Document.

3. Enter your name and address on the business card, then save the business card as **PR A-My Business Cards** to the location where you save the files for this book.

4. Apply formatting to selected text. For example, you may want your name to appear in a larger font and in bold.

5. Create an attractive WordArt logo based on your initials. Experiment with some of the many text effects available for formatting a WordArt object. For example, you can modify the shading and line color, add or remove a shadow, or add a 3-D effect.

6. Reduce the size of the logo, modify the Before Paragraph spacing, and position the logo attractively on the business card.

7. Insert a clip art picture that you modify in some way or draw a shape such as a triangle or circle. You can crop the clip art picture, and you can fill the shape with a fill color and modify the border style and color. Experiment until you are pleased that the graphic you include on your business card effectively communicates the image you want to project.

8. Modify the theme applied to the business cards.

9. Copy the contents of the upper-left cell to every cell in the table so that you have a full sheet of business cards.

10. If possible, print your sheet of business cards on a sheet of perforated business card stock. You may need to adjust the spacing of the various elements in the card.

11. Save the document, submit a copy to your instructor, then close all open documents.

Independent Challenge 4

Format a term paper in the APA style (American Psychological Association) according to the guidelines provided below. You are provided with the text of the term paper and information about what citations and sources to include. The APA style is most commonly used to format papers and cite sources in disciplines within the social sciences, such as psychology and sociology.

1. Start Word, open the file PR A-2.docx from the drive and folder where you store your Data Files, save it as **PR A-Sociology Term Paper** to the location where you save the files for this book, then format the paper according to the guidelines included in Table A-2.

TABLE A-2: Summary of general APA guidelines for formatting a term paper

guideline	description
Margins	Set all four page margins to 1".
Spacing	Double-space all content, including the list of references after it is generated.
Title page	Format the title page as shown in Figure A-23, including the text and page number in the first page header; start the title about 10 lines (press [Enter] five times) from the top margin.
Header on subsequent pages	On page 2, create a header that is different from page 1 and that includes only the title of the paper in uppercase at the left margin of the page header (without the text "Running Head:") and the page number (starting at page 2) at the right margin of the page header.
Abstract	Center "Abstract" on page 2 of the term paper, and indent each paragraph except paragraph 1. The indent should be one-half inch.
Term paper text	On the first page of the term paper following the abstract page, type the title of the paper above the first paragraph, and then center it.

Independent Challenge 4 (continued)

2. Use the Search function to find the text "participation in the wider society", then create a new source for a book as follows:
   Author: Denis McQuail
   Title: Audience Analysis
   Year: 1997
   City: Thousand Oaks, CA
   Publisher: Sage Publications

3. Insert a citation for Denis McQuail so that it immediately follows the closing quotation mark. (*Note*: In the APA style, a citation uses the author, date format and includes the page number preceded by "p." unless the author's name appears in the preceding sentence. Edit the citation so only the page number (p. 99) appears. You do not need to type the "p." because it is added automatically.)

4. Find "offline social skills," insert the citation for Zweerink (the source is included in the list of available sources associated with the paper), then edit the citation so it shows only "p. 12".

5. In the Source Manager, create a new source for a book as follows:
   Author: Matt Hills
   Title: Fan Cultures
   Year: 2002
   City: London
   Publisher: Routledge

6. Search for "cultural creativity" and insert citations after the closing quotation marks that include only page numbers (p. 90 for the first citation after "creativity or 'play'" and p. 106 after "between 'fantasy' and 'reality'" in the next line).

7. Find the text "ideals into practice" and edit the citation so that only the page number appears.

8. Add a new page at the end of the paper and generate a list of references. Enter "References" centered as the title of the page. (*Hint*: Select the Insert Bibliography option. Double space the list of references.)

9. Save the document, submit a copy to your instructor, then close the document.

FIGURE A-23

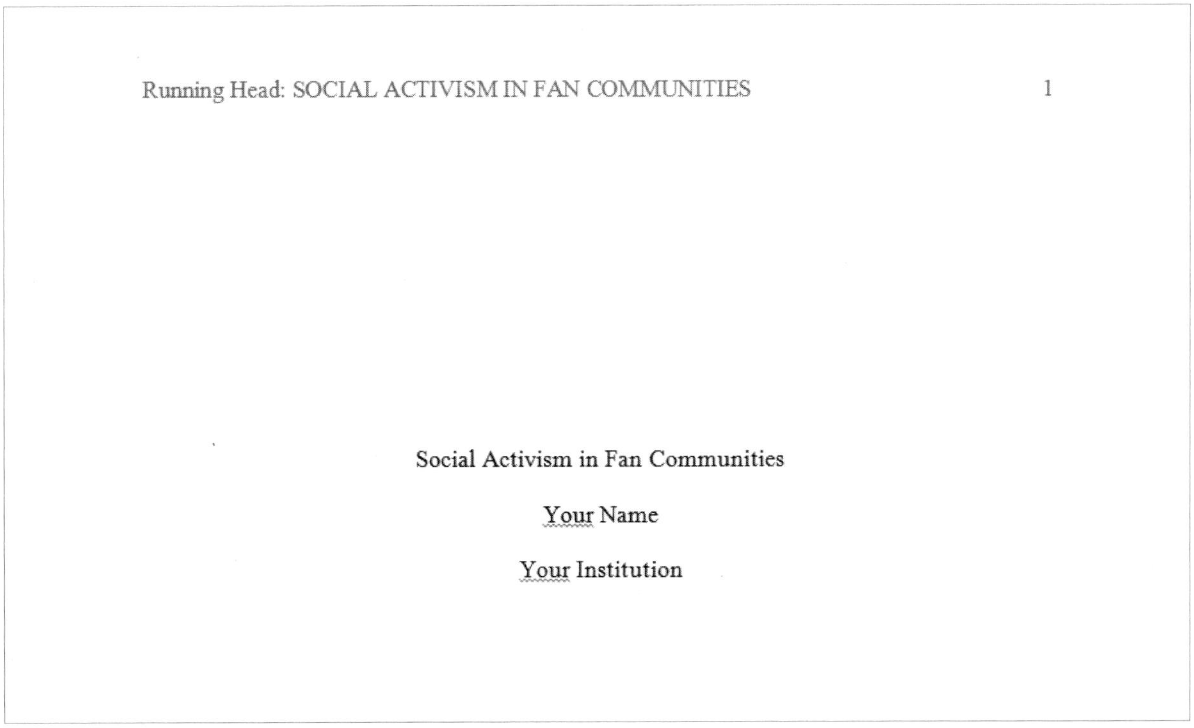

Running Head: SOCIAL ACTIVISM IN FAN COMMUNITIES   1

Social Activism in Fan Communities

Your Name

Your Institution

Visual Workshop

Create the letterhead shown in Figure A-24 in a new document. Save the document as **PR A-High Seas Adventures Letterhead** to the location where you save the files for this book. Use the Fill – Olive Green, Accent 3, Powder Bevel WordArt style. Find the clip art picture by searching the Clip Organizer. You need to rotate the picture so that it faces the direction shown in the figure. Change the text wrapping for the Clip Art picture to Square and the WordArt object to In Front of Text, and position them as shown in Figure A-24, along with the address text. Adjust the size of the WordArt text so it closely resembles the figure.

FIGURE A-24

High Seas Adventures

405 Palm Way, Maui, HI 96833 www.hawaiihighseasadventures.biz

Word Projects II

With Microsoft Word, you can design multiple-page documents such as proposals and reports that include page numbers, headers and footers, charts and diagrams, and an automatically generated table of contents. You can also use Word to create multipanel brochures containing text formatted in columns, and you can insert a variety of graphics, including screenshots, clip art pictures, drawn shapes, and SmartArt graphics. In this unit, you will apply your Microsoft Word skills to modify styles, create a new style, insert a footnote, create a SmartArt diagram, generate a table of contents and work with sections, format text in columns, remove the background from a photograph and add an artistic effect, insert drop caps, and modify clip art pictures.

In This Unit You Will Create the Following:

Five-Page Proposal

Six-Panel Brochure

One-Page Résumé

Five-Page Proposal for Lakeview College

The dean of Lakeview College in Chicago has asked the Business Department to submit a proposal for a new program to train office managers. You will **Set Up the Document**, **Create Page 1**, **Create Page 2**, **Create Page 3**, and **Create the Table of Contents and Cover Page**. Figures B-3 through B-7 on pages 29 through 35 show the five pages that you'll create for the proposal.

Set Up the Document

You need to insert a header and a footer, and then you need to modify styles associated with the Perspective Quick Styles set.

Steps:

1. Start Word, click the Insert tab, click the Header button in the Header & Footer group, click the Blank style, type Office Management Program, press [Tab] twice, click the Date & Time button in the Insert group, click the style that corresponds to June 20, 2013, then click OK

2. Click the Go To Footer button in the Navigation group, type your name, then press [Tab] twice

3. Click the Page Number button in the Header & Footer group, point to Current Position, click Plain Number, click the Close Header and Footer button in the Close group, then save the document as PR B-Lakeview College Proposal to the location where you save the files for this book

   The document now includes a header and a footer containing text that will appear at the top and bottom of every page.

4. Click the Change Styles button in the Styles group, point to Style Set, then click Perspective

5. Click Heading 1 in the Styles gallery, type Introduction, press [Enter], click the Change Styles button in the Styles group, point to Colors, then scroll to and click Slipstream

6. Select Introduction, click the Bold button **B**, increase the font size to 18 pt, click the Shading list arrow 🖌 in the Paragraph group, then click Turquoise, Accent 2, Lighter 40%

7. Right-click Heading 1 in the Styles gallery, then click Update Heading 1 to Match Selection as shown in Figure B-1

8. Click below "Introduction" to deselect it, click the More button 🔽 in the Styles group, right-click Heading 2 in the Styles gallery, click Modify, click the Font Color list arrow, click Turquoise, Accent 2, Darker 50%, click the Increase Indent button 🔄, click Format, click Border, click the Shading tab, click the Fill list arrow, click Turquoise, Accent 2, Lighter 80%, then click OK

   The Modify Style dialog box appears as shown in Figure B-2.

9. Click OK, then save the document

FIGURE B-1: Updating the Heading 1 style

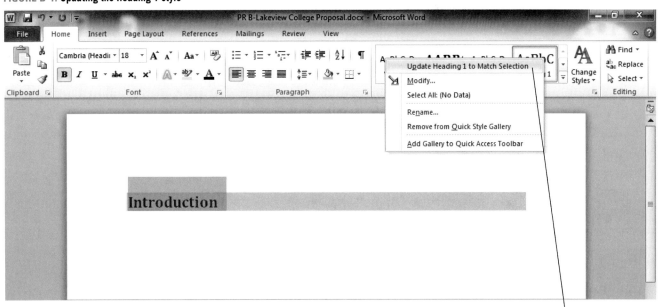

Heading 1 style is updated when you click Update Heading 1 to Match Selection

FIGURE B-2: Heading 2 style modified

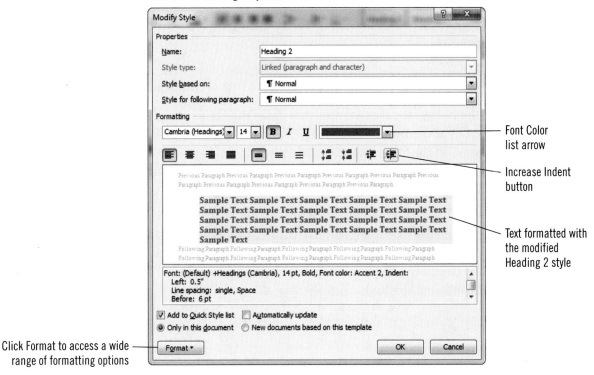

Font Color list arrow

Increase Indent button

Text formatted with the modified Heading 2 style

Click Format to access a wide range of formatting options

Create Page 1

First, you need to create a new style to format the proposal text. The new style, which you name Proposal Text, changes the text indent to .5, the line spacing to 1.5, and the before paragraph spacing to 6 pt. Then, you need to enter the text required for page 1 and create a footnote. The completed page 1 is shown in Figure B-3.

Steps:

1. Click the launcher 🔲 in the Styles group, click the New Style button 🔳 at the bottom of the task pane, then type Proposal Text as the style name

2. Click the 1.5 Space button ≡ (middle selection in the three line-spacing icons), click the Increase Paragraph Spacing button 🔳 once, click the Increase Indent button 🔳, then click OK

   All text formatted with the new Proposal Text style will have 1.5 spacing between lines, 6-pt spacing between paragraphs, and be indented .5".

3. Close the Styles task pane, then type the introductory paragraph as shown in Figure B-3

4. Press [Enter], select Heading 1 in the Styles gallery, type Scope of the Program, press [Enter], select Proposal Text in the Styles gallery, then type the next paragraph as shown in Figure B-3

5. Press [Enter], select Heading 2 in the Styles gallery, type Description of Need, then press [Enter]

6. Select Proposal Text in the Styles gallery, then type the next two paragraphs as shown in Figure B-3

7. Click the References tab, click the Insert Footnote button in the Footnotes group, then type the footnote text as shown in Figure B-3 (the text will be single-spaced at this point)

8. Click the Home tab, click the launcher 🔲 in the Styles group, click the Style Inspector button 🔳 at the bottom of the Styles task pane, then click the Reveal Formatting button 🔳 in the Style Inspector dialog box

   When text is formatted with a style that is not included in the Styles gallery, you can determine and then modify the formats in the Reveal Formatting task pane.

9. Click Paragraph Style in the Paragraph section of the Reveal Formatting task pane, click Modify, click the Increase Indent button 🔳, change the font size to 11 pt, click the 1.5 Space button ≡, click OK, click Apply, close all open task panes, click anywhere in the text to exit the footnote area, then save the document

   The footnote text is formatted as shown in Figure B-3.

Hint

As you make formatting changes, a description of your selections appears under the preview window. Use this information to verify your selections.

Trouble

if a heading style is not visible in the Styles gallery, click the Gallery's down scroll arrow or the More button 🔽.

Office Management Program   Current Date

Introduction

This proposal presents a request to develop the Office Management program to train students for employment as Office Administrators, Office Managers, and Office Coordinators. Included in the proposal is a discussion of three factors related to the development of the program: Scope of the Program, Proposed Courses, and Funding Requirements. If approved, the Coordinator of the Business Department will develop course outlines and begin to recruit students for entry into the program in September 2014.

Scope of the Program

The proposed program will provide students with extensive training in computer applications and business-related skills. The goal of the program is to train students for employment. The program will run for nine months from September to May and include a two-week work practicum. Students who graduate from the program will be prepared to enter the workforce.

Description of Need

At present, none of the local community colleges offers an Office Management program. West Side College, the closest competitor to Lakeview College, offers an Executive Assistant program that primarily attracts students who have just graduated from high school. The proposed Office Management program will target candidates who have either several years of college or considerable work experience. These candidates require practical skills that will help them gain employment in an office environment.

The marketing survey conducted by Gerry Kwan, Coordinator of the Business Department, is attached to this proposal.[1]

---

[1] Personnel agencies, human resources professionals, and businesspeople responded to the survey. The results show a need for candidates with the skills offered by the proposed Office Management program.

Your Name   1

Word 2010

Create Page 2

You need to insert a page break so that the text and headings you enter next appear on page 2. When you have finished entering the text and headings, you insert a table containing the list of courses and then enclose the table in a rounded rectangle. The completed page 2 is shown in Figure B-4.

Steps:

1. Click at the end of the last paragraph on page 1 after the footnote reference number, click the Page Layout tab, click Breaks in the Page Setup group, click Page, click the Home tab, select the Heading 1 style, type Proposed Courses, then press [Enter]

2. Select the Proposal Text style, then enter and format the text required for the rest of page 2, except the table in the Course Descriptions section, as shown in Figure B-4
   Remember to format the two subheadings with the Heading 2 style and the paragraphs of text with the Proposal Text style.

3. Verify that the insertion point appears at the end of the document text and following "Office Management program.", press [Enter], click the Insert tab, click Table, click Insert Table, type 2, press [Tab], type 9, click OK, then enter the text for the table as shown in Figure B-4
   The text will wrap to page 3. You'll fix this problem in the next step.

Hint

Use the screen tips to find the correct style.

4. Scroll up to the top of the table, move the pointer over the upper-left corner of the table to display the table move handle ⊞, then click ⊞ to select the entire table

5. Click the View Ruler button 🔲 at the top of the vertical scroll bar to the right of the document window to show the ruler bar if it is not already displayed, drag the left edge of the table to the right until the guide line crosses through the "u" in the Course Descriptions paragraph heading, double-click the right edge of the table to fit the contents of column 2, click the More button 🔽 in the Table Styles group to show the selection of table styles, then click Medium Shading 1 – Accent 2

6. Verify that the table is selected, click the Page Layout tab, reduce both the Before and After Paragraph Spacing in the Paragraph group to 0, click the Home tab, then click the Center button 🔳 in the Paragraph group

7. Click above the table to deselect it, click the View tab, click the Zoom button in the Zoom group, click the 75% option button, click OK, then scroll as needed so the entire table is visible
   In 75% view, you can easily see the entire table.

Hint

You can use your arrow keys to position the rectangle precisely.

8. Click the Insert tab, click the Shapes button in the Illustrations group, then click the Rounded Rectangle button in the Rectangles section

9. Drag the pointer to draw a rounded rectangle (any size) below the table, click the More button 🔽 in the Shapes Styles group, click Colored Outline – Turquoise, Accent 2, click the Shape Fill list arrow 🔽, click No Fill, use your mouse to adjust the size and position of the rounded rectangle so that it encloses the table like a border as shown in Figure B-4, then save the document

Office Management Program   Current Date

Proposed Courses

Peter Simpson, an instructor in the Business Department, developed eight new courses for the proposed Office Management program. He was assisted by Dr. Iris Kostas, a Management Consultant and former faculty member at Lakeview College.

Course Overview

Students in the proposed Office Management program will take eight courses over two terms: September to December and January to May. The courses are evenly divided between theory-based and application-based courses. During the program, students become proficient in several software applications. In addition, students improve their written and oral communication skills, develop project management skills, and learn how to plan and run special events.

Course Descriptions

The following table lists the eight courses offered to students in the proposed Office Management program.

Course	Description
Basic Business Skills	Learn the fundamentals of business
Document Design	Develop expert-level skills in Microsoft Word
Project Management	Learn the fundamentals of project management
Budgeting and Analysis	Develop spreadsheet skills using Microsoft Excel
Web Page Design	Use HTML to design Web pages
Event Planning	Organize special events
Data Management	Develop database skills using Microsoft Access
Communications	Develop written and oral communication skills

Your Name   2

Create Page 3

You need to include a radial diagram that illustrates the various sources of revenue required to run the Office Management program. In addition, you need to include information about estimated expenses and a conclusion. The completed page 3 is shown in Figure B-5.

Steps:

1. **Increase the zoom to 100%, insert a new page break below the table, apply the** Heading 1 style, **type** Funding Requirements, **then enter and format the text above the radial diagram as shown in Figure B-5**

   Remember to format the two subheadings with the Heading 2 style and the paragraphs of text with the Proposal Text style.

2. **Press** [Enter] **following "sources available.", click the** Insert tab, **click the** SmartArt button **in the Illustrations group, then click** Cycle

3. **Click the** Diverging Radial diagram **(third row, third column), then click** OK

   A diagram with five circles is inserted, and the SmartArt Tools Design and Format tabs appear, with the Design tab selected.

4. **Type** Funding Sources **in the middle circle, click the** Add Shape button **in the Create Graphic group to insert a new circle, then enter text in the five perimeter circles as shown in Figure B-5**

5. **Click the** More button ⮟ **in the SmartArt Styles group, click the** Inset style **in the 3-D section, click** Change Colors, **then click** Colorful – Accent Colors

6. **Click the gray border of the SmartArt graphic to deselect the currently selected circle, click the** SmartArt Tools Format tab, **click the** Size button **if you do not see the Shape Height and Shape Width text boxes, set the height at** 3.2", **then press** [Enter]

7. **Click the** Home tab, **click the** Bold button **B** **in the Font group, click the** Font Color list arrow **A ▾**, **then click** Automatic

   All the text in the SmartArt diagram is formatted with bold and black.

8. **Close the SmartArt text pane if it is open, double-click at the left margin below the SmartArt graphic, type** Conclusion **and apply the** Heading 1 style, **then enter the concluding paragraph formatted with the Proposal Text style as shown in Figure B-5**

Office Management Program

Current Date

Funding Requirements

Following is information about estimated costs for the program along with the estimated revenue.

Estimated Costs

The total estimated cost for the proposed program is $150,000 broken down as follows: $88,000 for faculty (based on an $11,000 cost per course), $40,000 for administrative support, $10,000 for advertising, and $12,000 for new software.

Estimated Revenue

The radial diagram shown below displays the various funding sources available.

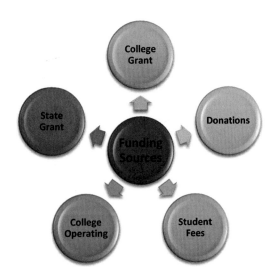

Conclusion

The Office Management program will enroll 30 students at a cost of $3,000 per student for total fees of $90,000. The remaining funding should break down as follows: College Grant: $15,000, Donations: $10,000, College Operating: $20,000, and State Grant: $15,000.

Your Name

3

Create the Table of Contents and Cover Page

You need to insert a section break above the first page of the proposal text, generate a table of contents, and create a cover page.

Steps:

1. Press [Ctrl][Home] to move to the top of the document, click the Page Layout tab, click Breaks, click Next Page, press [Ctrl][Home] again, click the Home tab, then click the Clear Formatting button in the Font group

   The Next Page command creates a new blank page and a section break. The document now contains two sections: section 1 is the new blank page and section 2 is the rest of the document.

2. Type Table of Contents, press [Enter] two times to move to the next line, then enhance "Table of Contents" with bold, a font size of 16 pt, and center alignment

3. Click below "Table of Contents", click the References tab, click the Table of Contents button in the Table of Contents group, click Insert Table of Contents, click the Formats list arrow, click Formal, then click OK

   The table of contents is automatically generated based on the styles you applied to the various headings.

4. Press [Ctrl][Home], insert another Next Page section break, move to the top of the document again, click the Insert tab, click the Header button, click Edit Header, then click the Different First Page check box in the Options group to select it

   This step creates a new section 1 and returns the header and footer on the first page to blank.

5. Click the Next button twice in the Navigation group to move to the header for section 3 (which contains the three pages of the proposal text), click the Link to Previous button in the Navigation group to deselect it, click the Go to Footer button, click the Link to Previous button to deselect it, click the Page Number button in the Header & Footer group, click Format Page Numbers, click the Start at option button, verify that 1 appears in the Start at text box, then click OK

   You deselected the Link to Previous buttons in Section 3 to ensure that changes you made to the header and footer in Section 3 do not affect the header and footer in Section 2.

6. Click the Previous button in the Navigation group to move to the footer for section 2 (the table of contents page), click the Link to Previous button to deselect it, click the Page Number button, click Format Page Numbers, click the Number format list arrow, click the i, ii, iii number format, click the Start at option button, verify that "i" appears in the Start at text box, then click OK

7. Go to the header, click to the left of the header text to select it, press [Delete], then click the Close Header and Footer button in the Close group

   The table of contents page appears in its own section, which is section 2. You can delete the header text without deleting it from the rest of the proposal text because you deselected Link to Previous in section 3.

8. Scroll to the table of contents page, right-click the table of contents, click Update Field, click the Update entire table option button, click OK, click below the table of contents to deselect it, then compare the table of contents to Figure B-6

9. Press [Ctrl][Home], click the Insert tab, click Cover Page in the Pages group, click Austin, enter text in the Abstract, Title, Subtitle, and Author content controls as shown in Figure B-7, check the spelling and grammar, save the document, submit a copy to your instructor, then close the document

Additional Practice

For additional practice with the skills presented in this project, complete Independent Challenge 1.

FIGURE B-6: Completed table of contents

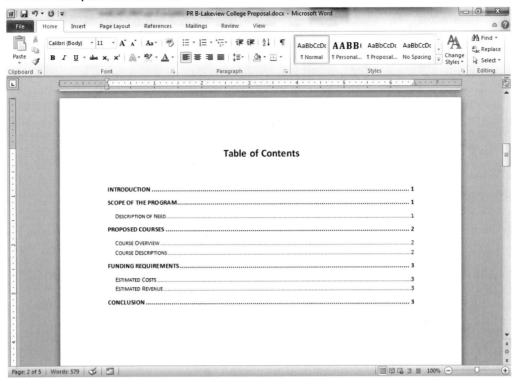

FIGURE B-7: Completed title page with the Austin style

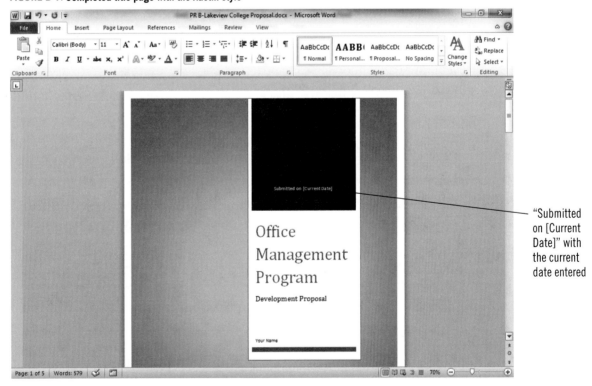

"Submitted on [Current Date]" with the current date entered

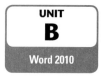

Six-Panel Brochure for French Country Tours

You need to create a six-panel brochure that describes a small group tour of France led by a tour operator based in Connecticut. Page 1 of the document consists of the inside three panels of the brochure (panels 1, 2, and 3), and page 2 consists of the folded-over panel, the back panel, and the front panel (panels 4, 5, and 6). To create the brochure for French Country Tours, you need to **Set Up the Brochure**, **Create Page 1**, and then **Create Page 2**. The completed brochure is shown in Figure B-10 and Figure B-11 on pages 39 and 41.

Set Up the Brochure

You need to set up the brochure in Landscape orientation, create a header and footer that appear only on the first page of the brochure, and then insert and modify a clip art picture in the footer.

Steps:

Hint

To set the Before Paragraph spacing to 0, click Format in the Modify Style dialog box, click Paragraph, select the contents of the Before text box, then type 0.

1. Open a new document in Word, click the Page Layout tab, select Landscape orientation, select the Narrow margin setting (all four margins at 0.5"), then save the document as PR B-French Country Tours Brochure to the location where you save the files for this book

2. Click the Home tab, right-click Normal in the Styles gallery, modify the Normal style so that the font is Arial, then modify the Heading 1 style so the font is Arial, the font size is 16 pt, and the Before Paragraph spacing is set to 0

3. Switch to Page Width view, insert a header using the Blank style, click the Different First Page check box in the Options group to select it, press [Enter] once, then press the ↑ once

4. Click the Insert tab, click the Shapes button, click the Line button, hold down [Shift], then draw a straight line in the header to the right margin as shown in Figure B-8
   You press and hold the [Shift] key while you draw the line to keep the line straight.

5. Verify that the line is selected, click the Shape Outline list arrow ✏️ ▾, click Blue, Accent 1, Darker 25%, click ✏️ ▾ again, point to Weight, click 6 pt, click Shape Effects, point to Shadow, then click Offset Bottom (top row, middle selection in the Outer category)

6. Click the Header & Footer Tools Design tab, click the Go to Footer button in the Navigation group, click the Clip Art button in the Insert group, then type France map in the Search for text box

7. Click the Results should be list arrow, click the Photographs check box to deselect it, click Go, then find and insert the picture of the map shown in Figure B-9
   When you insert the picture, it will appear left aligned and much larger than the picture shown in Figure B-9.

8. Select the contents of the Height text box in the Size group, enter 1 as the height, click the Wrap Text button in the Arrange group, click In Front of Text, then drag the clip art picture to position it as shown in Figure B-9

9. Double-click anywhere in the document to exit the footer, click the Results should be list arrow in the Clip Art task pane, click the Photographs check box to select it, close the Clip Art task pane, then save the document

FIGURE B-8: **Straight line drawn from the left to the right margin in the header**

Line button

Straight line

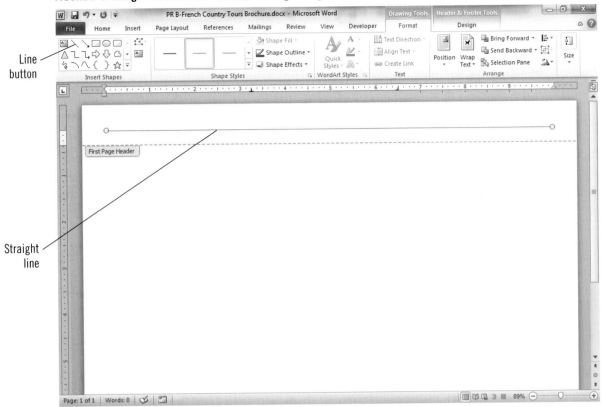

FIGURE B-9: **First page footer**

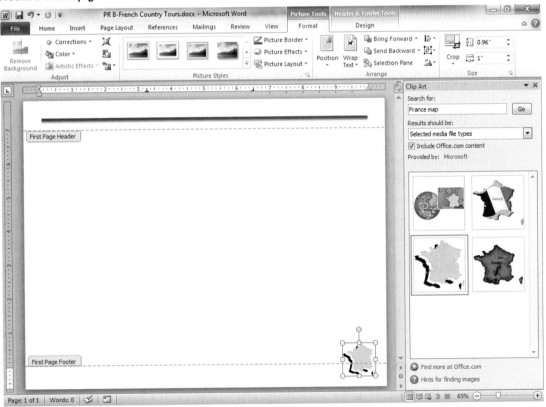

Create Page 1

Although many brochures display all information in a three-column format, you decide to create a more interesting effect by formatting the text in two columns of uneven width. Page 1 of the French Country Tours brochure appears in Figure B-10. As you can see, column 1 is about 3" wide, and column 2 is a little more than double that width. You need to format the columns, then enter the text for columns 1 and 2. After you create the text for column 1, you create an attractive graphic by removing the background from a photograph and then superimposing it over another photograph to which you add an artistic effect. Finally, you create the text for column 2 and insert drop caps to spell "France."

Steps:

1. Verify that the insertion point is positioned at the top of the document, click the Page Layout tab, click Columns in the Page Setup group, then click Left

   The Left column type formats the document in two uneven columns, with the narrower column to the left.

2. Switch to 100% view, click the Home tab, click Heading 1 in the Styles group, type Tour Description, press [Enter], then type the first three paragraphs of text (through "history of Provence.") shown in Figure B-10

3. Press [Enter], click the Insert tab, click the Picture button in the Illustrations group, navigate to the location where you store your Data Files, double-click PR B-1.jpg, click to the right of the picture to deselect it, then insert PR B-2.jpg

4. Double-click the flag picture, click Remove Background in the Adjust group, click Keep Changes, select the contents of the Width text box in the Size group, type 2, press [Enter], click the bridge picture, click Artistic Effects in the Adjust group, click the Pencil Sketch effect (top row, fourth column), verify the width of the picture is 3", click Wrap Text in the Arrange group, then click Through

Trouble

If the bridge picture hides the flag picture, click the Send Backward list arrow in the Arrange group, then click Send to Back.

5. Reduce the zoom to 75%, click the flag picture, change the wrapping to Through, then use your mouse to position the two pictures in relation to each other between paragraph 2 and 3 as shown in Figure B-10

6. Click after "Provence.", click the Page Layout tab, click Breaks, click Column, type the paragraph of text that appears at the top of column 2 in Figure B-10, press [Enter], apply Heading 1, type Moments to Remember, press [Enter], type the paragraph that begins "Here are just...", press [Enter], then type the remaining six paragraphs of text, typing the letters that appear as drop caps normally, and pressing [Enter] once between each paragraph

7. Select the text from "Find the time" to "Dordogne.", click the Page Layout tab, then change the After spacing to 24 pt

Trouble

If the text jumps to the next page, finish adding the drop caps, change the zoom to Two Pages view, use your mouse to move the flag picture from page 2 back to page 1, and then complete Step 9.

8. Click in the paragraph that begins "Find the time...", click the Insert tab, click Drop Cap in the Text group, click Dropped, then repeat the process to add drop caps to each of the paragraphs shown in Figure B-10

9. Click after Dordogne, insert a Next Page section break, return to One Page view, then save the document

   Page 1 of the brochure is shown in Figure B-10.

Tour Description

Let French Country Tours take you on a journey through the back roads of rural France. This tour will appeal to you if you are longing to experience the beauty and peace of the French countryside, but you don't want to worry about arranging transportation and accommodations and you don't want to spend your precious vacation time on a crowded tour bus.

Each French Country Tour is limited to just 15 people. To keep costs down and to make your travel experience as authentic as possible, you travel on local buses and trains and stay in comfortable, family-run pensions.

Monique Deville, our experienced guide and gourmet chef, takes care of all the travel details as she escorts you through the ancient hills of the Dordogne, along the serene rivers of the Loire Valley, and into the heart and history of Provence.

After a day touring the highways and byways of the French countryside, you can relax with a glass of local wine in a charming country restaurant and then take a stroll through a quaint French village. Sleep comfortably in cozy pensions and awake each morning to the smell of freshly baked croissants.

Moments to Remember

Here are just some of the moments you will share with other nature lovers on our French Country Tour:

Find the time to linger over a three-course lunch served under the plane trees in a village square.

Relax on the beaches of Provence with a good book, a view of the azure sea, and a cold drink.

Appreciate firsthand the warm hospitality of your French hosts at family-run pensions where the beds are comfortable and the company is cheerful.

Nurture your inner gourmet with tastings of local delicacies at farms deep in the French countryside

Chart a course through French history as you wander the opulent hallways of the chateaux in the Loire Valley.

Explore the prehistoric sites and ancient cave paintings left by people who lived over 30,000 years ago in the Dordogne.

Create Page 2

Page 2 of the French Country Tours brochure is shown in Figure B-11. You need to insert a column break at the top of the page and select the three-column format. The page includes a table, text enclosed by a border, a WordArt object, and a photograph.

Steps:

1. Return the zoom to 100%, click at the top of page 2, click the Page Layout tab, click Columns in the Page Setup group, click More Columns, click Three, click the Apply to list arrow, click This point forward, then click OK

2. Click the Home tab, click Heading 1 in the Styles group, type Tour Itinerary, press [Enter], then type the first two paragraphs of text as shown in Figure B-11

3. Press [Enter] after the second paragraph, insert a table consisting of 3 columns and 17 rows, select the table, change the font size of the table text to 9 pt and the line spacing to 1.5, enter the table text shown in Figure B-11, select the table, apply the Medium Shading 1 – Accent 4 table design (lavender), then use the pointer to modify the column sizes so the table appears as shown in Figure B-11

4. Click below the table, insert a column break, type the text as shown in the box at the top of column 2 in Figure B-11, press [Enter] twice, select all the text from "Tour Cost" through "... are not included.", click Page Borders in the Page Background group, click the Borders tab, click Box, click Options, set the From text Top and Bottom settings to 4 pt, then click OK twice

5. Click below the box, press [Enter] three times, then enter the remaining text for column 2 as shown in Figure B-11, pressing [Shift][Enter] after each line to insert manual line breaks, and including your name where indicated

6. Insert a column break following your name, click the Insert tab, click the WordArt button in the Text group, click Fill, – Blue, Accent 1, Metal Bevel, Reflection (last selection in the last row), then type French Country Tours (the text will appear on three lines)

7. Select the text, click the Text Fill list arrow in the WordArt Styles group, point to Gradient, click More Gradients, click the Preset colors list arrow, select Calm Water, then click Close

8. Reduce the zoom to 75%, use your mouse to position the WordArt object as shown in Figure B-11, click away from the object, press [Enter] until the insertion point appears below the object, click the Insert tab, click the Picture button in the Illustrations group, navigate to the location where you store your Data Files, double-click PR B-3.jpg, set the height of the picture at 3.4", then center it

9. Double-click in the header, click the Link to Previous button in the Navigation group to deselect it, click the line and delete it, click Go to Footer, click the Link to Previous button, click the graphic of France and delete it, close the header and footer areas, compare page 2 to Figure B-11, make any spacing adjustments required, check the spelling, save the document and submit a copy to your instructor, then close the document

   If possible, print the brochure on two sides of the same sheet of paper. You may need to adjust the positioning of the picture and WordArt on the front panel so they appear centered when the brochure is folded.

Hint

By inserting manual line breaks, you keep all the lines single-spaced with no Before or After spacing.

Trouble

To center the picture, click the Home tab, then click the Center button in the Paragraph group.

Additional Practice

For additional practice with the skills presented in this project, complete Independent Challenge 2.

Tour Itinerary

You can choose from four tour dates: May 16 to May 31, June 15 to June 30, July 16 to July 31, or September 15 to September 30.

The tour starts and ends in Paris. The following itinerary lists only those activities in which your guide accompanies you. You will also have plenty of time to explore on your own.

Day	Overnight	Sites
Day 1	Paris	Louvre Museum
Day 2	Paris	Notre Dame
Day 3	Blois	Chambord
Day 4	Tours	Amboise
Day 5	Tours	Chinon
Day 6	Limoges	Porcelain Museum
Day 7	Montignac	Caves of Lascaux
Day 8	Montignac	Dordogne Valley
Day 9	Albi	Cathedral
Day 10	Montpellier	At Leisure
Day 11	Arles	Glanum
Day 12	Arles	Les Baux
Day 13	Toulon	At Leisure
Day 14	Toulon	Guided Hike
Day 15	Antibes	Picasso Museum
Day 16	Paris	Train to Paris

Tour Cost: $3,800 per person

Cost includes travel insurance, accommodations, transportation, museum entrance fees, and six three-course dinners. Airfare to Paris and all additional meals except breakfast are not included.

Call (203) 555-6788 to book your French Country Tour

French Country Tours, Inc.
800 Main Street, Branford, CT 06402
www.frenchcountrytours.biz
Your Name

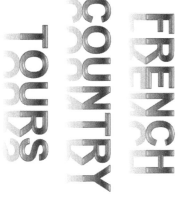

One-Page Résumé for Ian Robinson

Ian Robinson recently earned an Office Management certificate from North Shore College in Portland, Maine. Now he needs to create an attractive one-page résumé to include with his job applications. For this project, you will **Create and Enhance the Résumé**. The completed résumé is shown in Figure B-12.

Create and Enhance the Résumé

You need to modify styles, create a table, then enter and format the text.

Hint

Ian's name is enhanced with 18 pt and bold.

Hint

In the Modify Style dialog box, click Format, then click Paragraph to modify the Before and After spacing.

Steps:

1. Open a blank document in Word, change the Left and Right margins to 1.2", type and center the name and contact information as shown in Figure B-12 (press [Shift][Enter] between each line), press [Enter] following the e-mail address, click the Align Text Left button ▤ in the Paragraph group, type Objective, press [Enter], then save the résumé as PR B-Ian Robinson Resume to the location where you save the files for this book

2. Click the Change Styles button in the Styles group, click Distinctive, modify the Heading 1 style as follows: 16 pt, bold, italic, bottom border with a width of 1½ pt, the Before Spacing set to 12 pt, and the After Spacing set to 3 pt, then apply the Heading 1 style to "Objective"

3. Type the text for the objective as shown in Figure B-12, press [Enter], then insert a table consisting of 2 columns and 10 rows

4. Select the table, click the Table Tools Layout tab, click Properties in the Table group, click the Column tab, click the Next Column button, enter 1.5 as the preferred width of column 1, click the Next Column button, enter 4.8 as the preferred width of column 2, then click OK

5. Select the cells in the first row of the table, then click the Merge Cells button in the Merge group

6. Select the table, click the Table Tools Design tab, click the Bottom Border list arrow ⊞ ▾ in the Table Styles group, click No Border, click the Table Tools Layout tab, then click View Gridlines in the Table group to view the gridlines if they are not already visible

7. Using Figure B-12 as your guide, type Education in the merged row, apply the Heading 1 style, press [Tab], type 2012-2013 in column 1 of the new row, press [Tab], type North Shore College, Portland, ME in column 2, press [Enter], then type the text under "North Shore College" and format column 2 text as shown in Figure B-12

Additional Practice

For additional practice with the skills presented in this project, complete Independent Challenge 3.

8. Complete the résumé as shown in Figure B-12, adjust formatting and spacing as needed to match Figure B-12, check the spelling and grammar, type your name in the document footer, turn off the display of gridlines, save the résumé, submit a copy to your instructor, then close it

   Remember to merge the rows that contain headings (e.g., "Work Experience"), to apply the Heading 1 style to the headings, and to apply bold, italic, and bullets where required.

Ian Robinson

3400 Hammond Street

Bangor, ME 04402

Phone: (207) 555 1544

E-mail: ianrobinson@webplace.org

OBJECTIVE

An office manager in a fast-paced environment where I can apply my excellent computer skills to streamline office systems

EDUCATION

| 2012-2013 | **North Shore College**, Portland, ME |
| | *Office Management Certificate* |

- Computer skills: Microsoft Office 2010: Word, Excel, Access, PowerPoint, Project, and Publisher
- Business Communications and Organizational Behavior
- Accounting and Bookkeeping
- Project Management
- Supervisory Skills

| 2010 | **West Bangor High School** |
| | *Graduated Grade 12, with honors* |

WORK EXPERIENCE

2011-Date	**Watson Bookkeeping**, 3100 George Street, Bangor
	Office Assistant (part time)
	Responsibilities include:

- Maintain company records
- Format documents in Word 2010
- Organize company database with Access 2010

2008-2010	**Camp Atlantic**, Penobscot Bay, ME
	Camp Counselor (summers)
	Responsibilities included:

- Supervised groups of 10 campers aged 9 to 11
- Organized crafts and sports activities
- Assisted with general office duties

| 2008-2009 | **Gino's Pizza Palace**, Bangor |
| | *Pizza waiter and cashier (part time)* |

VOLUNTEER EXPERIENCE

2012-2013	**North Shore College Business Technology Department**
	Student Activities Coordinator
2010-2012	**Food Bank**, Bangor

Your Name

Independent Challenge 1

Write a multiple-page proposal that requests a significant change in a course, program, or company procedure. For example, you could request more hours of computer training as part of a college course or propose the setting up of a day care facility at your company. Alternatively, you could write a proposal to purchase new computer equipment or to establish a more equitable procedure for allocating holiday time. If you are a student, you may want to request that more classroom time be allocated to a specific topic such as the Internet or computerized accounting. If you are in the workplace, you could propose a new marketing strategy for a particular product or you could request new computer software (such as the latest Office upgrade). The possibilities are endless! Fill in the boxes provided below with information about your proposal and then follow the steps to create and format the proposal, a title page, and a table of contents page. The completed proposal should consist of approximately three pages of text (excluding the title page and table of contents).

1. Determine the subject of your proposal. To help you focus on a subject, ask yourself what changes you would like to see happen in your own workplace or at college. Write the principal request that your proposal will make in the box below:

Proposal Request: _____
_____
_____
_____

2. Determine the three or four principal sections of your proposal in addition to the introduction and conclusion. These sections will form the basis of your outline. For example, suppose you decide to write a proposal that requests changes to a college course on computer applications that you have just taken. You could organize your proposal into the following three sections:

    I. Recommended Software
    II. Laboratory Hours
    III. Learning Materials

    Under each of these headings you would describe the current situation in the course and then offer your recommendations for improvement. Write the three principal sections of your proposal in the box below:

    I. _____
    II. _____
    III. _____

3. After each of the principal subjects you listed above, add subheadings that further organize your proposal. Limit the number of additional headings to one or two for each section.

4. Start a new document in Word, create a header that includes the name of the proposal at the left margin and the current date aligned at the right margin.

5. Create a footer that includes your name at the left margin and the page number at the right margin.

6. Save the proposal as **PR B-My Proposal** to the location where you save the files for this book.

7. Select the Style Set you prefer, then modify the Heading 1 and Heading 2 styles. You choose the settings you prefer.

8. Create a new style called **Proposal Text** for the proposal text. This style is based on the Normal style and formats text with 1.15 line spacing, a left indent of .5", and 12-pt After paragraph spacing and 0-pt Before paragraph spacing.

9. Type **Introduction**, apply the Heading 1 style, press [Enter], apply the new Proposal Text style you created, then type the text for your introduction.

10. Enter headings and write the text required for your proposal. As you write, try to visualize your reader. What information does your reader need to make an informed decision concerning your request? How will your request directly affect your reader? What benefits will your reader gain by granting your request? What benefits will other people gain? All of these questions will help you to focus on communicating the information your reader needs in order to respond positively to the principal request your proposal makes.

Independent Challenge 1 (continued)

11. Insert at least one footnote in an appropriate place in your proposal. Remember that you can use a footnote to reference any books, periodicals, or Web sites you mention in your proposal or to add additional information.

12. Include a SmartArt graphic in an appropriate section of your proposal. For example, you could include a Target diagram that shows the steps toward a specific goal related to your proposal.

13. Insert a Next Page section break above page 1 of your proposal, clear formatting, enter and format **Table of Contents**, then generate a table of contents.

14. Double-click in the header area to show the Header & Footer Tools Design tab, move to the footer for the first page of the proposal (starts with "Introduction"), deselect the Link to Previous button, then start the page numbering at 1.

15. Show the footer for the table of contents page, change the page numbering style on the Table of Contents page to lowercase Roman numerals that start at "i", go to the header on the table of contents page, then click the Different First Page check box to select the box.

16. Add a Next Page section break above the table of contents page, then create an attractive cover page for your proposal. Use one of the built-in cover pages, remove any controls you don't use, and delete the blank page following the cover page if one is inserted with the cover page. At a minimum include the title of the proposal, the current date, and your name.

17. View the proposal in Two Pages view, make any spacing adjustments required, check spelling and grammar, save the document, submit a copy to your instructor, then close the document.

Independent Challenge 2

Create a two-page, six-panel brochure that advertises the products or services sold by a fictitious company of your choice. For example, you could create a brochure to advertise the programs offered by a public television station or to present the products sold by Quick Buzz, a company that sells high-energy snack foods. If you are involved in sports, your brochure could describe the sports training programs offered by a company called Fitness Forever, or if you are interested in art, your brochure could list the products sold by an art supply store called Painting Plus. For ideas, check out the pictures in the Clip Art task pane. A particular clip art picture or photograph may provide you with an idea for just the subject you require.

1. Determine the name of your company and the products or services that it sells. Think of your own interests and then create a company that reflects these interests.

2. Select two or three products or services that your brochure will highlight. For example, a brochure for a landscaping company called Greenscapes could present information about bedding plant sales, landscaping design, and garden maintenance services.

3. Allocate one of the three inside panels (1, 2, and 3) for each of the products or services you have selected. For example, if you want to create a brochure for the Painting Plus art supply store, you could devote one panel to each of the three main types of products sold: painting supplies, papers and canvases, and drawing supplies. Alternatively, you could include two sections in panels 1, 2, and 3 of a brochure that advertises the sports training programs offered by Fitness Forever. Panel 1 could describe the sports facilities, and the weekly program schedule could be spread over panels 2 and 3, similar to page one of the brochure you created in Unit B Project 2.

4. Determine the information required for page 2 of the brochure. This page includes panel 4 (usually a continuation of the information on page 1 of the brochure), panel 5 (the back panel), and panel 6 (the front panel). For example, you could include a price list on panel 4, contact information on panel 5, and just the company name and one or two enhancements on panel 6. Note that the readers of your brochure see panel 6 first, so you want to make it as attractive as possible to encourage readers to open the brochure and read the contents.

5. Before you start creating the brochure in Word, sketch the brochure layout on two blank pieces of paper. Put the sketch back-to-back and fold the brochure so that you can see how it will appear to readers. The more time you spend planning your brochure, the fewer problems you will encounter when you start creating your brochure in Word.

6. Refer to the brochure you created in Unit B Project 2. If you wish, you can adapt this brochure to advertise a tour that interests you.

Independent Challenge 2 (continued)

7. In Word, start a new document, select Landscape orientation and set the four margins to .5, create an attractive header and footer that appears only on page 1 of the brochure, then save the brochure as **PR B-My Brochure** to the location where you save the files for this book.

8. Set the number of columns for page 1, then enter the text and enhancements for panels 1, 2, and 3. Include attractively formatted section headings, and use drop caps to emphasize the first letter of several paragraphs. Alternatively, you can use drop caps to spell a word and then add appropriate text next to each letter. For ideas, refer to the "Moments to Remember" section of the brochure you created for Unit B Project 2.

9. Include on either page of your brochure a photograph from which you have removed the background and a photograph to which you have applied an artistic effect. You can superimpose one photograph over another as you did in Unit B Project 2, or you can remove the background from one photograph and apply an artistic effect to a separate photograph in another location in the document. Experiment with the many effects you can achieve working with the special picture effects such as background removal and artistic effects.

10. Insert a Next Page section break at the end of page 1, then format the columns for page 2 of the brochure. Note that page 2 must display the information in three columns of equal width because readers will usually see only one panel at a time. Remove the header and footer from page 2 of the brochure.

11. Enter the text and graphics for page 2 of the brochure.

12. View the brochure in Two Pages view, check the spelling and grammar, make any spacing adjustments required, add your name at the bottom of panel 5, save the document, submit a copy to your instructor, then close the document.

Independent Challenge 3

Create or modify your own résumé. To help you determine the information required for your résumé, fill in the boxes below and then create the résumé in Word as directed.

1. Determine your objective. What kinds of positions are you looking for that will match your qualifications and experience? How will your skills help the company that employs you? Refer to the objective you typed in Unit B Project 3, then enter your objective in the box below:

Resume Objective:
_____
_____

2. In the table below, list the components related to your educational background, starting with your most recent school or college. Note the name of the institution, the certificate or degree you received, and a selection of the courses relevant to the type of work you are seeking.

Year(s):	Institution:	Certificate/Degree:	Courses:

Independent Challenge 3 (continued)

3. In the table below, list the details related to your work experience. Use parallel structure when listing your responsibilities; that is, make sure that each element uses the same grammatical structure. For example, you can start each point with a verb, such as "maintain," "manage," or "use," and then follow it with the relevant object, for example, "maintain company records" and "use Microsoft Word 2010 to create promotional materials." Make sure you use the appropriate tense: present tense for your current position and past tense for former positions.

Year(s):	Company or Institution:	Responsibilities:

4. In the table below, describe any volunteer experience you have, awards you have received and, if you wish, your hobbies and interests:

Year(s):	Focus of Additional Information	Examples
	Volunteer Experience	
	Awards	
	Hobbies/Interests	

5. Set up your résumé in Word as follows:

   a. Type your name and format it attractively, then enter and enhance the appropriate contact information. Don't forget to include your e-mail address along with your Web site address, if you have one.

   b. Save the résumé as **PR B-My Resume** to the location where you save the files for this book.

   c. Create a new style called **Resume Heading Style** based on the Normal style with formatting you choose.

   d. Enter **Objective** formatted with the new Resume Heading Style, then type your objective.

   e. Create a table consisting of two columns, then enter the headings and text required for your résumé. Refer to Unit B Project 3 for ideas.

   f. Fit the résumé to one page, check spelling and grammar, save the document, submit a copy to your instructor, then close the document.

Independent Challenge 4

You have been asked to create a six-panel brochure to advertise a two-year intensive training program in drama and theatrical production offered by the San Diego School of Drama. The information you need to include in the brochure is provided in a Word document. The completed brochure is shown in Figure B-13. Following are the directions required to complete the brochure:

1. Open **PR B-4.docx** from the location where you store the Data Files, then save it as **PR B-San Diego School of Drama Brochure** to the location where you save the files for this book.

2. Change the orientation of the document to Landscape orientation with .5" margins.

3. Create a footer on the first page only that contains a 6 pt purple line (Purple, Accent 4, Darker 25%) formatted with the Half Reflection, 4 pt offset reflection style.

4. Format the text in three evenly spaced columns.

5. Change the Color Scheme to Composite, then modify the Heading 1 style so that it enhances text with 16 pt, Lavender, Accent 4, Darker 25%, bold, space before set to 0, and space after set to 10.

6. Apply the Heading 1 style as shown in Figure B-13.

7. Format the table in panel 3 attractively as shown in Figure B-13, then add 12-pt space before the Course Descriptions heading. (*Hint*: Be sure to deselect the Header Row check box in Table Style Options group on the Table Tools Design tab.)

8. Create a new paragraph style based on the Normal style called **Course** that applies bold and italics and changes the After spacing to 0. Apply the Course style to all the course names and the faculty names as shown in Figure B-13.

9. On panel 6, create a WordArt object using **San Diego School of Drama** and applying the style of your choice, then insert an appropriate clip art picture. (*Hint*: Search for "drama" or "theater" in the Clip Art task pane.)

10. View the brochure over two pages, adjust the formatting where required, such as adding columns breaks to match what you see in Figure B-13, check the spelling and grammar, type your name at the bottom of panel 5, save the document, submit a copy to your instructor, then close the document.

Program Objectives

The San Diego School of Drama offers students a wide range of courses in acting, directing, and stagecraft.

This two-year intensive program provides students with the training they need to develop professional-level skills in all areas of theatrical production.

Upon successful completion of the San Diego School of Drama program, graduates receive a certificate recognized as equivalent to 36 credits at the university level. Students may then enter university in the Junior year where they can fulfill the requirements for a Bachelor of Fine Arts in Drama.

Admission Procedures

Auditions for the San Diego School of Drama are held at the school in January and February of each year for admission to the school in September. Candidates may apply for an audition by calling the School Registrar at (619) 555-3321.

The following materials must be provided to the Audition Committee six months prior to the audition date:

- Resume detailing performance experience and drama-theater education
- Transcript from the last educational institution attended
- Reference letter from two or more instructors (one of which should be a drama instructor)
- Video of a recent performance (acting students only)
- Directing script of a recent production (directing students only)
- Costume, lighting, or set designs of a recent production (stagecraft students only)

The audition will consist of the following elements:

- Sight analysis of a selection from a contemporary play chosen by the audition committee.
- Thirty-minute interview

In addition, acting students must present two prepared speeches and perform one sight reading of a role chosen by the audition committee.

Program Content

The San Diego School of Drama program is divided into two 8-month terms.

Year 1:	
DRA 100	History of Theater 1
DRA 101	Dramatic Theory 1
DRA 102	Elective 1
DRA 103	Elective 2
DRA 104	Year 1 Production
Year 2:	
DRA 200	History of Theater 2
DRA 201	Dramatic Theory 2
DRA 202	Elective 3
DRA 203	Career Choices
DRA 204	Year 2 Production

Course Descriptions

DRA 100: History of Theater 1
Evolution of theater from the Greeks to the English Restoration; special emphasis on Shakespearean drama

DRA 101: Dramatic Theory 1
The fundamentals of dramatic theory, including techniques for dramatic criticism

DRA 102: Elective 1
Choice of Acting 1, Directing 1, or Stagecraft 1

DRA 103: Elective 2
Choice of Improvisation 1, Production 1, or Graphic Design 1

DRA 104: Year 1 Production
Participation in a full-length production of a play selected by the students

DRA 200: History of Theater 2
Development of the theater from the 19th century in England and the United States with special emphasis on contemporary American playwrights

DRA 201: Dramatic Theory 2
In-depth analysis of selected plays from a variety of genres and historical periods

DRA 202: Elective 3
Choice of Acting 2, Directing 2, or Stagecraft 2

DRA 203: Career Choices
Development of job search skills to obtain employment in theater or film

DRA 204: Year 2 Production
Participation in a full-length production of a musical selected by the students

Faculty

All the instructors at the San Diego School of Drama continue to work professionally in theaters throughout North America. In addition to our regular faculty, we are proud to welcome the following artists-in-residence for the 2013 program:

Tamsin Montcalm: Acting
Ms. Montcalm has won acclaim for her performances on and off Broadway. Her most recent triumph was playing Gertrude in the recent production of *Hamlet* staged by the New Shakespeare Theater.

Gerrie Levine: Directing
In 2012, Mr. Levine won the coveted Players Trophy for his production of *The Glass Menagerie* at the Covent Theater in London, England.

Ruth Vinton: Stagecraft
Ms. Vinton has won numerous awards for her costume and set designs. Recently, she designed the costumes for the Oscar-winning film adaptation of *Jane Eyre*.

SAN DIEGO SCHOOL OF DRAMA

San Diego School of Drama
180 Pacific Crest Road
San Diego, CA 92102
Phone: (619) 555-3321
www.SanDiegoDrama.com

Your Name

Visual Workshop

As part of a report you've prepared for Rosemary Designs about the development of its new e-business initiative, you need to create the Process SmartArt graphic shown in Figure B-14. Match the graphic by experimenting with inserting shapes and applying SmartArt styles. Apply the Fancy Style Set and change the color scheme to Perspective. Format the title with the Title style and the subtitle with the Subtitle style. Save the diagram as **PR B-Rosemary Designs Web Development Graphic** to the location where you save the files for this book, type your name where indicated, submit the file to your instructor, then close the document.

FIGURE B-14

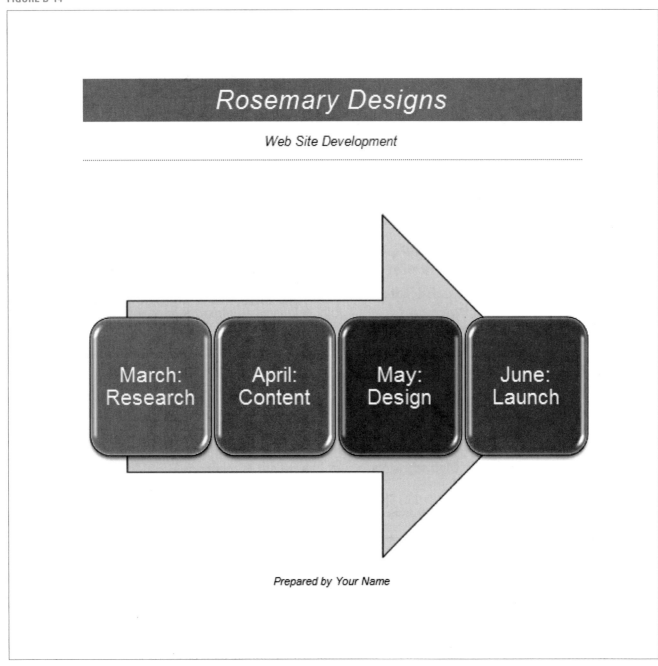

Excel Projects I

Microsoft Excel provides the tools you need to make effective planning decisions. For example, suppose you plan to take a two-week vacation to Florida and you have allocated $3,000 to cover all your trip expenses. To find out if you have allocated enough money, you can set up a simple worksheet that lists anticipated expenses for airfare, accommodations, food, and entertainment. Once you total the expenses, you may find that they exceed the budgeted amount of $3,000. Rather than cancel your trip, you can ask "What if?" questions to help you determine which expenses you can decrease. For example, you can ask "What if I stay at a less expensive hotel?" and then modify values in the worksheet to determine how much money you can save. In this unit, you create and format worksheets that include arithmetic formulas and functions and modify data by asking relevant what-if questions. You also use absolute references in formulas and create sparklines to display relationships between data.

In This Unit You Will Create the Following:

Projected Budget

Expense Report

Trip Planning Budget

Projected Budget for Camp Orca

Each year, teens from all over North America come to Camp Orca near Anacortes in Washington State to enjoy kayaking, sailing, and camping. As the assistant to the director of the camp, you need to create Camp Orca's budget for the 2013 summer season and then ask a series of what-if questions to determine realistic goals. For this project, you **Enter and Enhance Labels**, **Calculate Totals**, **Ask What-If Questions**, and **Format and Print the Budget**. The completed budget appears in Figure C-9 on page 59.

Enter and Enhance Labels

You need to enter and enhance the name and address of the organization, the worksheet title, the current date, and the first series of labels.

Steps:

1. **Start Excel to open a new blank workbook, click the** Select All button **to the left of the "A" at the upper-left corner of the worksheet frame to select the entire worksheet, click the** Font Size list arrow **in the Font group, then click** 12

2. **Click cell** A1, **type** Camp Orca, **press** [Enter], **type the remaining labels as shown in Figure C-1, then save the workbook as** PR C-Projected Budget for Camp Orca **to the location where you save the files for this book**

3. **Click cell** A1, **click the** Page Layout tab, **click** Themes **in the Themes group, click** Austin, **click the** Home tab, **click the** Font Size list arrow **in the Font group, change the font size to** 20, **then click the** Bold button **B** **in the Font group**

Hint

Although the text extends into columns B and C, you need to select only cells A4 and A5—the place where the text originated.

4. **Select cells** A4 **and** A5, **then change the font size to** 16

5. **Select cells** A1:G5, **right-click the selection, click** Format Cells, **click the** Alignment tab, **click the** Horizontal list arrow, **click** Center Across Selection, **then click** OK

6. **Select cells** A4:G5, **click the** Fill Color list arrow ⬛▾ **in the Font group, click** Green, Accent 1, Darker 25%, **click the** Font Color list arrow **A**▾ **in the Font group, click** White, Background 1, **then click the** Bold button **B**

7. **Click cell** B7, **type** May, **position the pointer over the lower-right corner to show the** Fill Handle pointer ✛, **drag** ✛ **to cell** F7, **click the** Center button ☰ **in the Alignment group, click cell** G7, **then type** Totals **and center it**

   The five months from May to September are added and centered.

8. **Point to** B **on the worksheet frame, click and drag to select** columns B through G **as shown in Figure C-2, click** Format **in the Cells group, click** Column Width, **type** 14, **then click** OK

9. **Click cell** A8, **enter the labels required for cells** A8:A23 **as shown in Figure C-3, click the** Review tab, **click the** Spelling button **in the Proofing group, correct any spelling errors, then save the workbook**

FIGURE C-1: Labels for cells A1 to A5

Font Size list arrow

Select All button; click to select the entire worksheet

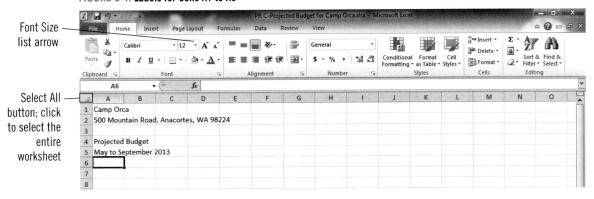

FIGURE C-2: Selecting columns

Columns B through G selected

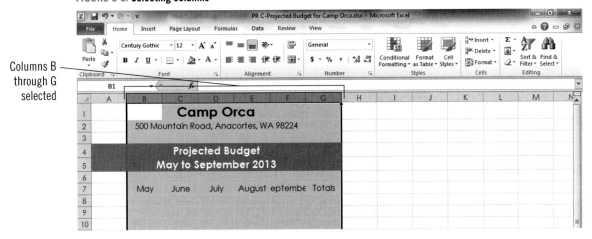

FIGURE C-3: Labels for budget categories

Labels for cells A8 to A23

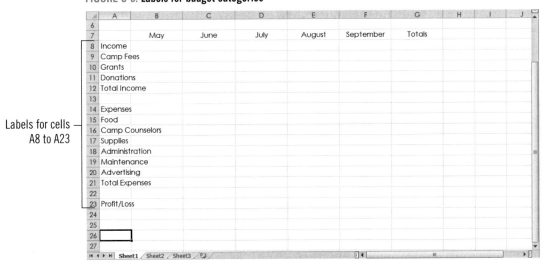

Merging cells

A merged cell is created by combining two or more cells into a single cell. The cell reference for the merged cell is the upper-left cell of the originally selected range. When you merge a range of cells containing data, only the data in the upper-left cell of the range is included in the merged cell. If you want to merge cells in a single row quickly, use the Merge and Center button in the Alignment group on the Home tab and then adjust the alignment as needed. If you want to merge cells in several consecutive rows, use the Alignment tab in the Format Cells dialog box.

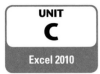
Calculate Totals

You need to enter the income and expenses that Camp Orca anticipates in 2013. Then, you need to calculate the camp fees and the total income and expenses.

Steps:

Hint

You use a new worksheet to avoid cluttering the first worksheet with data that will not be printed.

1. **Double-click the** column divider **between columns** A **and** B **on the worksheet frame to increase the width of column A to fit all the labels**

2. **Click cell** B10, **enter the values for May as shown in Figure C-4, select cells** B10:B20, **position the pointer over the lower-right corner of cell** B20, **then drag ✛ to cell** F20

3. **Double-click the** Sheet1 tab **at the bottom of the worksheet, type** Budget, **press** [Enter], **double-click the** Sheet2 tab, **type** Fees, **then press** [Enter]

   In the previous year (2012), you know that approximately 200 teens attended camp each month in three payment categories: one-week, two-week, and three-week. You use this data as the basis for your calculations for the 2013 budget.

4. **Enter and format the labels and values in the Fees worksheet as shown in Figure C-5**

   Double-click or drag the column divider to widen column A so that the labels are clearly visible, and then center and bold the labels in cells A1:D1.

5. **Click cell** D2, **type the formula** =B2*C2, **then press** [Enter]

   You should see 55000 in cell D2. If not, check your formula and try again.

6. **Click cell** D2 **again, drag ✛ down to cell** D4 **to copy the formula into the next two cells, click cell** D5, **then double-click the** Sum button Σ **in the Editing group**

   The camp fees collected should be 164000.

7. **Click the** Budget sheet tab, **click cell** B9, **type** =, **click the** Fees sheet tab, **click cell** D5, **press** [Enter], **click cell** B9 **again, then drag the pointer across to cell** F9 **to copy the formula to the other months**

   Oops! Cells C9 through F9 contain zeroes. Why? Excel changed the copied formula because it uses relative references by default. However, you need to enter a formula that designates cell D5 as an absolute value to ensure that the formula always contains a reference to cell D5, no matter where in the worksheet the formula is copied.

Trouble

You may need to press [Fn][F4] on your computer to insert the dollar signs.

8. **Click cell** B9, **select** D5 **in the formula bar, press** [F4] **to insert dollar ($) signs to make D5 an absolute reference, press** [Enter], **click cell** B9 **again, then drag ✛ to fill cells C9:F9 with the new formula**

   The exclamation mark (!) following Fees indicates that the formula comes from a worksheet other than the active worksheet.

9. **Select cells** B9:G12, **click** Σ, **select cells** B15:G21, **click** Σ **again, click cell** G22, **then save the workbook**

   The total income displayed is 857500, and the total for expenses shown is 534000, as shown in Figure C-6.

FIGURE C-4: Values for cells B10 to B20

	A	B	C	D	E	F	G	H	I
7		May	June	July	August	September	Totals		
8	Income								
9	Camp Fees								
10	Grants	5000							
11	Donations	2500							
12	Total Income								
13									
14	Expenses								
15	Food	75000							
16	Camp Counselors	22000							
17	Supplies	4000							
18	Administration	3000							
19	Maintenance	1800							
20	Advertising	1000							
21	Total Expenses								
22									
23	Profit/Loss								
24									
25									
26									

FIGURE C-5: Labels and values for Fees sheet

Labels centered and bold →

	A	B	C	D	E
1	**Category**	**Campers**	**Cost**	**Total Fees**	
2	One-Week	50	1100		
3	Two-Week	30	1900		
4	Three-Week	20	2600		
5					

FIGURE C-6: Worksheet completed with totals

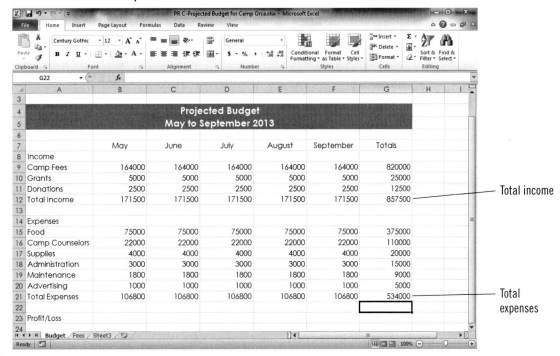

Total income

Total expenses

Understanding relative and absolute references

By default, Microsoft Excel considers all values entered in formulas as relative values. That is, Excel automatically changes all cell addresses in a formula when you copy the formula to a new location. If you do not want Excel to change the cell address of a value when you copy it, you must make the value absolute. To do this, you enter a dollar sign ($) before both the column and the row designation in the address. You can also press [F4] to insert $. For example, $C$26 tells Excel that the reference to cell C26 must not change, even if you copy the formula to a new location in the worksheet.

Ask What-If Questions

You need to calculate the profit you expect to make in each of the five months of the 2013 season, and then perform the calculations required to answer several what-if questions. You also create a sparkline to give you a quick visual review of the profit earned by the camp over the five months.

Steps:

1. **Click cell B23, enter the formula =B12-B21, press [Enter], copy the formula across to cell G23, then click cell G23 to deselect the range**

   The total projected profit for the 2013 camp season is 323500. The first what-if question is: "What if you raise the one-week course fee to $1,200?"

2. **Click the Fees sheet tab, click cell C2, type 1200, press [Enter], then click the Budget sheet tab**

   By changing the value in C2, you answer the what-if question and see that your total profit in cell G23 increases to 348500. Next, you want to know, "What if an increase in the one-week camp fee results in a 30-percent drop in the number of campers you can expect in 2013?"

3. **Click the Fees sheet tab, click cell B2, replace "50" with the formula =50-(50*.3) as shown in Figure C-7, press [Enter], then click the Budget tab**

   The formula you entered in the Fees sheet subtracts 30 percent of 50 from the number of teens expected to take a one-week course (50). The new profit in cell G23 is 258500—quite a reduction from 323500! Perhaps you shouldn't raise the one-week camp fee to $1,200 if the result is a 30-percent drop in the number of teens who enroll.

4. **Return to the Fees sheet, change the cost of the one-week camp fee in cell C2 to 1100 and the number of campers in cell B2 to 50, then return to the Budget sheet**

   The value in cell G23 is again 323500. Next, you want to know, "What if you launch an $8,000 advertising campaign in May?"

5. **Click cell B20 in the Budget sheet, type 8000, then press [Enter]**

   If you increase your advertising cost, you reduce your total profit for the summer season (cell G23) to 316500. Next, you want to know, "What if the May advertising campaign leads to a 30-percent increase in revenue from camp fees in August and September?" You edit the formula in cells E9 and F9 to reflect a potential increase.

Trouble

If a green triangle appears in cell E9, move the pointer over the triangle to read the comment. When you copy the formula, the triangle disappears.

6. **Click cell E9, click at the end of the formula in the formula bar, type *1.3, press [Enter], then copy the formula to cell F9**

   The new total profit shown in cell G23 is 414900, a significant increase. As a result of this what-if analysis, you decide to keep the advertising campaign in place. Finally, you want to know, "What if you hire a full-time executive assistant for $22,000?" You divide this amount by 5 to determine the monthly rate for the five months the camp is open and then you add the total to the values entered in the Administration row.

7. **Click cell B18, enter the formula =(22000/5)+3000, press [Enter], then copy the formula across to cell F18**

   Based on this what-if analysis, your total profit as shown in cell G23 is now 392900.

8. **Click cell A25, type Growth, press [Tab], click the Insert tab, click Line in the Sparklines group, type B23:F23, then click OK**

   You insert a Line sparkline to provide a visual representation of the growth in profits over the five months the camp is in operation.

9. **Click the Zoom Out button ⊖ in the lower-right corner of the worksheet window until 80% appears, compare your worksheet to Figure C-8, then save the workbook**

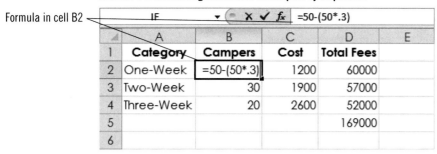

FIGURE C-7: Decreasing the number of campers by 30 percent

Formula in cell B2 —— Formula bar: =50-(50*.3)

	A	B	C	D	E
1	Category	Campers	Cost	Total Fees	
2	One-Week	=50-(50*.3)	1200	60000	
3	Two-Week	30	1900	57000	
4	Three-Week	20	2600	52000	
5				169000	
6					

FIGURE C-8: Worksheet with completed budget

August and September camp fees income reflects ad campaign

Administration expense reflects new executive assistant position

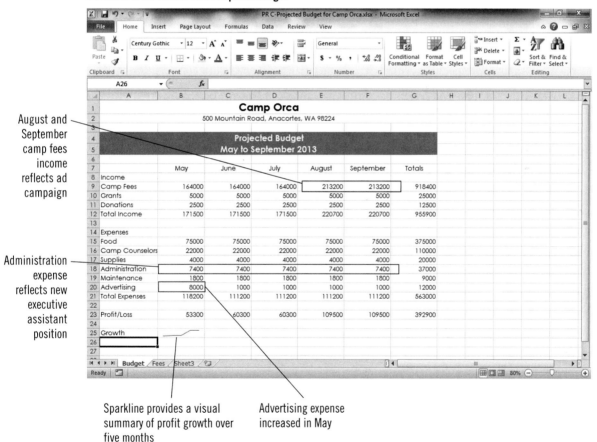

Sparkline provides a visual summary of profit growth over five months

Advertising expense increased in May

Format and Print the Budget

To make the worksheet easier to read, you need to format values using either the Accounting Number Format or the Comma Style (depending on their location in the worksheet), add border lines to selected cells, and use a variety of Page Setup features. Then you need to print a copy of your budget.

Steps:

Hint

Refer to Figure C-9 as you work.

1. Click the Home tab, **select cells** B9:G9, **click the** Accounting Number Format button $ **in the Number group, then click the** Decrease Decimal button ⬚ **in the Number group two times**

2. **Select cells** B12:G12, **press and hold** [Ctrl], **select cells** B15:G15, **cells** B21:G21, **and cells** B23:G23, **click** $, **click** ⬚ **twice, then click cell** A25 **to deselect the cells**

   You use the [Ctrl] key to select a series of nonadjacent cells.

3. **Use** [Ctrl] **to select cells** B10:G11 **and cells** B16:G20, **click the** Comma Style button ⬚ **in the Number group, click** ⬚ **twice, then click cell** A25 **to deselect the cells**

4. **Select cells** B12:G12, **click the** Bottom Border list arrow ⬚ **in the Font group, select the** Top and Double Bottom Border style, **then click outside the selected cells to see the change**

   A single line appears above cells B12 through G12 and a double line appears below them.

5. **Add the** Top and Double Bottom Border style **to cells** B21:G21, **then add the** Bottom Double Border style **to cells** B23:G23

6. **Select cells** B7:G7, **click the** Bold button **B** **in the Font group, click cell** A8, **press and hold** [Ctrl], **select cells** A12, A14, A21, A23:G23, **and** A25, **then click** **B** **to format all the cells at once**

7. **Click cell** A1, **click the** File tab, **click** Print, **click** Portrait Orientation, **then click** Landscape Orientation

8. **Click the** Page Setup link **at the bottom of the Print pane, click the** Margins tab, **click the** Horizontally **and** Vertically **check boxes to select them, click the** Header/Footer tab, **click** Custom Header, **type** Camp Orca Budget **in the left section, press** [Tab] **twice, type your name in the right section, click** OK, **then click** OK **again**

9. **Click the** Print button **if your computer is connected to a printer and if your instructor has directed you to print**

Additional Practice

For additional practice with the skills presented in this project, complete Independent Challenge 1.

10. **Click** Save, **submit the file to your instructor, then close the workbook**

    The printed budget for Camp Orca is shown in Figure C-9.

FIGURE C-9: Completed budget

Camp Orca Budget

Your Name

Camp Orca

500 Mountain Road, Anacortes, WA 98224

Projected Budget
May to September 2013

	May	June	July	August	September	Totals
Income						
Camp Fees	$ 164,000	$ 164,000	$ 164,000	$ 213,200	$ 213,200	$ 918,400
Grants	5,000	5,000	5,000	5,000	5,000	25,000
Donations	2,500	2,500	2,500	2,500	2,500	12,500
Total Income	$ 171,500	$ 171,500	$ 171,500	$ 220,700	$ 220,700	$ 955,900
Expenses						
Food	$ 75,000	$ 75,000	$ 75,000	$ 75,000	$ 75,000	$ 375,000
Camp Counselors	22,000	22,000	22,000	22,000	22,000	110,000
Supplies	4,000	4,000	4,000	4,000	4,000	20,000
Administration	7,400	7,400	7,400	7,400	7,400	37,000
Maintenance	1,800	1,800	1,800	1,800	1,800	9,000
Advertising	8,000	1,000	1,000	1,000	1,000	12,000
Total Expenses	$ 118,200	$ 111,200	$ 111,200	$ 111,200	$ 111,200	$ 563,000
Profit/Loss	**$ 53,300**	**$ 60,300**	**$ 60,300**	**$ 109,500**	**$ 109,500**	**$ 392,900**
Growth	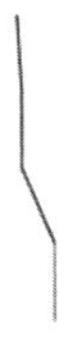					

Excel 2010

Travel Expense Report for Bright Lights Learning

The three sales representatives at Bright Lights Learning have each submitted their travel expenses for May. You need to record these expenses and prepare an expense report. For this project, you **Create the Expenses Form, Calculate Expenses**, and **Prepare the Expense Report**. The completed report is shown in Figure C-17 on page 65.

Create the Expenses Form

You need to create a form to record expenses in Sheet1 of a new workbook and then copy the form to Sheet2 and Sheet3. The completed form is shown in Figure C-12.

Steps:

Trouble

To apply the Perspective theme, click the Page Layout tab, then click Themes in the Themes group.

1. **Open a new workbook in Excel, apply the** Perspective **theme, enter and format the labels as shown in Figure C-10, then save the workbook as** PR C-Expense Statements for Bright Lights Learning **to the location where you save the files for this book**
   Be sure to follow the formatting directions in Figure C-10.

2. **Fill cell** A1 **with** Dark Purple, Accent 4, Lighter 60%, **click cell** A30, **type** Current mileage, **press [Tab], type** $.35, **then press [Enter]**
   When you enter expenses in the expense form, you will use the value in cell B30 in calculations for mileage. You use cell addresses in formulas rather than typing values in order to minimize errors and provide flexibility.

3. **Click cell** H12, **click the** Formulas **tab, click the** AutoSum **button in the Function Library group, select cells** B12:G12, **press [Enter], copy the formula to cell** H25, **click cell** B26, **click the** AutoSum **button, select cells** B12:B25, **press [Enter], then copy the formula to cell** H26
   Zeroes appear in the cells that contain formulas.

Hint

You entered a formula to add a sales representative's total expenses and then you entered a formula that subtracts the total expenses from any advance a sales representative may have received.

4. **Type the text for cells** G27:G29 **as shown in Figure C-11, click cell** H27, **enter the formula** =SUM(H12:H25), **press [Enter], click cell** H29, **enter the formula** =H27-H28, **press [Enter], select cells** B12:H29, **click the** Home **tab, then click the** Accounting Number Format **button** $ **in the Number group**

5. **Select rows 6, 7, and 8, click the** Format **button in the Cells group, click** Row Height, **type** 25, **click OK, select columns B through H, click the** Format **button in the Cells group, click** Column Width, **type** 12, **click OK, then increase the width of column A to** 18

6. **Select cells** B6:G6, **click the** Bottom Border list arrow ⊞▾ **in the Font group, click** Bottom Border, **then add a bottom border to cells** B7:G7, **cells** C8:D8, **and cells** F8:G8

7. **Select cells** A11:H26, **click the** Bottom Border list arrow ⊞▾, **click** All Borders, **then format text and add borders to cells** G27:H29 **as shown in Figure C-11**

Hint

Press the Select All button just to the left of the Column A heading.

8. **Double-click the** Sheet1 **tab, type** Wong, **press [Enter], name the Sheet2 tab** Martin, **name the Sheet3 tab** Goldberg, **go to the** Wong **sheet, select the entire worksheet, click the** Copy **button** , **show the** Martin **worksheet, then click the** Paste **button**

9. **Show the** Goldberg **worksheet, click the** Paste **button, click cell A1, reduce the zoom to 80%, compare the worksheet to Figure C-12, then save the workbook**

FIGURE C-10: Labels entered and enhanced

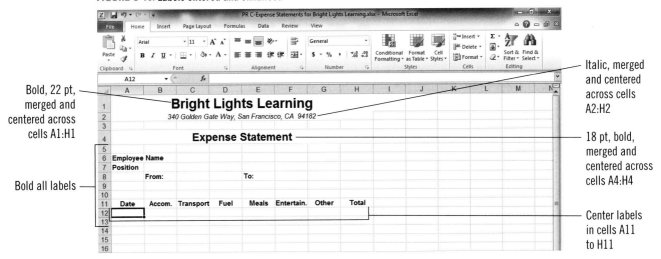

Bold, 22 pt, merged and centered across cells A1:H1

Italic, merged and centered across cells A2:H2

18 pt, bold, merged and centered across cells A4:H4

Bold all labels

Center labels in cells A11 to H11

FIGURE C-11: Formatting for cells G27 to H29

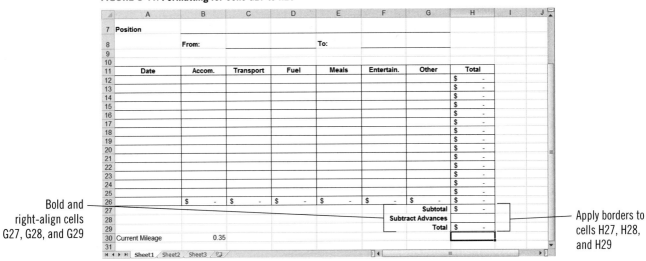

Bold and right-align cells G27, G28, and G29

Apply borders to cells H27, H28, and H29

FIGURE C-12: Formatted form

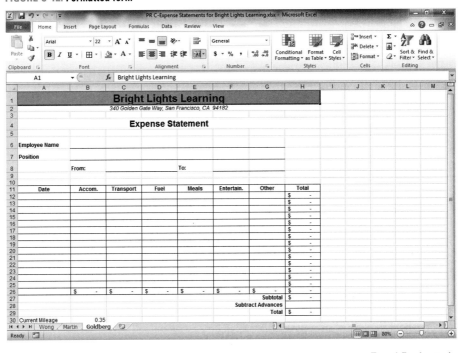

Expense Report (continued)

Calculate Expenses

The three sales representatives have provided you with receipts from the various business trips they took in May. You need to enter these expenses in the expense form.

Steps:

1. **Click the** Wong sheet tab, **click cell** B6, **type** Abigail Wong, **press** [Enter], **then type** Sales Representative

2. **Click cell** C8, **type** May 15, 2013, **press** [Tab] **three times, type** May 18, 2013, **then press** [Enter]

   When you enter the dates, Excel automatically changes the format to 15-May-13.

3. **Click cell** C8, **press and hold** [Ctrl], **click cell** F8, **click the** Number Format list arrow **in the** Number group, **click** More Number Formats, **click** Date **in the Category list, select the date format that corresponds to** March 14, 2001 **in the Type list (you'll need to scroll down), then click** OK

4. **Click cell** A12, **type** May 15, 2013, **press** [Tab], **type** =420/3, **press** [Tab], **type** =190*1.09, **press** [Tab], **type** =12*, **click cell** B30, **press** [Tab], **type** =14+45, **then press** [Enter]

   You've entered the expenses that Abigail incurred on May 15. She stayed one of three nights in Denver ($420/3), she flew to Denver ($190 + 9 percent tax), she drove 12 miles to the airport (12*B30), and she bought lunch and dinner ($14 + $45). The total in cell H12 should be $410.30.

Hint

Remember to use B30 in formulas that include the mileage reimbursement.

5. **Enter the remaining expenses for Abigail Wong according to the following information:** On May 16 and 17, Abigail stayed two more nights at the Denver Hilton Hotel at the same rate she paid on May 15. From May 16 to 17, she rented a car @ $42.50/day + $14.30/day for insurance. On May 16, she drove 25 miles; she spent $10 on breakfast, $25 on lunch, and $50 on dinner; in the evening she spent $72 on a theater ticket. On May 17, she drove 35 miles, she spent $105 on meals, and she spent $12 on other expenses. On May 18, she paid $15 for breakfast, she drove 15 miles from the airport back to her home, and she spent $13 on other expenses.

6. **Check your work against Figure C-13 to verify that the total in cell H29 is $1,132.15**

Hint

Remember to format the dates in cells C8 and F8 in the same way you formatted the date in Step 3.

7. **Click the** Martin sheet tab, **then refer to Figure C-14 to enter the information and expenses for Harry Martin**

8. **Verify that Martin's total expenses (less his advance) are $747.10 in cell H29**

9. **Click the** Goldberg tab, **refer to Figure C-14 to enter the information and expenses for Rachel Goldberg, verify that Rachel's total expenses (less her advance) are $950.45 in cell H29, then save the workbook**

FIGURE C-13: Expenses for Abigail Wong

	Date	Accom.	Transport	Fuel	Meals	Entertain.	Other	Total
6	**Employee Name**	Abigail Wong						
7	**Position**	Sales Representative						
8		**From:**	May 15, 2013		**To:**	May 18, 2013		
9								
10								
11	**Date**	**Accom.**	**Transport**	**Fuel**	**Meals**	**Entertain.**	**Other**	**Total**
12	15-May-13	$ 140.00	$ 207.10	$ 4.20	$ 59.00			$ 410.30
13	16-May-13	$ 140.00	$ 56.80	$ 8.75	$ 85.00	$ 72.00		$ 362.55
14	17-May-13	$ 140.00	$ 56.80	$ 12.25	$ 105.00		$ 12.00	$ 326.05
15	18-May-13			$ 5.25	$ 15.00		$ 13.00	$ 33.25
16								$ -
17								$ -
18								$ -
19								$ -
20								$ -
21								$ -
22								$ -
23								$ -
24								$ -
25								$ -
26		$ 420.00	$ 320.70	$ 30.45	$ 264.00	$ 72.00	$ 25.00	$ 1,132.15
27							**Subtotal**	$ 1,132.15
28							**Subtract Advances**	
29							**Total**	$ 1,132.15

Wong / Martin / Goldberg

FIGURE C-14: Expenses for Harry and Rachel

Harry Martin

Harry Martin, Sales Representative, incurred his expenses from May 8 to May 16, 2013, and has already been advanced $150. On May 8, Harry drove 40 miles, flew to Seattle for $120 + 9% tax, stayed overnight at the Pikes Place Inn for $150 + 7% tax, and spent $60 on meals. On May 9, he took a ferry ride for $50, drove 40 miles, and spent $45 on meals and $25 on other expenses. On May 15, he drove 40 miles, flew to Los Angeles for $110 + 9% tax, stayed overnight at the Pacific Heights Motel for $110 + 9% tax, and spent $75 on meals. On May 16, he drove 40 miles and spent $35 on meals and $20 on other expenses.

Rachel Goldberg

Rachel Goldberg, Sales Representative, incurred her expenses from May 5 to May 11, 2013, and has already been advanced $200. On May 5, Rachel drove 27 miles and spent $40 on meals. On May 9, Rachel flew to Chicago for $275 + 9% tax, spent $70 on meals, and drove 18 miles. On May 9 and 10, she stayed at the Lakeside Hotel for $225/night + 11% tax. On May 10, she spent $90 on meals, $50 on entertainment, and $43 on other expenses. On May 11, she drove 27 miles and spent $33 on meals.

Prepare the Expense Report

You need to consolidate data from the Wong, Martin, and Goldberg worksheets to create the May expense report. Then, you need to enhance the report attractively. The completed expense report is shown in Figure C-17.

Steps:

1. Click the Insert list arrow in the Cells group, click Insert Sheet, double-click the Sheet4 tab, type Report, press [Enter], right-click the Report tab, click Move or Copy, click (move to end), then click OK

2. Click the Wong sheet tab, copy cells A1:A4, click the Report tab, click the Paste button in the Clipboard group, click cell A4, then change "Expense Statement" to May Expense Report

3. Enter and format the labels as shown in Figure C-15

4. Click cell B7, type =, click the Wong sheet tab, click cell B26, press [Enter], click cell B7, copy the formula through cell G7, click cell B8, type =, click the Martin sheet tab, click cell B26, press [Enter], copy the formula through cell G8, then repeat the process to enter the amounts for Rachel Goldberg in cells B9:G9

5. Select cells B7:H9, click the Sum button Σ in the Editing group, click cell H10, double-click Σ, click cell H11, type =, click the Wong sheet tab, click cell H28, click in the formula bar, type +, click the Martin sheet tab, click cell H28, type +, click the Goldberg sheet tab, click cell H28, then press [Enter]

   The formula in cell H11 is =Wong!H28+Martin!H28+Goldberg!H28. The total advances are $350.00.

6. Click cell H12, calculate Reimbursement Total, verify that the Reimbursement Total is $2,829.70, click the Wong sheet tab, enter an advance of $300, then verify that the Reimbursement Total in the Report tab is now $2,529.70

7. Select cells H7:H9, click Conditional Formatting in the Styles group, point to Icon Sets, then select the 3 Traffic Lights (Unrimmed) icon set (first row, first column in the Shapes section)

Trouble

If you press [Enter] and the New Formatting Rule dialog box closes, repeat Step 8.

8. Click Conditional Formatting, point to Icon Sets, click More Rules, click Reverse Icon Order, click the top Type list arrow, click Number, type 1000 in the Value text box, press [Tab], complete the New Formatting Rule dialog box as shown in Figure C-16, click OK, then widen column H as needed to fit content

   The conditional formatting rules highlight which sales representatives have spent the most money on expenses.

9. Select rows 6 through 12, click Format in the Cells group, click Row Height, type 20, click OK, click the Page Layout tab, click Margins, click Custom Margins, set the top margin at 1.5, set the left and right margins at 0.45, then click OK

Additional Practice

For additional practice with the skills presented in this project, complete Independent Challenge 2.

10. Click the File tab, click Print, click Page Setup, click the Fit to Option button, click the Margins tab, center the worksheet horizontally, click the Header/Footer tab and include the custom header shown in Figure C-17, save the workbook, submit a copy to your instructor, then close the workbook

FIGURE C-15: **Labels for the Expense report**

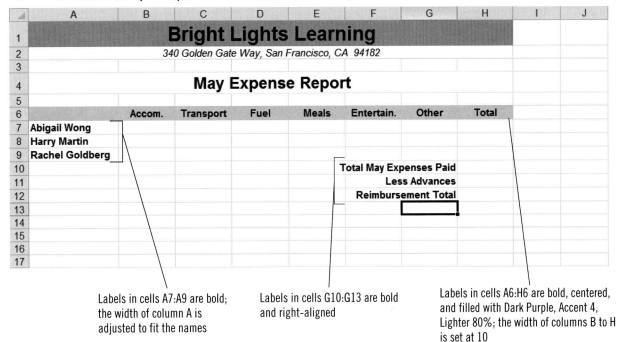

Labels in cells A7:A9 are bold; the width of column A is adjusted to fit the names

Labels in cells G10:G13 are bold and right-aligned

Labels in cells A6:H6 are bold, centered, and filled with Dark Purple, Accent 4, Lighter 80%; the width of columns B to H is set at 10

FIGURE C-16: **Setting conditional formatting rules**

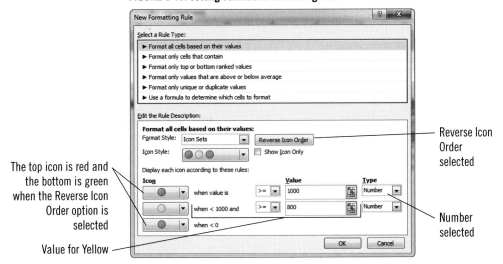

Reverse Icon Order selected

The top icon is red and the bottom is green when the Reverse Icon Order option is selected

Value for Yellow

Number selected

FIGURE C-17: **Completed May Expense Report**

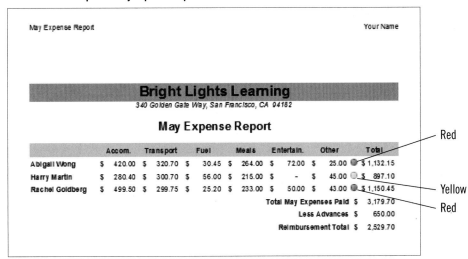

Red

Yellow

Red

Planning Budget for a European Vacation

You have a budget of $5,000 for a three-week trip to Europe with a friend. Before you buy your plane ticket, you need to determine how much you can spend on airfare, accommodations, food, entertainment, and transportation. You want to stay in first-class hotels, but your $5,000 budget may not extend that far. What kind of trip can you really afford? For this project you need to **Set Up the Budget** and then **Calculate Options**. The completed budget appears in Figure C-20 on page 69.

Set Up the Budget

Trouble

Click the More button ⬇ in the Styles group if you do not see Cell Styles.

Steps:

1. **Create a blank workbook in Excel, apply the** Pushpin theme, **type** Budget, **press** [Enter], **click cell** A1, **click the** Home tab, **click** Cell Styles **in the Styles group, click** Accent2, **then apply bold and increase the font size to** 20 pt

2. **Enter and format the labels and values as shown in Figure C-18, adjust column widths as needed to fit the content, then save the workbook as** PR C-European Trip Budget **to the location where you save the files for this book**

3. **Select cells** B3:E3, **click the** Orientation button **in the Alignment group, then click** Rotate Text Up

4. **Click cell** E4, **enter the formula** =C4*D4, **press** [Enter], **then copy the formula through cell** E9

5. **Click cell** E10, **then double-click the** Sum button Σ **in the Editing group to calculate the subtotal**

    The expense subtotal is $7,345.00.

Trouble

The required formula is =E10*.1.

6. **Click cell** E11, **calculate a 10% contingency on the subtotal, then press** [Enter]

    The value in the Contingency cell is $734.50.

7. **Enter a formula in cell** E12 **to add the** subtotal **to the** contingency **to determine your** total expenses

    Your total expenses in cell E12 are $8,079.50. You are $3,079.50 over your budget of $5,000.

8. **Change the font size to** 14 pt **for cells A3:E12, then adjust column widths as shown in Figure C-19**

9. **Save the workbook**

FIGURE C-18: **Worksheet setup**

Merge cells and center text across A1:E1

Merge cells and center text across A2:E2, then apply the Heading 1 style

Bold and center labels in row 3

Apply Accounting Number Format to values in column C

Bold and right-align labels in cells D10:D12

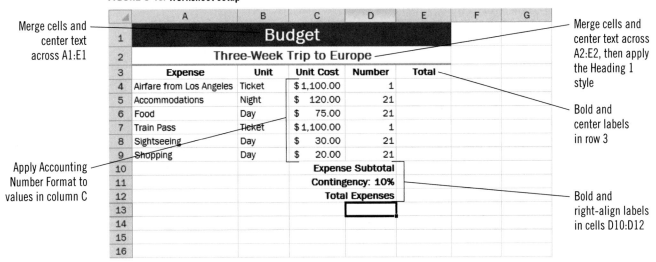

FIGURE C-19: **Worksheet with expenses**

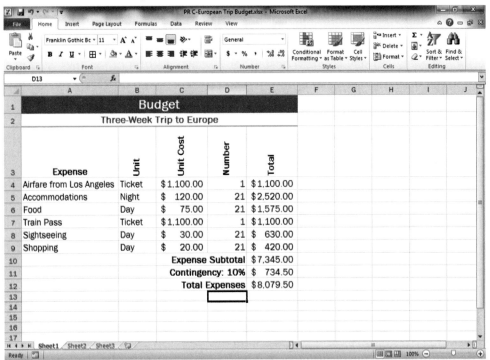

Calculate Options

You need to reduce the trip cost to $5,000. You decide to perform a variety of calculations to answer several what-if questions. As you enter data to answer the what-if questions in Steps 2 through 7, check the value in the Total Expenses cell against the total expenses value provided in the text. You will need to think carefully about the calculations required. For some steps, you need to insert new rows. The completed budget is shown in Figure C-20.

Steps:

1. Rename the Sheet1 tab Budget 1 and rename the Sheet2 tab Budget 2, return to the Budget 1 sheet, click the Select All button ◢ in the upper-left corner of the worksheet frame, click the Copy button 🗈 in the Clipboard group, click the Budget 2 tab, then click the Paste button in the Clipboard group

   Now you have two copies of the budget—your original copy and a new copy that you can modify by changing values to calculate responses to what-if questions.

2. Perform the calculation required to answer the question "What if you reduce your sightseeing allowance to $20 a day?"

   The total for sightseeing is $420, and the total expenses are now $7,848.50.

3. What if you do not buy a train pass but instead lease a car for two weeks at a cost of $800 per week and share the cost of the car lease with your friend?

   Total expenses are now $7,518.50. Remember to divide the car lease cost by two because you are sharing the expense with your friend.

4. What if you stay at youth hostels for 10 days ($30/night for one), stay in small pensions for 8 days ($80.00/night for one), and then stay in moderately priced hotels for the remaining 3 days ($200/night for two)?

   You will need to insert two new rows for the various accommodation options. See Figure C-20 for the three labels that replace the Accommodations label. You will also need to copy the formula required to calculate the Youth Hostel, Pension, and Hotel expenses. The total expenses are now $6,110.50. Getting there!

5. What if you buy and cook your own food on the days that you stay in youth hostels, thereby reducing your food costs on those days to $20 a day?

   The total expenses are now $5,505.50.

6. If you lease a car, you will split gas costs with your friend during the two weeks that you have the car. You plan to drive approximately 1,200 kilometers; the car you plan to rent gets 15 kilometers to the liter; gas costs approximately $1.50 a liter

   The total expenses are now $5,571.50.

7. What if you book a charter flight that costs $250 less than the current airfare and you further reduce your shopping allocation to $10/day?

   Total expenses are now $5,065.50. You are still $65.50 over your budget of $5,000. You decide that you can just afford to pay the shortfall, but realize that you will need to stick very carefully to your budget.

8. Add border lines to selected cells as shown in Figure C-20

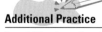

Additional Practice

For additional practice with the skills presented in this project, complete Independent Challenge 3.

9. Click Print on the File tab to view the worksheet in the Preview pane, center the worksheet horizontally (click the Margins tab in the Page Setup dialog box), add the header text shown in Figure C-20, save the workbook and submit a copy to your instructor, then close the workbook

FIGURE C-20: Completed European Trip Budget

European Trip Budget   Your Name

Budget
Three-Week Trip to Europe

Expense	Unit	Unit Cost	Number	Total
Airfare from Los Angeles	Ticket	$ 850.00	1	$ 850.00
Accommodations: Youth Hostels	Night	$ 30.00	10	$ 300.00
Accommodations: Pensions	Night	$ 80.00	8	$ 640.00
Accommodations: Hotels	Night	$ 100.00	3	$ 300.00
Food	Day	$ 75.00	11	$ 825.00
Food: Hostels	Day	$ 20.00	10	$ 200.00
Car Lease	Week	$ 400.00	2	$ 800.00
Gas	Liter	$ 1.50	40	$ 60.00
Sightseeing	Day	$ 20.00	21	$ 420.00
Shopping	Day	$ 10.00	21	$ 210.00
			Expense Subtotal	$4,605.00
			Contingency: 10%	$ 460.50
			Total Expenses	$5,065.50

Independent Challenge 1

Create your own personal budget for the next six months, then ask a series of what-if questions to help you make decisions regarding how you will spend your money. To help you get started, fill in the boxes below with the required information, then set up your budget in an Excel worksheet and perform the calculations required to answer several what-if questions. If you wish, adapt the workbook you created in Unit C Project 1 to show labels and values relevant to your own situation.

1. You need to determine the goal of your budget. Even a personal budget should be created for a specific purpose. For example, you may wish to save for a vacation or to buy a car, or you may just want to live within a set income. Identify the goal of your budget in the box below:

Budget goal: _____
_____
_____

2. Determine your sources of income. You may receive money from a paycheck, from investment dividends, or from a student loan. Each income source requires a label and a row on your budget worksheet. In the box below, list the income labels you will require:

Income labels:

1. _____
2. _____
3. _____
4. _____
5. _____

3. Determine your expenses. At the very least, you will probably need to list your rent, food, utilities, phone, and transportation costs such as car payments, gas, insurance, and bus fares. In addition, include labels for entertainment, clothing, incidentals, and savings. In the box below, list the expense labels you have identified:

Expense labels:

1. _____   6. _____
2. _____   7. _____
3. _____   8. _____
4. _____   9. _____
5. _____   10. _____

4. Create a new workbook in Excel, save it as **PR C-My Personal Budget** to the location where you save the files for this book, then set up your budget in Excel as follows:

a. Select a theme, then enter and enhance a title for your budget in cell A1.

b. Enter the current date.

c. Enter the Income and Expenses labels and appropriate subcategory labels in column A.

d. Determine the time frame of your budget (e.g., monthly or weekly), then enter the appropriate labels starting in column B.

e. Enter the values associated with your income and expenses categories. Adjust expenses according to the time of year. For example, your utilities costs will probably be less in the summer than in the winter if you live in the north, while your entertainment and travel expenses may occur mostly in the summer.

Independent Challenge 1 (continued)

    f. Calculate your total income and expenses.

    g. Add a row to the worksheet with a label and cells that calculate any surplus income remaining after expenses are subtracted.

5. Copy Sheet1 to Sheet2 of your budget, name Sheet1 **Budget** and Sheet2 **What If**, and then type at least five what-if questions at the bottom of the What If sheet. Try to formulate questions that will help you plan your finances to achieve the goal you set. Here are some sample what-if questions:

    a. What if I buy a car with payments of $250/month? (Remember to factor in costs for insurance and gas.)

    b. What if I move in March to a new apartment where my rent is $30 less than the current rent?

    c. What if I join a fitness club with monthly dues?

    d. What if I put 10 percent of my income in savings each month?

    e. What if I start taking violin lessons?

6. Make the necessary calculations and modifications to the copy of your budget to answer your five questions.

7. Format both worksheets attractively, be sure your name is on the worksheets, save the workbook and submit a copy to your instructor, then close the workbook.

Independent Challenge 2

Create expense records related to business travel for three consecutive months. Then, prepare an expense report that totals the expenses you incurred in each category for each month, shows the total for all expenses for each month, and calculates the total for the three-month expenses minus the advances.

1. Set up Sheet1 with a theme and an attractive heading including the name and address of the company as well as labels for dates and each expense category. Categories include accommodations, transportation, fuel/mileage (determine the mileage rate your company will pay; e.g., $.25/mile or $.16/kilometer), meals, entertainment, and miscellaneous (or other) expenses. If you wish, adapt the expense form you created for Unit C Project 2.

2. At the end of the column that shows the total for each row, include formulas to calculate the subtotal, the advances for each month, and the total. Be sure to include a label to identify each value.

3. Save the workbook as **PR C-My Travel Expenses** to the location where you save the files for this book.

4. Copy your expense form to the next two sheets, and then name the sheet tabs with the months you traveled (e.g., March, April, May).

5. Enter realistic expenses for each month. For example, a flight from New York to Los Angeles should cost more than a flight from Montreal to Toronto. Assume that each time you fly, you drive your own car to the airport from your home town. Include the mileage calculation. Also include taxes where applicable.

6. In a new worksheet, set up an attractive expense report for the three months. Include the name of the company you work for.

7. Enter the formulas required to calculate your total expenses for each category in each of the three months, as well as the totals for the months. Calculate the total expenses paid, then calculate the reimbursement total for the three months by subtracting any advances you were given.

8. Use conditional formatting to highlight totals that are below or above a limit you determine. Modify the formatting rules applied by the conditional formatting you selected.

9. Format the worksheet containing the expense report attractively, include your name in the header, save the workbook and submit a copy to your instructor, then close the workbook.

Independent Challenge 3

Create a planning budget to help you determine your expenses for a vacation of your choice. Adapt the budget you created for Unit C Project 3 if you wish. The following tasks will help you get started.

1. Before you create the worksheet in Excel, answer the questions listed below:
   a. Where do you plan to go for your vacation?
   b. What is your proposed budget?
   c. How long is your planned vacation?
   d. What kind of activities do you plan to do on your vacation (e.g., sightseeing, guided tours, horseback riding, skiing)?
2. Set up your worksheet with labels for transportation costs (airfare, car rental, train fares, etc.), accommodations, food, sightseeing, shopping, and any other expense categories appropriate to the kind of vacation you plan to take. Save your vacation planning budget as **PR C-My Vacation Budget** to the location where you save the files for this book.
3. Apply a style to at least one heading in the worksheet (for example, you could apply the Heading 1 style to the location of the trip).
4. Include a contingency amount for emergency expenses that is 10 to 15 percent of your total expenses.
5. Try to make your budget as realistic as possible. You can choose to base your budget on a vacation you have already taken or on a vacation you hope to take.
6. Format the worksheet attractively, be sure your name is on the worksheet, save the workbook and submit a copy to your instructor, then close the workbook.

Independent Challenge 4

You're planning a trip to Quebec and Ontario in Canada in May and decide to include your vacation budget as part of your personal budget for the six months from January to June. To make the budget as dynamic as possible, you include formulas that reference a Web query that contains a table of currency exchange rates copied from a currency conversion Web site. You can then refresh the worksheet data periodically to see how the latest exchange rates are affecting your six-month budget.

1. Create the worksheet shown in Figure C-21, change the name of the Sheet1 tab to **Budget**, then save the workbook as **PR C-Canada Trip Budget** to the location where you save the files for this book.
2. Use AutoFill to fill in the months from February through June, then center the labels.
3. Copy the values for January through June.
4. Add a column labeled **Totals**, then calculate the row totals. Verify that all the values are formatted in the Comma Style.
5. Calculate the monthly and total income (row 5), the monthly and total expenses (row 18), and the total savings (row 20). Your total income is $22,860.00, your total expenses are $11,310.00, and your total savings are $11,550.00.
6. Click the Data tab, click the From Web button in the Get External Data group, click No if a warning message appears, type the Web site address **www.x-rates.com** in the Address text box, then click Go. The x-rates.com Currency Conversion Web site opens in the New Web Query dialog box.

FIGURE C-21

	A	B	C
1		January	
2	Income		
3	Pay Check	3,250.00	
4	Investment Dividends	560.00	
5	Total Income		
6			
7	Expenses		
8	Rent	800.00	
9	Food	400.00	
10	Phone	40.00	
11	Utilities	90.00	
12	Car Payment	275.00	
13	Gas	80.00	
14	Car Insurance	100.00	
15	Entertainment	100.00	
16	Vacation Hotels		
17	Vacation Food		
18	Total Expenses		
19			
20	Total Savings		
21			
22			

Independent Challenge 4 (continued)

7. Scroll down the dialog box, then click the table select arrow next to the table shown in Figure C-22. Note that the table select arrow button turns green, and a check mark appears when you click it to indicate that the entire table has been selected.

FIGURE C-22

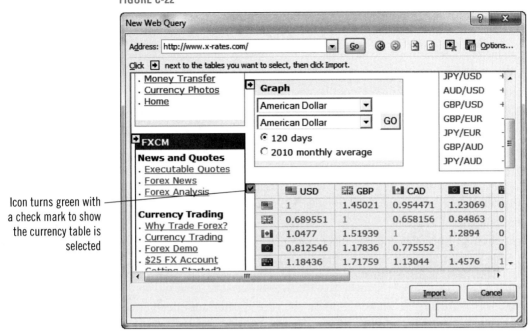

Icon turns green with a check mark to show the currency table is selected

8. Click the Import button at the bottom of the dialog box, click the New worksheet option button, then click OK. The formatted data appears in a new worksheet. Note that image files are not included.

9. Rename the new worksheet **Currency**.

10. Return to the Budget worksheet, then click cell F16. You will be staying at hotels in Montreal and Toronto for eight days. You've checked out hotels on the Internet and decided that 200 Canadian dollars (CAD) per night is a reasonable amount to pay. You'd like to know what this amount converts to in U.S. dollars so you can include the hotel cost in your worksheet. You can also choose to convert the amount to euros or to another currency. However, the following steps relate to U.S. dollars.

11. In cell F16 of the Budget worksheet, enter the formula =8*200* and leave the insertion point in the cell. Switch to the Currency worksheet, click cell D2 (which contains the exchange rate for Canadian dollars to U.S. dollars), then press [Enter] to add the value from cell D2 to your formula in the Budget worksheet. The value entered in cell F16 represents the cost of hotels for eight days in U.S. dollars, presuming you spend 200 CAD per night.

12. Click cell F17, enter the formula =8*100* and leave the insertion point in the cell. Switch to the Currency worksheet, click cell D2, and then press [Enter]. The value in cell F17 represents the cost of food for eight days in U.S. dollars, presuming you spend 100 CAD per day. Note the total savings entered in cell H20.

13. Format the worksheet attractively with border lines in the appropriate areas, include **Canada Trip Budget** and your name in the header, format the worksheet in landscape orientation with the data centered horizontally and vertically, then save and close the workbook.

14. On another day, open the workbook, click Refresh All in the Connections group on the Data tab, then check if the total savings in cell H20 has changed to reflect the updated exchange rate. On the x-rates.com Web site, the exchange rates are updated every 24 hours.

Visual Workshop

Create the six-month budget shown in Figure C-23 for Home on the Web, a company that creates Web sites for small businesses. Set up the workbook in Landscape orientation, apply the Apothecary theme, fill cell A1 with Gold, Accent 5, Lighter 60%, enter the required formulas to calculate total revenue, expenses, and profit (the results will be 0s until you add values), then apply the Comma Style to all cells that contain or will contain values. Save the budget as **PR C-Home on the Web Budget** to the location where you save the files for this book, then answer the following four questions:

1. In July, you estimate that 10 new businesses will contract Home on the Web to create a Web site at an average cost of $2,200 per Web site. You project that the contract revenue generated in July will increase by 5 percent in August, 10 percent in September, then 20 percent for each of the remaining months. Calculate all increases based on July revenue. What is the total revenue for Web site design contracts in cell H6? Enter the cell address H6 in cell B20.
2. In July, you estimate that 15 businesses will contract Home on the Web to program their Web sites with animations and other interactive elements at an average cost of $1,500 per Web site. Each month through December, the revenue increases by 10 percent over the previous month. (*Hint:* Enter =B7*1.1 in cell C7, then copy the formula through cell G7.) What is the total revenue in cell H8? Enter the cell address of the value in cell B21.
3. Make the salaries expense for both November and December $35,000. What is the total salaries expense in cell H11? Enter the cell address of the value in cell B22.
4. Make the equipment leases for November and December four times the current equipment leases for October. What is the total projected profit in cell H18? Enter the cell address of the value in cell B23.

Format the values in rows 6, 8, 11, 16, 18, and cells B20:B23 with the Accounting style, then add border lines where appropriate. Save the workbook, preview it, make sure the worksheet fits on one page in landscape orientation and is centered horizontally and vertically, add your name to the header, save the workbook and submit a copy to your instructor, then close the workbook and Excel.

FIGURE C-23

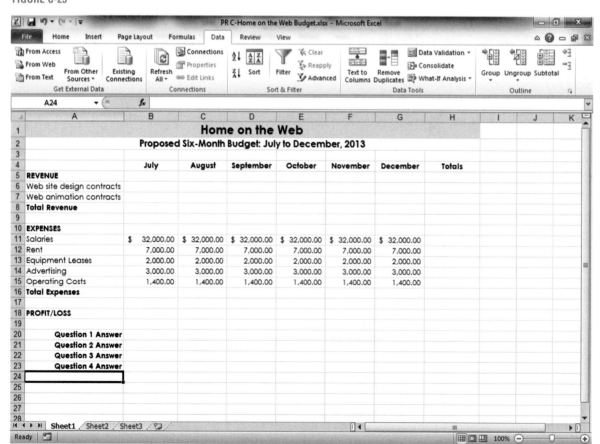

Excel Projects II

Files You Will Need:

PR D-1.xlsx

PR D-2.xlsx

With Microsoft Excel, you can analyze numerical data and identify patterns and trends. For example, you can use the powerful Scenario function to make predictions based on a current set of data. You can then use these predictions to plan business and sales ventures, analyze current sales patterns, and create sales forecasts. You can also create lookup tables to create complex "IF" formulas that enter values in a cell based on specified criteria. For example, you can create a formula to enter the grade a student earns IF the student earns a specific number of points (such as an "A" for 85 points). You can display the results of an analysis visually in the form of pivot tables, slicers, and charts. In this unit, you will create scenarios to forecast sales, create a lookup table and use the Lookup function, build a pie chart from a PivotTable, and use a PivotTable and slicers to analyze sales.

In This Unit You Will Create the Following:

Sales Forecast

Course Grades Analysis

Sales Report

Sales Forecast for Central Green Consulting

You own Central Green Consulting, a small consulting firm that advises businesses on how to develop environmentally friendly work environments through the use of recycling programs, walk-to-work initiatives, and so on. The firm also sells recycled paper products. Business is good, so you are thinking about moving from your home office to a commercial office space and then hiring an executive assistant and a sales representative. To help you decide what course of action you should take, you use scenarios in Excel to help you perform different what-if analyses. For this project, you **Set up the Workbook**, **Create Current Scenarios**, **Create Best and Worst Case Scenarios**, and **Format the Scenarios**. The completed reports showing the Best Case and Worst Case scenarios are shown in Figures D-8 and D-9 on page 83.

Set Up the Workbook

You need to enter the labels and values for the six-month revenue and expenses statement for Central Green Consulting, and then calculate the total revenue, expenses, and net income.

Hint

The result of each calculation appears in parentheses in the text.

Steps:

1. Start Excel, enter data and format the worksheet as shown in Figure D-1, then save the workbook as PR D-Central Green Consulting Sales Forecasts to the location where you save the files for this book

2. Click cell B15, then enter a formula that calculates 60 percent of cell B6 (1800)

   The formula in cell B15 calculates the cost of goods sold as 60 percent of the total revenue. Note that returns and the cost of goods sold are calculated as a percentage of the total monthly revenue (usually 3 percent for returns and 60 to 70 percent for cost of goods sold).

3. Fill cells C15:G15 with the formula in cell B15

4. Select cells B6:H8, then click the Sum button Σ in the Editing group (52000 in cell H8)

5. Select cells B11:H16, click Σ, then click cell B18 (48600 in cell H16)

6. In cell B18, enter a formula that subtracts the total expenses in cell B16 from the total revenue in cell B8 (1300)

7. Fill cells C18:H18 with the formula in cell B18

   The total net profit for January to June 2013 is 3400 in cell H18.

Hint

You can use the Ctrl key to select nonadjacent rows to speed up the process.

8. Select cells B6:H6, click the Accounting Number Format button $ in the Number group, select cells B7:H7, then click the Comma Style button ' in the Number group

9. Refer to Figure D-2 to format the remaining rows with the appropriate formats, then save the workbook

Set the width of column A to 21   24 pt and bold   14 pt and bold   Set the widths of columns B:H to 12

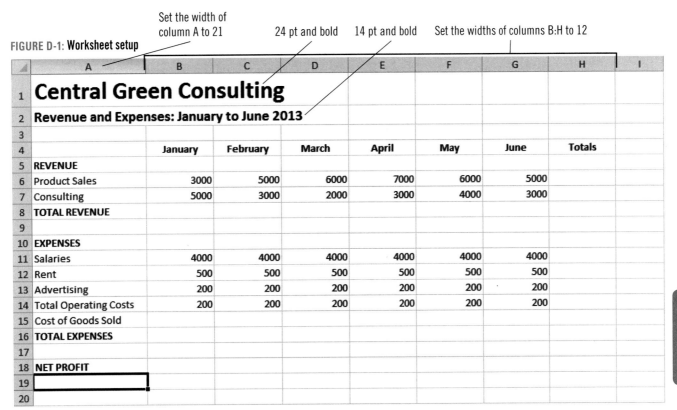

	A	B	C	D	E	F	G	H	I
1	**Central Green Consulting**								
2	**Revenue and Expenses: January to June 2013**								
3									
4		January	February	March	April	May	June	Totals	
5	REVENUE								
6	Product Sales	3000	5000	6000	7000	6000	5000		
7	Consulting	5000	3000	2000	3000	4000	3000		
8	TOTAL REVENUE								
9									
10	EXPENSES								
11	Salaries	4000	4000	4000	4000	4000	4000		
12	Rent	500	500	500	500	500	500		
13	Advertising	200	200	200	200	200	200		
14	Total Operating Costs	200	200	200	200	200	200		
15	Cost of Goods Sold								
16	TOTAL EXPENSES								
17									
18	NET PROFIT								
19									
20									

Excel 2010

FIGURE D-2: Formatted worksheet with totals calculated

	A	B	C	D	E	F	G	H	I	J
1	**Central Green Consulting**									
2	**Revenue and Expenses: January to June 2013**									
3										
4		January	February	March	April	May	June	Totals		
5	REVENUE									
6	Product Sales	$ 3,000.00	$ 5,000.00	$ 6,000.00	$ 7,000.00	$ 6,000.00	$ 5,000.00	$ 32,000.00		
7	Consulting	5,000.00	3,000.00	2,000.00	3,000.00	4,000.00	3,000.00	20,000.00		
8	TOTAL REVENUE	$ 8,000.00	$ 8,000.00	$ 8,000.00	$ 10,000.00	$ 10,000.00	$ 8,000.00	$ 52,000.00		
9										
10	EXPENSES									
11	Salaries	$ 4,000.00	$ 4,000.00	$ 4,000.00	$ 4,000.00	$ 4,000.00	$ 4,000.00	$ 24,000.00		
12	Rent	500.00	500.00	500.00	500.00	500.00	500.00	3,000.00		
13	Advertising	200.00	200.00	200.00	200.00	200.00	200.00	1,200.00		
14	Total Operating Costs	200.00	200.00	200.00	200.00	200.00	200.00	1,200.00		
15	Cost of Goods Sold	1,800.00	3,000.00	3,600.00	4,200.00	3,600.00	3,000.00	19,200.00		
16	TOTAL EXPENSES	$ 6,700.00	$ 7,900.00	$ 8,500.00	$ 9,100.00	$ 8,500.00	$ 7,900.00	$ 48,600.00		
17										
18	NET PROFIT	$ 1,300.00	$ 100.00	$ (500.00)	$ 900.00	$ 1,500.00	$ 100.00	$ 3,400.00		
19										
20										
21										
22										
23										
24										

Sheet1 / Sheet2 / Sheet3

Sales Forecast (continued)

Create Current Scenarios

You create scenarios so you can engage in what-if analysis, which is the process of changing values in selected cells so you can see how the changes affect formula results, such as total revenue, total expenses, and total profit. A scenario is a set of values that you name and save. You can apply various combinations of scenarios to see how formula results are affected. In this project, you will create three sets of scenarios: Current, Best Case, and Worst Case. First, you highlight the cells that contain the values you plan to change when you create the three scenario sets. Although highlighting the cells is not a required step when you create scenarios, you do so in order to quickly and easily identify which rows contain the data that will change when you show different scenarios. Second, you use the Scenario Manager to create scenarios that represent the current values for product sales, rent, salaries, and operating costs.

Steps:

1. **Select cells** B6:G6, **press and hold** [Ctrl], **select cells** B11:G12, **then select cells** B14:G14
   You have selected the cells containing the values you will include in the set of Current scenarios.

2. **Click the** Fill Color list arrow ⬇ **in the Font group, click** Yellow **in the Standard Colors area, then click cell** B6
   The cells for Product Sales, Salaries, Rent, and Operating Costs are filled with color, as shown in Figure D-3, so you can easily see which values change each time you show a new scenario.

3. **Select cells** B6:G6, **click the** Data tab, **click the** What-If Analysis button **in the Data Tools group, click** Scenario Manager, **then click** Add
   In the Add Scenario dialog box, you enter a name for the scenario and designate which cells will change when you add new data.

4. **Type** Current Sales, **then click** OK **to accept** B6:G6 **as the cells to change**
   In the Scenario Values dialog box, you can keep values currently entered or you can enter new values.

5. **Click** OK **again to accept the values currently entered in cells** B6:G6
   The Current Sales scenario consists of the values currently entered in cells B6:G6.

6. **Click** Add, **type** Current Salaries, **click the** Collapse Dialog Box button ⬚ **at the far right of the Changing cells text box, then select cells** B11:G11 **in the worksheet**
   These cells contain the values for the current salaries you are paying each month from January to June.

7. **Click the** Expand Dialog Box button ⬚, **click** OK, **then click** OK **to accept the values currently entered in cells** B11:G11

8. **Add a scenario called** Current Rent **based on cells** B12:G12, **then add a scenario called** Current Operating Costs **based on cells** B14:G14

9. **Compare the Scenario Manager dialog box to Figure D-4**

10. **Click** Close **to exit the Scenario Manager dialog box, then save the workbook**

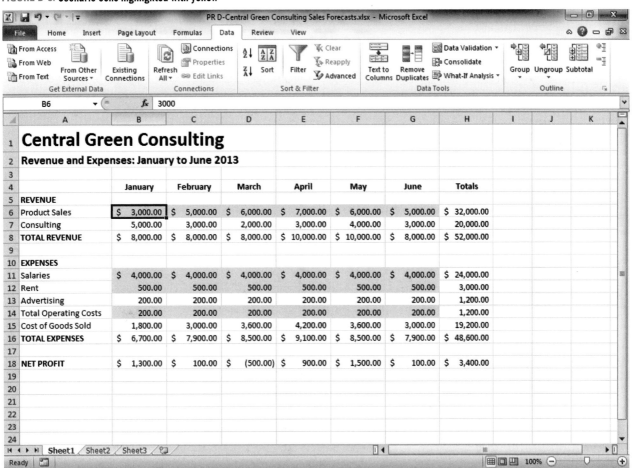

FIGURE D-4: Scenario Manager dialog box

Create Best and Worst Case Scenarios

You need to change the values in the worksheet to reflect your best case projections, and then you need to change the values again to reflect your worst case projections.

Steps:

Trouble

Figure D-5 shows only the values required for C6:G6. The value for B6 is not shown because the dialog box shows only five items at once.

Trouble

If the correct value does not appear in cell H18, find the yellow shaded cell(s) that does not contain the correct value(s) based on the information entered in the preceding steps, then edit the value for that cell in the Scenario Manager dialog box.

1. Click the What-If Analysis button in the Data Tools group, click Scenario Manager, click Current Sales, click Add, type Best Case Sales, then click OK

2. Type 20000, press [Tab], enter the values for cells C6:G6 of Best Case Sales as shown in Figure D-5, then click OK

   These values represent the sales that you hope to generate if you move to a commercial space and hire additional help.

3. Click Current Salaries, click Add, type Best Case Salaries, click OK, type 9000, press [Tab], enter 9000 for cells C11:G11, then click OK

   You estimate the monthly salaries expense will more than double when you hire a new sales representative and an assistant.

4. Click Current Rent, add a scenario called Best Case Rent that changes all the values in cells B12:G12 to 1500, click Current Operating Costs, then add a scenario called Best Case Operating Costs that changes all the values in cells B14:G14 to 800

   You hope to obtain office space for $1,500 a month and generate operating costs of no more than $800 a month.

5. Click Best Case Sales, click Show, click Best Case Salaries, click Show, show the remaining Best Case scenarios, then click Close

   The value in cell H18 is $7,800. This value represents your net profit after six months if you move to a commercial space and hire new personnel to help you sell Central Green Consulting products. But what happens if you move and things don't go as planned?

6. Click the What-If Analysis button in the Data Tools group, click Scenario Manager, click Current Sales, click Add, type Worst Case Sales, click OK, type 15000, press [Tab], enter the values for cells C6:G6 of Worst Case Sales as shown in Figure D-6, then click OK

7. Add the Worst Case Salaries, Worst Case Rent, and Worst Case Operating Costs scenarios based on the values displayed below:

Worst Case Salaries	10000
Worst Case Rent	2000
Worst Case Operating Costs	900

8. Show all the Worst Case scenarios, then close the Scenario Manager dialog box

   The total net income displayed in cell H18 is now $(18,600.00) as shown in Figure D-7. The Worst Case scenarios are based on your projection of lower sales paired with higher expenses for salaries, rent, and operating costs.

9. Click What-If Analysis in the Data Tools group, click Scenario Manager, click Current Sales, click Show, show all the remaining Current scenarios, click Close, then fill cell H18 with yellow and apply bold

   You should see $3,400.00 in cell H18.

FIGURE D-5: Best Case Sales values

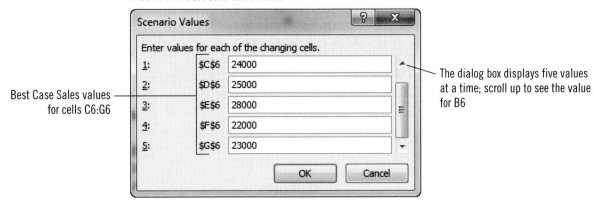

Best Case Sales values
for cells C6:G6

The dialog box displays five values
at a time; scroll up to see the value
for B6

FIGURE D-6: Worst Case Sales values

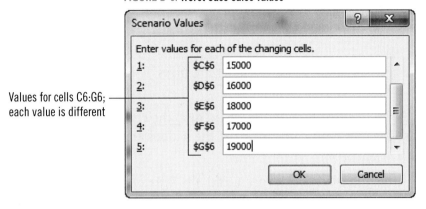

Values for cells C6:G6;
each value is different

FIGURE D-7: Worksheet with Worst Case Scenarios shown

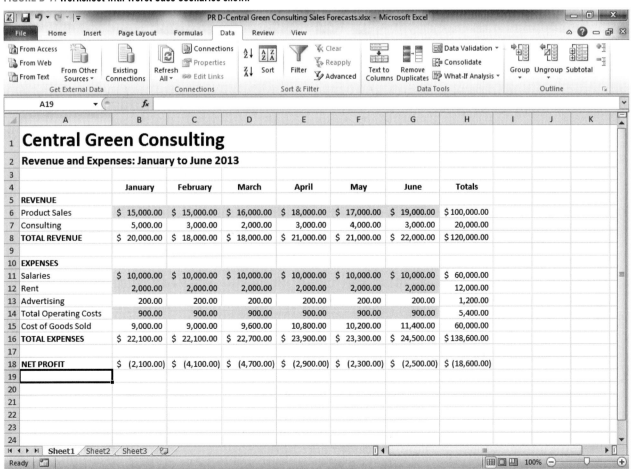

Central Green Consulting

Revenue and Expenses: January to June 2013

	January	February	March	April	May	June	Totals
REVENUE							
Product Sales	$ 15,000.00	$ 15,000.00	$ 16,000.00	$ 18,000.00	$ 17,000.00	$ 19,000.00	$ 100,000.00
Consulting	5,000.00	3,000.00	2,000.00	3,000.00	4,000.00	3,000.00	20,000.00
TOTAL REVENUE	$ 20,000.00	$ 18,000.00	$ 18,000.00	$ 21,000.00	$ 21,000.00	$ 22,000.00	$ 120,000.00
EXPENSES							
Salaries	$ 10,000.00	$ 10,000.00	$ 10,000.00	$ 10,000.00	$ 10,000.00	$ 10,000.00	$ 60,000.00
Rent	2,000.00	2,000.00	2,000.00	2,000.00	2,000.00	2,000.00	12,000.00
Advertising	200.00	200.00	200.00	200.00	200.00	200.00	1,200.00
Total Operating Costs	900.00	900.00	900.00	900.00	900.00	900.00	5,400.00
Cost of Goods Sold	9,000.00	9,000.00	9,600.00	10,800.00	10,200.00	11,400.00	60,000.00
TOTAL EXPENSES	$ 22,100.00	$ 22,100.00	$ 22,700.00	$ 23,900.00	$ 23,300.00	$ 24,500.00	$ 138,600.00
NET PROFIT	$ (2,100.00)	$ (4,100.00)	$ (4,700.00)	$ (2,900.00)	$ (2,300.00)	$ (2,500.00)	$ (18,600.00)

Format the Scenarios

To highlight the differences among the three sets of scenarios, you create a column chart for each set of scenarios that shows the net profit generated from January to June, then print each set of scenarios. Figure D-8 shows a printout of the worksheet with the Best Case scenarios displayed and Figure D-9 shows a printout of the worksheet with the Worst Case scenarios displayed.

Steps:

1. Select cells B4:G4, press and hold [Ctrl], select cells B18:G18, click the Insert tab, click the Column button in the Charts group, click the far-left selection in the top row to insert a Clustered Column chart, click the More button ⊡ in the Chart Styles group, then select Style 26 (second column, fourth row)

2. Click the Chart Tools Layout tab, click the Chart Title button in the Labels group, click Above Chart, type Current Monthly Net Profit, press [Enter], click the Legend button in the Labels group, then click None

3. Click the gray frame that encloses the chart, drag the chart down to row 23, then resize the chart so the upper-left corner starts at the midpoint of cell A23 and the lower-right corner ends in cell G43

Hint

To use a keystroke command to show a scenario, click the scenario in the Scenario Manager, then press [Alt][S].

4. Click away from the chart to deselect it, click the Data tab, open the Scenario Manager dialog box, show all the Best Case scenarios, close the Scenario Manager dialog box, then verify that $3,000 appears as the top value of the value axis (y-axis)

5. Show all the Current scenarios again, close the dialog box, right-click the value axis (contains the dollar amounts), click Format Axis, verify that Axis Options is active, click the Maximum Fixed option button, select the contents of the Maximum text box, type 3000, then click Close

    You change the top value of the value axis to match the top value ($3,000) of the value axis when the Best Case scenarios are active to ensure that each chart provides a meaningful comparison of the scenarios.

6. Click away from the chart to deselect it, click the File tab, click Print, click Page Setup, click the Fit to option button to fit the worksheet on one page, click the Margins tab, click the Horizontally check box to select it, click the Header/Footer tab, click Custom Header, type Current Scenarios at the left and your name at the right, click OK twice, then click Print

7. Click the Data tab, open the Scenario Manager dialog box, show all the Best Case scenarios, close the dialog box, then verify that $7,800 appears in cell H18

8. Click the chart title, click in the formula bar, type Best Case Forecast, click outside the chart, click the Page Layout tab, click the Print Titles button in the Page Setup group, click the Header/Footer tab, change the custom header text to Best Case Scenarios, then print a copy

    Figure D-8 shows a printout of the worksheet with the Best Case scenarios active.

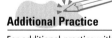

Additional Practice

For additional practice with the skills presented in this project, complete Independent Challenge 1.

9. Click the Data tab, open the Scenario Manager dialog box, show all the Worst Case scenarios, verify that $(18,600.00) appears in cell H18, change the chart title to Worst Case Forecast, change the custom header to show Worst Case Scenarios, print a copy, then save and close the workbook

    Figure D-9 shows a printout of the worksheet with the Worst Case scenarios active. Now that you have created scenarios, you can mix and match them to try out new predictions. The net profit in cell H18 changes with each combination.

Best Case Scenarios   Your Name

Central Green Consulting
Revenue and Expenses: January to June 2013

	January	February	March	April	May	June	Totals
REVENUE							
Product Sales	$ 20,000.00	$ 24,000.00	$ 25,000.00	$ 28,000.00	$ 22,000.00	$ 23,000.00	$ 142,000.00
Consulting	5,000.00	3,000.00	2,000.00	3,000.00	4,000.00	3,000.00	20,000.00
TOTAL REVENUE	$ 25,000.00	$ 27,000.00	$ 27,000.00	$ 31,000.00	$ 26,000.00	$ 26,000.00	$ 162,000.00
EXPENSES							
Salaries	$ 9,000.00	$ 9,000.00	$ 9,000.00	$ 9,000.00	$ 9,000.00	$ 9,000.00	$ 54,000.00
Rent	1,500.00	1,500.00	1,500.00	1,500.00	1,500.00	1,500.00	9,000.00
Advertising	200.00	200.00	200.00	200.00	200.00	200.00	1,200.00
Total Operating Costs	800.00	800.00	800.00	800.00	800.00	800.00	4,800.00
Cost of Goods Sold	12,000.00	14,400.00	15,000.00	16,800.00	13,200.00	13,800.00	85,200.00
TOTAL EXPENSES	$ 23,500.00	$ 25,900.00	$ 26,500.00	$ 28,300.00	$ 24,700.00	$ 25,300.00	$ 154,200.00
NET PROFIT	$ 1,500.00	$ 1,100.00	$ 500.00	$ 2,700.00	$ 1,300.00	$ 700.00	**$ 7,800.00**

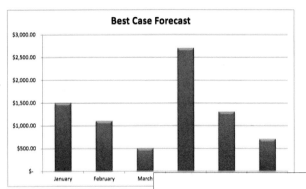

Worst Case Scenarios   Your Name

Central Green Consulting
Revenue and Expenses: January to June 2013

	January	February	March	April	May	June	Totals
REVENUE							
Product Sales	$ 15,000.00	$ 15,000.00	$ 16,000.00	$ 18,000.00	$ 17,000.00	$ 19,000.00	$ 100,000.00
Consulting	5,000.00	3,000.00	2,000.00	3,000.00	4,000.00	3,000.00	20,000.00
TOTAL REVENUE	$ 20,000.00	$ 18,000.00	$ 18,000.00	$ 21,000.00	$ 21,000.00	$ 22,000.00	$ 120,000.00
EXPENSES							
Salaries	$ 10,000.00	$ 10,000.00	$ 10,000.00	$ 10,000.00	$ 10,000.00	$ 10,000.00	$ 60,000.00
Rent	2,000.00	2,000.00	2,000.00	2,000.00	2,000.00	2,000.00	12,000.00
Advertising	200.00	200.00	200.00	200.00	200.00	200.00	1,200.00
Total Operating Costs	900.00	900.00	900.00	900.00	900.00	900.00	5,400.00
Cost of Goods Sold	9,000.00	9,000.00	9,600.00	10,800.00	10,200.00	11,400.00	60,000.00
TOTAL EXPENSES	$ 22,100.00	$ 22,100.00	$ 22,700.00	$ 23,900.00	$ 23,300.00	$ 24,500.00	$ 138,600.00
NET PROFIT	$ (2,100.00)	$ (4,100.00)	$ (4,700.00)	$ (2,900.00)	$ (2,300.00)	$ (2,500.00)	**$ (18,600.00)**

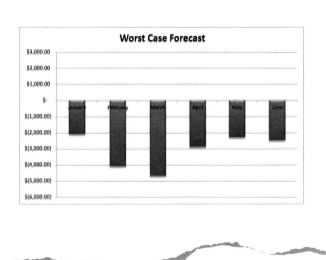

Excel 2010

Course Grades Analysis for Psychology 200

As the instructor of Psychology 200, a course in the history of psychology, you need to calculate a final grade for each student and then create a chart to help you analyze how well your students performed. To complete the course grades analysis, you need to **Calculate Totals and Grades**, **Create a Subtotals List and Chart**, and then **Format the Course Grades Analysis**. The completed course grades analysis is shown in Figure D-15 on page 89.

Calculate Totals and Grades

To calculate a student's grade for the course, you need to enter totals for each grade category (Assignments, Quizzes, and Exams), and then enter a formula to weight the grades earned by the students according to type. Assignments are worth 35 percent, quizzes 25 percent, and exams 40 percent.

Hint

Press [Ctrl][S] to save frequently as you work.

Trouble

You may need to press [Fn][F4] on your computer to insert the dollar signs.

Hint

Be sure to make cells H20, I20, and L21 absolute references.

Trouble

Be careful to enter "A," "B," and "C" where indicated; Excel adds the minus sign (–), which you will need to delete.

Steps:

1. Open a new Excel workbook, save the workbook as PR D-Course Grades Analysis to the location where you save the files for this book, then set up and format the worksheet so that it appears as shown in Figure D-10

2. Click cell J4, enter the formula =(B4+C4+D4+E4)/(B20+C20+D20+E20)*J21, press [Enter], then verify that 30.625 appears in cell J4

3. Click cell J4, click B20 in the formula on the formula bar, press [F4] to make the cell reference absolute, click C20 in the formula bar, press [F4], then use [F4] to make D20, E20, and J21 absolute

   You use the [F4] command to insert the dollar signs ($) because you want to make the cell references in cells B20, C20, D20, E20, and J21 absolute. When you copy the formula to the cells for the rest of the students, you want each formula to divide the total assignment score in cells B4:E4 by the total value in cells B20:E20, and then multiply the result of that calculation by the weighted value in cell J21.

4. Press [Enter], copy the formula through cell J18, then click the Comma Style button in the Number group

5. Click cell K4, enter the formula =(F4+G4)/(F20+G20)*K21, make the references to F20, G20, and K21 absolute, press [Enter], copy the formula through cell K18, then click

6. Click cell L4, enter the formula that calculates the weighted score for exams, copy the formula through cell L18, then click

   Lisa Braund earned 24.00 out of 25 for quizzes and 33.60 out of 40 for exams.

7. Select cells J4:M18, then click the Sum button Σ in the Editing group

   Lisa's total score is 88.23.

8. Double-click the Sheet1 tab, type Grades, press [Enter], double-click the Sheet2 tab, type Lookup, then press [Enter]

9. Set up the Lookup worksheet so that it appears as shown in Figure D-11, then save the workbook

FIGURE D-10: **Course Grades Analysis worksheet**

Set the width of columns B through I to 6

Merge and center across columns A through N; format with bold and 20 pt

Bold row 3

Center labels in columns B through N

Psychology 200

	A	B	C	D	E	F	G	H	I	J	K	L	M	N	O
1															
2															
3	Name	A1	A2	A3	A4	Q1	Q2	E1	E2	Assn	Quiz	Exam	Total	Grade	
4	Braund, Lisa	15	18	18	19	25	23	44	40						
5	Chow, Jason	18	20	19	19	22	20	45	46						
6	Denby, Elizabeth	13	19	12	14	22	21	42	40						
7	Ellis, Ron	15	15	15	12	15	14	40	37						
8	Kim, Joan	12	10	11	12	10	8	27	29						
9	Klein, Elaine	8	20	20	20	23	21	40	45						
10	Knutson, Ivan	12	18	18	19	22	23	33	39						
11	Leung, Grace	15	15	15	17	20	21	44	46						
12	Merton, George	18	19	20	20	22	24	46	42						
13	Mirelli, Maria	17	20	15	16	20	18	42	38						
14	Raulston, Jon	15	18	8	14	18	19	40	32						
15	Singh, Mansoor	20	15	19	20	15	14	45	47						
16	Stanfield, Wanda	15	18	14	19	25	22	40	38						
17	Waite, Sally	20	20	18	20	24	25	49	50						
18	Zagrev, Lance	18	20	18	20	20	16	40	42						
19															
20	Total Possible Points	20	20	20	20	25	25	50	50						
21	Weighted Values									35	25	40	100		
22															
23															
24															
25															

Sheet1 / Sheet2 / Sheet3

Right-align and bold labels in rows 20 and 21

FIGURE D-11: **Lookup table**

	A	B	C
1	Lookup Table		
2	0	F	
3	60	D	
4	65	C-	
5	70	C	
6	75	C+	
7	80	B-	
8	84	B	
9	87	B+	
10	90	A-	
11	95	A	
12	97	A+	
13			
14			
15			

This lookup table lists the grades corresponding to score values

Enter "A," "B," and "C" where indicated; delete the minus sign that Excel adds automatically

Course Grades Analysis (continued)

Create a Subtotals List and Chart

First you need to enter a formula that refers to the lookup table you created in the Lookup sheet. Then you need to create a Subtotals list that counts the number of times that each letter grade appears in column N of the Grades sheet. You create a Subtotals list when you want a quick way to sort, subtotal, and total a series of values. Once you have completed the Subtotals list from the list of student grades, you need to create a pie chart that compares how many students earned each letter grade.

Steps:

1. **Click the** Grades sheet tab, **click cell** N4, **click the** Formulas tab, **click the** Lookup & Reference button **in the Function Library group, click** LOOKUP, **click** lookup_value,array, **click** OK, **type** M4 **in the Lookup_value text box, then press** [Tab]

   You've entered the cell address of the value that the lookup table must use to assign a grade. This value represents Lisa's total score out of 100 for the course.

2. **Click the** Collapse Dialog Box button  **next to "Array", click the** Lookup sheet tab **to show the Lookup worksheet, select cells** A2:B12, **press** [F4], **then click the** Expand Dialog Box button

   The Function Arguments dialog box appears as shown in Figure D-12. Lisa earned a B+ for Psychology 200.

3. **Click** OK, **copy the formula in cell** N4 **down through cell** N18, **select cells** N3:N18, **click the** Home tab, **then click the** Copy button  **in the Clipboard group**

Trouble

If you do not see Grade in cell A1, repeat step 3 and be sure to select cell N3.

4. **Double-click the** Sheet3 tab, **type** Subtotals, **press** [Enter], **click the** Paste list arrow **in the Clipboard group, then click the** Values button **in the Paste Values section**

   Only the values themselves ("A," "B+," etc.) are pasted and not the underlying formulas.

5. **Select cells** A2:A16, **click the** Sort & Filter button **in the Editing group, then click** Sort A to Z

   Before you create a Subtotals list, you sort data so that the data you want to subtotal is arranged in groups. However, the results of the default sort are not correct. You want the grades sorted from A+ to F, and at present the first grade is A-.

6. **With cells** A2:A16 **still selected, click the** Sort & Filter button, **click** Custom Sort, **click the** Order list arrow, **click** Custom List, **click in the List entries box, enter the grades in the order shown in Figure D-13, click** Add, **click** OK, **then click** OK

Hint

The list needs to include a header row ("Grade", in this example) when you work with the Subtotals function.

7. **Select cells** A1:A16, **click the** Data tab, **click the** Subtotal button **in the Outline group, click** OK, **then click** OK

   The Subtotals function counts the number of times each grade appears. You can create a chart from this data.

8. **Click** 2 **in the Grouping pane (see Figure D-14) to collapse the Subtotals list to level 2, select cells** A1:B24, **click the** Insert tab, **click the** Pie button **in the Charts group, click the far-left selection in the top row to insert a Pie chart, click the** More button **in the Chart Styles group, then select** Style 29 **(green selection in the fourth row)**

9. **Select** Grade A+ **in the chart title, type** Breakdown of Final Grades, **click above the chart, then save the workbook**

   The pie chart appears as shown in Figure D-14.

FIGURE D-12: Function Arguments dialog box

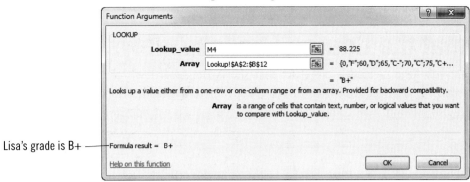

Lisa's grade is B+

FIGURE D-13: Creating a Custom List

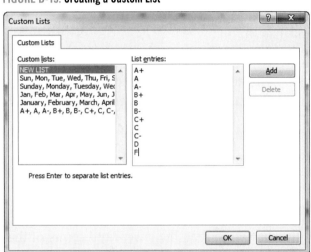

FIGURE D-14: Pie chart created

Click 2 in the Grouping pane to collapse the Subtotal list to level 2

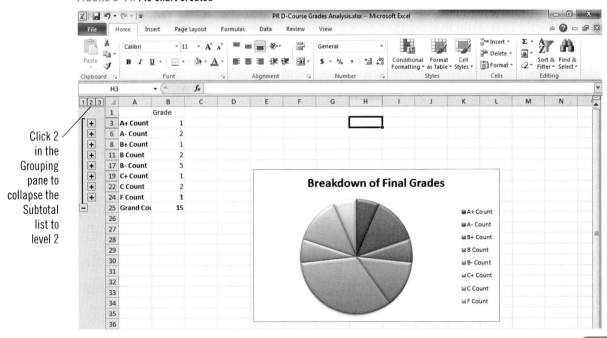

Format the Course Grades Analysis

Now that you have created a pie chart that shows the breakdown of grades for the students in Psychology 200, you need to format the chart, copy it into the Grades worksheet, and then format the worksheet for printing. Your completed course grades analysis will appear as shown in Figure D-15.

Steps:

1. **Click cell** A1, **click the** Find & Select button **in the Editing group, click** Replace, **type** Count, **press** [Tab], **click** Replace All, **click** OK, **then click** Close

   The "Count" label is removed from each of the entries on the worksheet and in the chart legend.

2. **Notice that the data is accurately shown in the pie chart, click** 3 **in the Grouping pane, notice how the pie chart data is no longer correct, then click** 2 **in the Grouping pane**

   When you create a chart from grouped data in a Subtotals list, you need to keep the data grouped to maintain the integrity of the chart.

3. **Click the** pie chart, **click the** Chart Tools Layout tab, **click the** Data Labels button **in the** Labels group, **click** More Data Label Options, **click the** Category Name check box **to select it, click the** Value check box **to deselect it, click the** Percentage check box **to select it, click the** Outside End option button, **then click** Close

4. **Click the** Legend button **in the Labels group, then click** None

5. **Click a** white area **of the chart, click the** Home tab, **click the** Copy button **in the** Clipboard group, **click the** Grades sheet tab, **click cell** A24, **click the** Paste button **in the** Clipboard group, **then click away from the chart to deselect it**

6. **Scroll to the chart, then drag the lower-right corner of the chart to cell N48**

7. **Scroll up, select cells** A3:N21, **click the** Format as Table button **in the Styles group, select** Table Style Medium 18 **(a green style), click** OK, **then apply bold to the grades in column N**

8. **Click the** File tab, **click** Print, **click** Page Setup, **format the worksheet so that it fits on one page, is centered horizontally, and includes a custom header that displays** Course Grades Analysis **at the left and your name at the right, then print a copy if directed to do so by your instructor or click the** Home tab **to return to the worksheet**

9. **Save the workbook, submit a copy to your instructor, then close the workbook**

   When printed, your worksheet should appear similar to Figure D-15.

Additional Practice

For additional practice with the skills presented in this project, complete Independent Challenge 2.

Course Grades Analysis   Your Name

Psychology 200

Name	A1	A2	A3	A4	Q1	Q2	E1	E2	Assn	Quiz	Exam	Total	Grade
Braund, Lisa	15	18	18	19	25	23	44	40	30.63	24.00	33.60	88.23	B+
Chow, Jason	18	20	19	19	22	20	45	46	33.25	21.00	36.40	90.65	A-
Denby, Elizabeth	13	19	12	14	22	21	42	40	25.38	21.50	32.80	79.68	C+
Ellis, Ron	15	15	15	12	15	14	40	37	24.94	14.50	30.80	70.24	C
Kim, Joan	12	10	11	12	10	8	27	29	19.69	9.00	22.40	51.09	F
Klein, Elaine	8	20	20	20	23	21	40	45	29.75	22.00	34.00	85.75	B
Knutson, Ivan	12	18	18	19	22	23	33	39	29.31	22.50	28.80	80.61	B-
Leung, Grace	15	15	15	17	20	21	44	46	27.13	20.50	36.00	83.63	B-
Merton, George	18	19	20	20	22	24	46	42	33.69	23.00	35.20	91.89	A-
Mirelli, Maria	17	20	15	16	20	18	42	38	29.75	19.00	32.00	80.75	B-
Raulston, Jon	15	18	8	14	18	19	40	32	24.06	18.50	28.80	71.36	C
Singh, Mansoor	20	15	19	20	15	14	45	47	32.38	14.50	36.80	83.68	B-
Stanfield, Wanda	15	18	14	19	25	22	40	38	28.88	23.50	31.20	83.58	B-
Waite, Sally	20	20	18	20	24	25	49	50	34.13	24.50	39.60	98.23	A+
Zagrev, Lance	18	20	18	20	20	16	40	42	33.25	18.00	32.80	84.05	B
Total Possible Points	20	20	20	20	25	25	50	50					
Weighted Values									35	25	40	100	

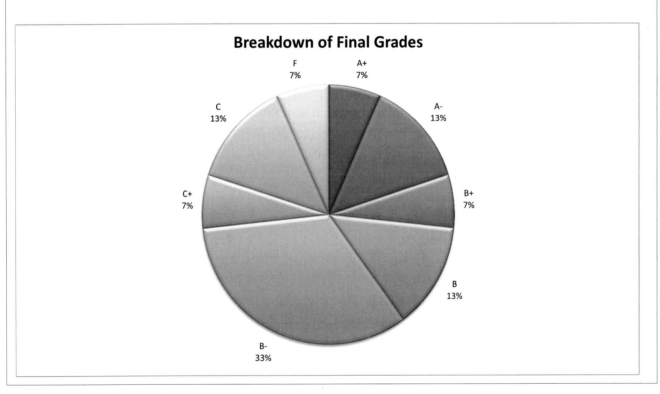

Breakdown of Final Grades

F 7%
A+ 7%
A- 13%
C 13%
C+ 7%
B+ 7%
B 13%
B- 33%

Excel 2010

Sales Report for Home Organics

As an analyst for Home Organics, you work with a product list already created in Excel to produce a report that analyzes sales over a three-year period. To create the Sales Report, you need to **Create a PivotTable** and **Filter and Chart Results**.

Create a PivotTable

You open the product list, then use the PivotTable function to create a PivotTable that shows yearly sales of each product category ("Appetizer," "Entree," etc.) sold by Home Organics.

Hint

The worksheet contains the total sales in each year from 2011 to 2013 of all the Home Organics products. Each product is allocated to a category such as "Appetizer" or "Dessert."

Steps:

1. Start Excel, open PR D-1.xlsx from the location where you store your Data Files, save it as PR D-Home Organics Sales Analysis to the location where you save the files for this book, double-click the Sheet1 tab, type Sales Data, then press [Enter]

2. Select cells A1:E1, click the Bold button **B** in the Font group, click the Center button ≡ in the Alignment group, select cells A1:E30, click the Bottom Border list arrow ⊞ ▾ in the Font group, then click All Borders

3. With cells A1:E30 still selected, click the Insert tab, click PivotTable in the Tables group, verify that the New Worksheet option button is selected, then click OK

   A new worksheet opens with the PivotTable Tools Options and Design tabs available and with the PivotTable task pane open on the right side of the window.

4. Click the Product check box in the PivotTable Field List, notice how all the products are added to the PivotTable starting in cell A3, then click each of the remaining check boxes in the PivotTable Field List as shown in Figure D-16

   All the data from the list is added to the PivotTable, with each product assigned to a different row.

Hint

You make each category a row label so you can analyze how much money each product category makes in each of the three years.

5. Click Product in the Row Labels area of the PivotTable task pane, then click Move Down

   The products are sorted and summarized by category.

6. Click cell B3, click Field Settings in the Active Field group on the PivotTable Tools Options tab, scroll the options in the Summarize value field by list, click Count, then click OK

   You have data for five appetizers, five desserts, ten entrées, and nine salads.

7. Click Field Settings, click Sum, click the Show Values As tab, click the Show values as list arrow, scroll the list of options to view how you can show values in the PivotTable report, scroll up and click % of Grand Total as shown in Figure D-17, then click OK

   The setting % of Grand Total shows each category of sales as a percentage of total sales.

Hint

Notice that sales of Appetizers in 2011 were 8.56 percent of total 2011 sales.

8. Click the Field Settings button, click the Show Values As tab, click the Show values as list arrow, click No Calculation, then click OK

9. Select cells B3:D37, click the Home tab, click the Accounting Number Format button $ in the Number group, then name the sheet tab Product Sales

10. Click cell A1, type Home Organics Sales Report, merge and center the title across cells A1:D1, click the Cell Styles button in the Styles group, click Heading 1, click the Align Text Left button ≡ in the Alignment group, click cell B3, then save the workbook

    The worksheet appears as shown in Figure D-18.

Trouble

Click the More button ▾ in the Styles group if you do not see the Cell Styles button.

FIGURE D-16: Selecting fields for the PivotTable

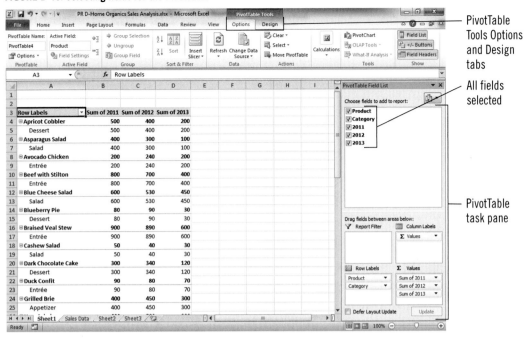

PivotTable Tools Options and Design tabs

All fields selected

PivotTable task pane

FIGURE D-17: Value Field Settings dialog box

Show values as list arrow

FIGURE D-18: Worksheet title and formatted PivotTable

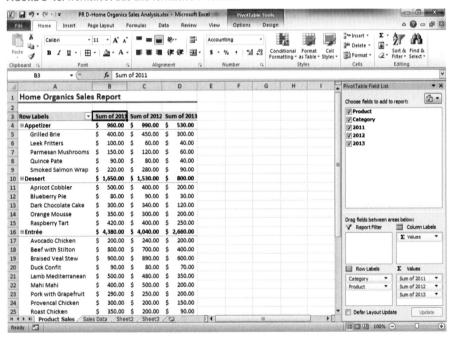

Excel 2010

Filter and Chart Results

You create a chart to represent the data in the PivotTable and then use the slicer to filter data. The completed sales report appears as shown in Figure D-21.

Steps:

1. As shown in Figure D-19, click the Collapse Outline button ⊟ to the left of Appetizer to collapse the list of appetizers so only the category name shows, then click ⊟ next to Dessert, Entrée, and Salad

2. Select cells A4:D8, click the Insert tab, click the Column button in the Charts group, then click Clustered Cylinder

3. Drag the chart down so that its upper-left corner is positioned in cell A11, then click the 2012 check box in the PivotTable Field List to deselect it

   Only data for 2011 and 2013 is shown. As you can see, Home Organics experienced a significant reduction in sales of entrées and salads between 2011 and 2013.

4. Click anywhere in the PivotTable (for example, cell B4), click the PivotTable Tools Options tab, click Insert Slicer in the Sort & Filter group, click the Category check box, click OK, click Dessert in the slicer, then move the slicer so you can see the chart and PivotTable as shown in Figure D-20

   Only the sales of items in the Dessert category are shown in the PivotTable and the chart. The slicer provides you with a quick and easy way to show only the data you want to study. You use options in the PivotTable to view the data related to specific products.

5. Click the Clear Filter button 🍲 to restore the slicer, click anywhere in the PivotTable, click Product in the lower-left corner of the chart, click the (Select All) check box to deselect it, click the check box next to "Asparagus Salad", "Cashew Salad", and "Dark Chocolate Cake", click OK, click the Expand button ⊞ next to "Dessert" in the PivotTable, then click ⊞ next to "Salad"

   You can quickly compare the drop in sales for any combination of products and categories.

6. Click the Collapse Outline button ⊟ next to "Dessert", click ⊟ next to "Salad", click Product in the chart, click the (Select All) check box, then click OK

   The chart again compares the sales for 2011 and 2013 in all four categories.

7. Click the Sales Data sheet tab, click cell E6, type 100, press [Enter], click the Product Sales tab, click anywhere in the PivotTable, click the PivotTable Tools Options tab, then click the Refresh button in the Data group

   Each time you change the data used to build the PivotTable, you need to refresh the PivotTable.

8. Click the chart, click the PivotChart Tools Analyze tab, click the Field Buttons list arrow in the Show/Hide group, then click Hide All

Additional Practice

For additional practice with the skills presented in this project, complete Independent Challenge 3.

9. Click the Page Layout tab, click Themes, select Oriel, click the slicer, press [Delete], type your name in cell A26, save the workbook, submit a copy to your instructor, then close the workbook

   The completed Sales Report appears as shown in Figure D-21.

FIGURE D-19: Collapsing the Appetizer group

The plus sign next to "Appetizer" indicates the Appetizer group is collapsed

The minus sign next to "Dessert" indicates the Dessert group is expanded

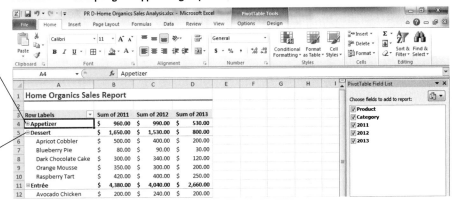

FIGURE D-20: Positioning the slicer

Only data related to the Dessert category is shown in the PivotTable

Only data related to the Dessert category is charted

Clear Filter button

Slicer positioned in the worksheet

Dessert selected

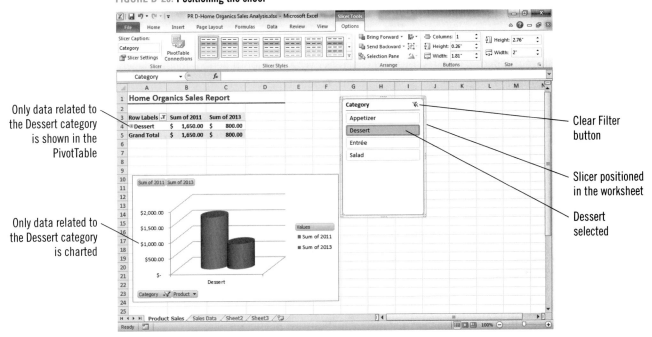

FIGURE D-21: Completed sales report

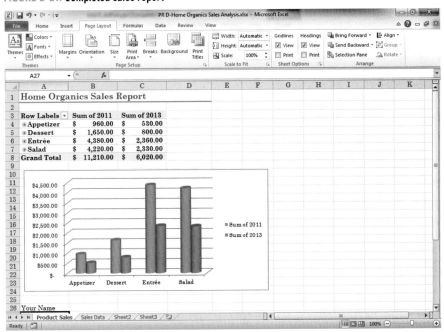

Independent Challenge 1

As the owner of a small business, you decide that you need to expand your operations in order to generate more income. To help you make an informed decision, you use the Scenario Manager to see the effect of your plans on a current revenue and expenses worksheet.

1. Determine the name of your company, the type of business it conducts, and your plans for expansion. For example, you could run a home-based catering service that has grown big enough to warrant moving the business out of your home and into a commercial location. Alternatively, you could run a snow removal business from a small commercial office and decide to move into a larger office and buy several new pieces of snow removal equipment. Write the name of your company and a short description of your expansion plans in the box below:

Company Name: _____

Description of Expansion Plans: _____

_____

2. Create a worksheet that shows your revenue and expenses over a six-month period. Include labels for each of six months (e.g., July to December), insert labels for the various types of revenue you generate (e.g., Catering Sales and Consulting), and insert labels for your various expenses (e.g., Rent, Salaries, Advertising, Equipment, and Operating Costs). Note that returns and cost of sales sold are calculated as a percentage of your total monthly revenue (usually 3 percent for returns and 60 percent to 70 percent for cost of sales). Calculate your monthly revenue and expenses and your total profit/loss for each month and at the end of six months.

3. Format the worksheet attractively, then save the workbook as **PR D-My Predictions** to the location where you save the files for this book.

4. Fill the rows containing the data you plan to change when you create your Best and Worst Case scenarios with the color of your choice.

5. Use the Scenario Manager to create Current scenarios from the data currently entered in the worksheet. Note that you only need to create scenarios for the rows that contain the values you will change when you create a Best Case scenario and a Worst Case scenario.

6. Select a Current scenario, click Add, rename the Current Scenario as the Best Case scenario for that category, then change values using the Scenario Manager to reflect your best case predictions should you carry out your expansion plans. For example, if you decide to move to a new office, your Rent expense may increase, and if you hire an assistant, your Salaries expense will increase. Make sure you also increase your income to reflect the increased revenue you expect to make as a result of expanding your operations.

7. Repeat Step 6, but this time enter values to reflect your worst case predictions, should your expansion plans fail to proceed as well as you hope.

8. Show the Best Case scenarios, create a column chart or bar chart that displays the Best Case monthly income, apply the chart style of your choice, add **Best Case Forecast** as the chart title, then format and print a copy of the worksheet. Make sure you include your name and text that identifies this report as the Best Case Forecast in the header along with a similar descriptive text in the subtitle on the worksheet.

9. Note the upper limit of the value axis (y-axis) in the chart. You want the printed charts with the Current, Best, and Worst Case scenarios worksheets to display the same upper limit on the value axis so that the differences in the three charts are readily apparent.

10. Show the Current scenarios, change the subtitle on the worksheet, change the title of the chart, change the upper limit on the value axis to the same upper limit displayed in the Best Case column chart, change the header to reflect the worksheet content, then print a copy of the worksheet.

11. Show the Worst Case scenarios, change the subtitle on the worksheet, change the title of the chart, change the upper limit on the value axis to the same upper limit displayed in the Best Case chart, change the header to reflect the worksheet content, then print a copy.

12. Save and close the workbook, then submit your files to your instructor.

Independent Challenge 2

You have been working all term as a teaching assistant for a course of your choice. The instructor you work for has given you the grade sheet she has kept by hand and has asked you to transfer the data to Excel and then calculate each student's grade. Complete the steps below to create a course grades analysis for a course of your choice.

1. Determine the name of the course. For example, the course could be Philosophy 100, History 210, or Biology 301.
2. Determine the grade categories (such as assignments, presentations, exams) and the percentage of scores (weighted scores) allocated to each category. Create at least three grade categories and make sure the percentages (weighted values) you assign add up to 100 percent. For example, you could allocate 40 percent of the total grade to Assignments, 30 percent to Exams, and 30 percent to Presentations.
3. Start Excel, name Sheet1 **Grades**, then set up the worksheet with the name of the course, a list of at least 15 students, and labels for the various assignments, presentations, quizzes, exams, and so on. Make sure you include at least two items (such as A1 and A2 for assignment 1 and assignment 2) in each of the three grade categories you have selected.
4. Save the workbook as **PR D-My Grades Analysis** to the location where you save the files for this book.
5. Determine the total score possible for each item in each grade category (such as 20 points for A1) and enter the totals two rows below the last student name. To check the setup of your course grades analysis worksheet, refer to the course grades analysis you created for Unit D Project 2.
6. Enter the points for each graded item (such as points for A1 and points for A2) for each student. Make sure you refer to the total you entered for each graded item to ensure that each score you enter for each student is equal to or less than the total points possible for that graded item.
7. Calculate the points for each grade category, divide the total points the student received by the total possible points for that category, then multiply the result by the percentage (weighted value) you assigned to the grade category. The formula required is: =(Sum of Student's Points)/(Sum of Total Points)*Weighted Value. Make sure you use absolute references for the Sum of Total Points values and for the Weighted Value reference so that you can copy the formula without errors. For example, if the Assignment points are entered in cells C4, D4, and F4, the total possible points are entered in cells C25, D25, and F25, and the weighted value of Assignments is entered in cell J26, the formula required is =(C4+D4+F4)/($C$25+$D$25+$F$25)*$J$26
8. Calculate the total points for all graded items earned by the first student on your list. (Hint: Add the total for each grade category to calculate the overall point total. The overall point total should be equal to or less than 100.)
9. Copy the formula you used to calculate the first student's weighted score in each grade category down the column for that grade category for the remaining students, then copy the formula you used to calculate the first student's overall points down the column for the remaining students.
10. Name Sheet2 **Lookup**, then create a Lookup table in that worksheet that lists the letter grades and ranges you specify.
11. Enter the LOOKUP formula in the appropriate cell in the Grades worksheet, then copy the formula down for the remaining students.
12. Name Sheet3 **Subtotals**, then copy the grades from the Grades worksheet and paste them as values.
13. Sort the grades in alphabetical order. (Note that you will need to create a custom list if your grades include grades such as A- and B+.)
14. Create a Subtotals list that counts the occurrences of each grade, then collapse the Subtotals list to level 2.
15. Remove "Count" where needed, create a pie chart from the data in the Subtotals list to show the scores by letter grade, format the chart attractively with an appropriate title, percentages, and the chart style of your choice, then copy it to the Grades worksheet.
16. Apply the table style of your choice to the Grades worksheet, format the worksheet so that both the table and the chart fit on one page, create a custom header that includes the name of the course and **Grades** (for example, History 100 Grades) and your name, save the workbook, submit a copy to your instructor, then close the workbook.

Independent Challenge 3

As the manager of a local video store, you have decided to evaluate the popularity of the classic film titles your clientele rents and buys. The data you need is already included in an Excel file. You open this file and then use the PivotTable feature to create a report and chart that analyzes the data.

1. Start Excel, open **PR D-2.xlsx** from the location where you store your Data Files, save it as **PR D-Classic Films Report** to the location where you save the files for this book, then name the Sheet1 tab **Unit Sales and Rentals**.

2. Format the worksheet so that the header row is bold and centered and all rows are enclosed by border lines.

3. Create a PivotTable in a new worksheet from the data, then add all the fields to the PivotTable by clicking each of the check boxes in the PivotTable Field list.

4. Move Title below Genre in the Row Labels area.

5. Name the sheet tab **Product Report**, then enter **Classic Films** as the title in cell A1 and **Rentals by Genre** as the subtitle in cell A2. Format the titles attractively. For example, you can merge and center the titles across columns A to C, add shading to one or both cells, increase the font sizes of the titles, and add bold.

6. Collapse the list so only the genres appear, show only the data for 2013 Unit Rentals, then create a pie chart that shows the breakdown of Unit Rentals by genre. (*Note:* If necessary, enlarge the chart until you see all of the categories listed.)

7. Format the chart attractively using chart layout 6 and chart style 26. Include **Breakdown of Rentals** as the chart title.

8. Show the slicer, then use it to view the total rentals of each title in the Comedy genre. (*Hint:* Click the Expand button next to Comedy to include the titles of each of the movies in the Comedy genre in the chart. If all of the Comedy titles do not appear, increase the height of the pie chart so that all the titles are visible.) Experiment with some other views and notice how the pie chart changes, depending on which data you select. Remove the slicer, then click Genre and (Select All) so that all seven legend entries (Adventure, Comedy, etc.) appear in the chart. If some entries are missing, increase the height of the chart.

9. In the Unit Sales and Rentals worksheet, search for **Classic** and replace with **Drama**, then update the PivotTable in the Product Report worksheet.

10. Show the 2013 Unit Sales field, apply the theme of your choice, set up the document so that it fits on one page, is centered horizontally, and includes **Classic Films Report** and your name in the header, save the workbook, submit a copy to your instructor, then close the workbook.

Independent Challenge 4

You run a sailboat rental business in the Bahamas that caters to adventure-based travelers who rent sailboats for up to two weeks to explore the Bahamas and other Caribbean islands. During the previous winter, you failed to make a profit on the business. Now you want to project sales for the coming winter months based on your plan to acquire more sailboats, increase advertising costs, and move into an attractive new boathouse.

1. Create the worksheet shown in Figure D-22, then save the workbook as **PR D-Winter Sailboat Rentals**. Fill cell A1 with Aqua, Accent 5, Lighter 60%, and highlight the cells as shown in Figure D-22.

2. Calculate the Cancellations (4 percent of Rental Income), Net Revenue (=B5-B6), Cost of Rentals (75 percent of Rental Income), Gross Profit on Rentals (=B7-B8), Total Expenses, and Net Income.

3. Ensure that your total net income in cell E18 is (2,490.00).

4. Create Current scenarios of the data for Rental Income, Rent, and Advertising. Call the scenarios **Current Rental Income**, **Current Rent**, and **Current Advertising**.

5. Create the following Expansion scenarios for the Rental Income, Rent, and Advertising data:

Expansion Rental Income:	**November: 106,000**
	December: 135,500
	January: 177,450
Expansion Rent:	**$2,200 per month**
Expansion Advertising:	**$3,000 per month**

Independent Challenge 4 (continued)

FIGURE D-22

	A	B	C	D	E	F
1		**Aqua Marine Sailing**				
2		**Winter Rentals**				
3		November	December	January	Totals	
4	REVENUE					
5	Rental Income	$ 54,000.00	$ 62,000.00	$ 75,000.00		
6	Cancellations: 4% of Rental Income					
7	NET REVENUE					
8	Cost of Rentals: 75% of Rental Income					
9	GROSS PROFIT ON RENTALS					
10						
11	EXPENSES					
12	Salaries	$ 8,200.00	$ 8,200.00	$ 8,200.00		
13	Rent	1,500.00	1,500.00	1,500.00		
14	Advertising	2,500.00	2,500.00	2,500.00		
15	Operating Costs	2,000.00	2,000.00	2,000.00		
16	Total Expenses					
17						
18	NET INCOME					
19						
20						

6. Show all the Expansion scenarios, and verify that your net income in cell E18 is $41,779.50.

7. With the Expansion scenarios still displayed, create a bar chart that displays the monthly net income. Note the upper limit of the value axis (x-axis) ($25,000). Format the bar chart attractively as shown in Figure D-23.

8. As shown in Figure D-23, insert a custom header, then center the worksheet horizontally. Be sure the worksheet fits on one page. Print a copy of the worksheet.

9. Show the Current scenarios, modify the header and chart title as shown in Figure D-24, then change the upper limit of the value axis (x-axis) to $25,000 so that it matches the bar chart that shows the Expansion net income.

10. Print a copy of the Current scenarios worksheet, then save and close the workbook.

FIGURE D-23

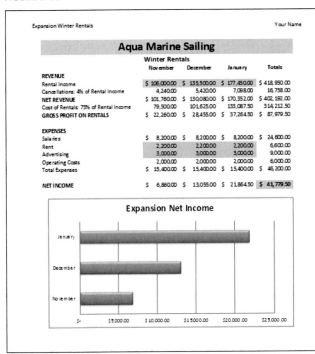

FIGURE D-24

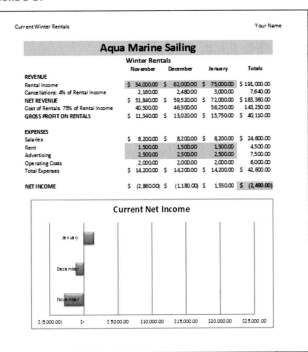

Visual Workshop

You have just completed a survey of the leisure activities preferred by your classmates in the animation program at Garden State College. Now you want to create a chart to display the results of your survey. Create the worksheet shown in Figure D-25, sort the items in alphabetical order by Activity, then create a Subtotals list that counts the number of times each activity appears in column B of Sheet1. (*Hint*: Be sure to select Activity in two places in the Subtotals dialog box.) Once you have created the Subtotals list, use Find and Replace to remove each instance of "Count," then create the pie chart shown in Figure D-26. (*Hint*: Select cells A6:A26, press and hold [Ctrl], then select cells B6:B26.) Apply the Essential theme and chart style 26, add a chart title, add your name below the chart, save your workbook as **PR D-Leisure Activities** to the location where you save the files for this book, submit a copy to your instructor, then close the workbook.

FIGURE D-25

FIGURE D-26

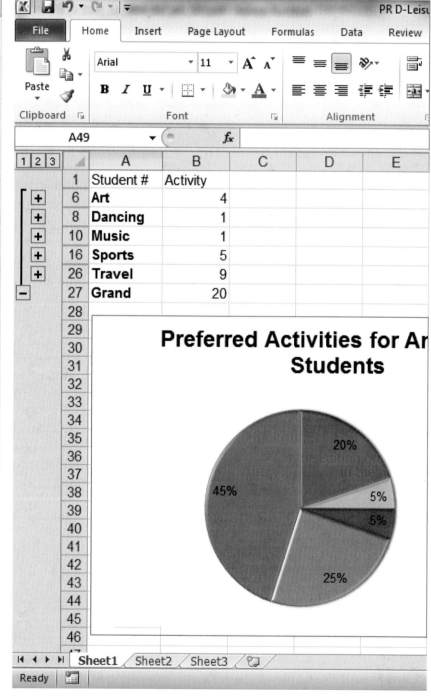

Integration Projects I

You can use the integration capabilities of Microsoft Office 2010 to combine text you create in Word with numerical data that you analyze in Excel. For example, suppose you have created a report in Word that references a variety of charts and other data created in Excel. You can copy selected data from Excel and paste it into the Word report as a link. Every time you make a change to the data in Excel, the changes are also made to the data you copied and pasted as a link into the Word report because the two files are linked. In this unit, you will learn how to link documents that combine elements created in both Word and Excel.

In This Unit You Will Create the Following:

Job Performance Reviews

Sales Report

Marketing Update

Job Performance Reviews

Lana Malek and Peter Cooper have worked for Maritime Properties for one year as a service agent and a sales manager, respectively. They are now due to be evaluated. As their supervisor, you need to create a form that you can use to compile the results of each employee's performance review. To complete the performance reviews, you **Create the Form in Word**, **Add Form Content Controls in Word**, **Compile Results in Excel**, and then **Link the Form and Results** for each employee. The completed performance review for Peter is shown in Figure E-10 on page 107.

Create the Form in Word

You set up the performance review form in Word and then create the form.

Steps:

1. **Start a new blank document in Word, click the** Page Layout tab, **click** Margins **in the** Page Setup group, **click** Custom Margins, **change the top and bottom margins to** .6", **click** OK, **then save the document as** PR E-Performance Review Form **to the location where you save the files for this book**

2. **Click the** Home tab, **click** Change Styles **in the Styles group, point to** Style Set, **click** Simple, **right-click** Normal **in the Styles gallery, click** Modify, **click the** Font list arrow, **select** Arial Rounded MT Bold, **click the** Decrease Paragraph Spacing button ⬍ **two times, then click** OK

3. **Type** Maritime Properties, **press** [Enter], **type** Job Performance Review, **press** [Enter] **twice, select** Maritime Properties, **click the** More button ⬍ **in the Styles group, click** Title, **select** Job Performance Review, **then apply the** Subtitle style

4. **Click the last** blank line **below "Job Performance Review", click the** Insert tab, **click** Table, **click** Insert Table, **type** 4, **press** [Tab], **type** 13, **click** OK, **then type the text for the table as shown in Figure E-1**

Hint

You use the [Ctrl] key to select the five nonadjacent rows in a table quickly so that you can apply formatting all at once.

5. **Click to the left of row 1 (contains "Employee Information") to select the entire row, press and hold** [Ctrl], **click to the left of "Rankings", click to the left of "Ranking Summary", "Ranking Chart", and "Written Evaluation" to select them, then release** [Ctrl]

6. **Click the** Shading list arrow **in the Table Styles group, select** Purple, Accent 4, Darker 25%, **click the** Home tab, **click the** Font Color list arrow ⬍ **in the Font group, click the** White, Background 1 color, **click the** Grow Font button ⬍ **in the Font group once, then click the** Center button ⬍ **in the Paragraph group**

7. **Select** row 1, **click the** Table Tools Layout tab, **click the** Merge Cells button **in the Merge group, then use Figure E-2 as your guide to merge cells and adjust cell widths to fit content**

8. **Select rows 1 through 6 ("Employee Information" through "Rankings"), press and hold** [Ctrl], **then select the rows containing "Ranking Summary", "Ranking Chart", and "Written Evaluation" to select a total of nine rows**

9. **Click** Properties **in the Table group, click the** Row tab, **click the** Specify height check box, **type** .3 **in the Specify height text box, click the** Cell tab, **click the** Center option **in the Vertical alignment section, click** OK, **click the document title to deselect the table, then save the document**

The document appears as shown in Figure E-2.

MARITIME PROPERTIES

JOB PERFORMANCE REVIEW

Employee Information			
Employee Name		Date	
Job Title		Employee ID	
Department		Manager	
Review Period		To	
Rankings			
Ranking Summary			
Ranking Chart			
Written Evaluation			
Supervisor Comments			

These rows are left blank

FIGURE E-2: Table cells merged and formatted

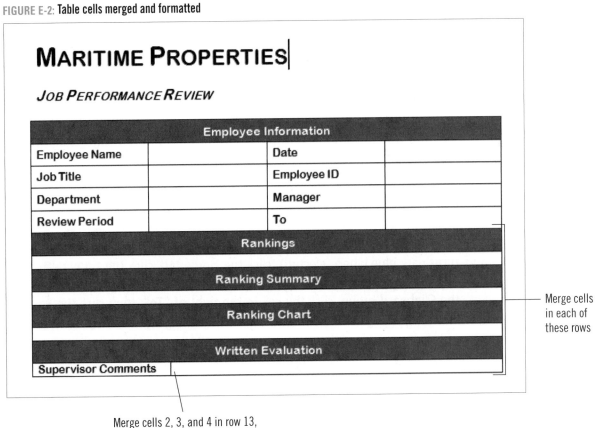

MARITIME PROPERTIES

JOB PERFORMANCE REVIEW

Employee Information			
Employee Name		Date	
Job Title		Employee ID	
Department		Manager	
Review Period		To	
Rankings			
Ranking Summary			
Ranking Chart			
Written Evaluation			
Supervisor Comments			

Merge cells in each of these rows

Merge cells 2, 3, and 4 in row 13, then drag the column divider to the right as shown

Add Form Content Controls in Word

You plan to use the same performance review form to record the performance reviews of numerous employees. You want the form to be an electronic one that you can complete on the computer. To make the form reusable, you need to insert form content controls. Your first step is to show the Developer tab so you can access the tools used to create forms.

Steps:

1. Click the File tab, click Options, click Customize Ribbon, click the Developer check box in the list of Main Tabs to select it, click OK, then click the cell to the right of "Employee Name"

2. Click the Developer tab, then click the Rich Text Content Control button Aa in the Controls group to insert a Rich Text content control as shown in Figure E-3

3. Press [Tab] twice to move to the blank cell to the right of "Date", click the Date Picker Content Control button 🖼 in the Controls group, click the Properties button in the Controls group, select the date format that corresponds to April 23, 2013, then click OK
   When you fill in the form, you will only be able to enter a date in the cell to the right of "Date".

4. Click the cell to the right of "Employee ID", click the Legacy Tools button 🖳 in the Controls group, click the Text Form Field button abl in the Legacy Forms area, double-click the shaded area to open the Text Form Field Options dialog box, click the Type list arrow, click Number, select the contents of the Maximum Length text box, type 4, compare the Text Form Field Options dialog box to Figure E-4, then click OK
   When you fill in the form, you will only be able to enter up to four digits in the cell to the right of Employee ID.

5. Add a Rich Text content control in the cells to the right of "Job Title" and "Manager", click the cell to the right of "Department", click the Combo Box Content Control button 🖼 in the Controls group, click Properties, click Add, type Administration, press [Enter], click Add, add Finance, Human Resources, Marketing, and Production as shown in Figure E-5, then click OK

6. Click the Date Picker content control to the right of Date, click the selection handle (it turns dark blue when selected), click the Home tab, click the Copy button 🖳 in the Clipboard group, click the cell to the right of "Review Period", click the Paste button in the Clipboard group, click the cell to the right of "To", then click the Paste button
   You can copy and paste fields that contain special formatting to save time.

7. Click the Developer tab, click to the right of "Supervisor Comments", insert a Rich Text content control, save the document, then save the document again as PR E-Performance Review Form_Lana Malek

8. Click the cell to the right of "Employee Name", type Lana Malek, press [Tab] twice, click the Date Picker content control list arrow to show the calendar, scroll to April 2013, then click 23

9. Enter the remaining data for Lana Malek as shown in Figure E-6, then save the document

FIGURE E-3: Rich Text content control inserted

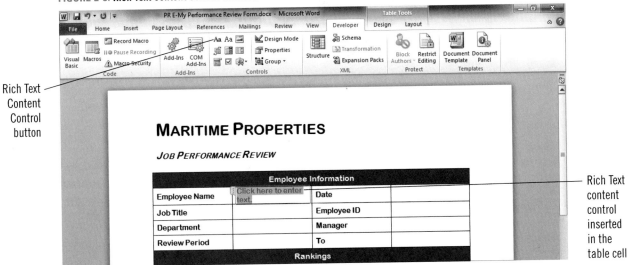

Rich Text Content Control button

Rich Text content control inserted in the table cell

FIGURE E-4: Text Form Field Options dialog box

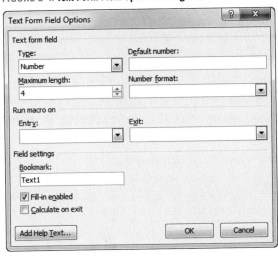

FIGURE E-5: Drop-Down List Properties

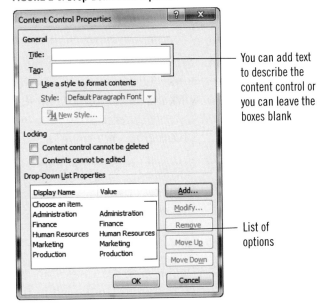

You can add text to describe the content control or you can leave the boxes blank

List of options

FIGURE E-6: Form text for Lana Malek

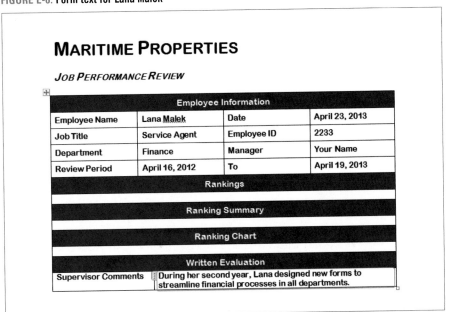

Compile Results in Excel

You need to create a worksheet in Excel into which you can enter the numerical results of the performance review. You also need to create a chart in Excel that summarizes the results.

Steps:

1. Start a new blank workbook in Excel, type Supervisor Rating in cell A1, select cells A1:B1, click the Merge and Center button ⊞ in the Alignment group, apply bold, enter and enhance the text as shown in Figure E-7, then save the workbook as PR E-Job Performance Reviews to the location where you save the files for this book

2. Double-click the Sheet1 tab, type Lana, press [Enter], click cell B8, double-click the Sum button Σ in the Editing group, click cell D8, then double-click Σ

3. Click cell B10, type =(B2+D2)/2, press [Enter], click cell B10, then fill cells B11:B15 with the formula in cell B10

    This formula determines the average score between the Supervisor Rating and the Peer Rating.

4. Select cells A10:B15, click the Insert tab, click Column in the Charts group, click the upper-left chart type (Clustered Column), click Layout 1 in the Chart Layouts group, click the More button ▾ in the Chart Styles group, select Style 30, click the Chart Tools Layout tab, click Chart Title in the Labels group, click None, click Legend in the Labels group, then click None

5. Size and position the chart so that it extends from cell C10 through cell J26

6. Right-click the value axis (y-axis), click Format Axis, click the Fixed option button for Maximum, verify that 5.0 appears in the Maximum text box, then click Close

    You set the maximum scale for the value axis at 5 so that the scale remains the same regardless of the data entered in the chart.

7. Double-click the Sheet2 tab, type Peter, press [Enter], click the Lana tab, click the Select All button ◢ to the left of the "A" in the upper-left corner of the worksheet frame to select the entire worksheet, click the Copy button 🖺 in the Clipboard group, click the Peter tab, then click the Paste button in the Clipboard group

8. Enter values for Peter in cells B2:B7 and cells D2:D7 as shown in Figure E-8, then verify that the totals are updated

9. Right-click the chart, click Select Data, click the Collapse button 🏢 next to "Chart data range", click the Peter tab, verify that cells A10:B15 are selected, click the Expand button 🖼, click OK, then save the workbook

    The chart appears as shown in Figure E-9. When you copied the chart from the Lana worksheet to the Peter worksheet, the chart still referenced the cells in the Lana worksheet. You changed the reference so that the chart shows data related to Peter's rankings.

FIGURE E-7: Worksheet labels and values

	A	B	C	D	E	F
1	**Supervisor Rating**		**Peer Rating**			
2	Knowledge	5	Knowledge	4		
3	Work Quality	5	Work Quality	3		
4	Attendance	4	Attendance	4		
5	Initiative	5	Initiative	4		
6	Communication	3	Communication	1		
7	Dependability	4	Dependability	4		
8						
9	**Average Rating**					
10	Knowledge					
11	Work Quality					
12	Attendance					
13	Initiative					
14	Communication					
15	Dependability					
16						
17						
18						

FIGURE E-8: Values for Peter

	A	B	C	D	E
1	**Supervisor Rating**		**Peer Rating**		
2	Knowledge	2	Knowledge	1	
3	Work Quality	3	Work Quality	1	
4	Attendance	1	Attendance	3	
5	Initiative	1	Initiative	2	
6	Communication	2	Communication	2	
7	Dependability	2	Dependability	1	
8		11		10	
9	**Average Rating**				

FIGURE E-9: Peter's chart updated

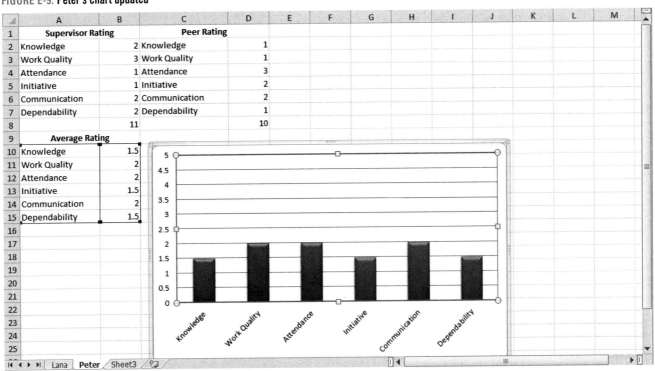

Link the Form and Results

You copy Lana's performance results from Excel and paste them into the Word form as linked objects. You save the document as Peter's, and then edit the text and object links so the form reflects Peter's information.

Steps:

1. Click the Lana tab, select cells A1:D8, click the Copy button in the Clipboard group, switch to Word, click the cell below "Rankings", click the Home tab, click the Paste list arrow in the Clipboard group, click Paste Special, click the Paste link option button, click Microsoft Excel Worksheet Object, click OK, click the worksheet object, then click the Center button ≡ in the Paragraph group

2. Switch to Excel, select cells A9:B15, click 📋, switch to Word, click the cell below "Ranking Summary", click the Paste list arrow, click Paste Special, click the Paste link option button, click Microsoft Excel Worksheet Object, click OK, then center the copied worksheet object

3. Switch to Excel, click the chart, click 📋 in the Clipboard group, switch to Word, click the cell below "Ranking Chart", click the Paste list arrow, click the Use Destination Theme & Link Data button 🖼 in the selection of Paste Options, click the chart, click the Chart Tools Format tab, click the launcher 🔲 in the Size group, click the Lock aspect ratio check box to select it, select the contents of the Height Absolute text box, type 2.3, click OK, then center the chart in Word

Trouble

If the value for attendance is not 5, right-click the object under Rankings, click Update Link, right-click the object under Ranking Summary, then click Update Link.

4. Switch to Excel, change Lana's ranking for Attendance to 5 in both the Supervisor and the Peers cells (cell B4 and cell D4), save and close the Excel workbook, switch to Word, verify that the value for attendance is "5" and the top of the Attendance column is even with "5" on the value axis, then save the document

Lana's rankings for Attendance and the column chart are both updated in the Word document.

5. Use Save As on the File tab to save the document again as PR E-Performance Review Form_Peter Cooper, scroll to and click the Employee Name cell, press [Tab], then enter text for Peter in the Employee Information and Written Evaluation sections as shown in the completed form in Figure E-10 (the values in the Excel objects will not match Figure E-10 yet)

6. Click the File tab, click Edit Links to Files in the lower-right corner under Related Documents, click the top link, click Change Source, click Item, select Lana and type Peter in the Enter Text dialog box as shown in Figure E-11, click OK, click PR E-Job Performance Reviews.xlsx in the list of files, then click Open

7. Repeat the process to change the source for the second link listed in the Links dialog box, then click OK

8. Click the Home tab, click the chart, click the Chart Tools Design tab, click Select Data in the Data group, select Lana in the Chart data range text box, type Peter, click OK, add your name to the Lana worksheet in cell A17, then close the Excel workbook

Additional Practice

For additional practice with the skills presented in this project, complete Independent Challenge 1.

9. Save the document, submit a copy of the Excel workbook and all performance review documents to your instructor, then close the document

The completed performance review for Peter appears as shown in Figure E-10. To make changes to a Word document linked to an Excel workbook, you open the Excel workbook first and then open the Word document and click Yes in response to the message that appears asking if you wish to maintain the link between the files.

MARITIME PROPERTIES

JOB PERFORMANCE REVIEW

Employee Information			
Employee Name	Peter Cooper	Date	May 23, 2013
Job Title	Sales Manager	Employee ID	4455
Department	Marketing	Manager	Your Name
Review Period	May 14, 2012	To	May 17, 2013

Rankings

Supervisor Rating		Peer Rating	
Knowledge	2	Knowledge	1
Work Quality	3	Work Quality	1
Attendance	1	Attendance	3
Initiative	1	Initiative	2
Communication	2	Communication	2
Dependability	2	Dependability	1
	11		10

Ranking Summary

Average Rating	
Knowledge	1.5
Work Quality	2
Attendance	2
Initiative	1.5
Communication	2
Dependability	1.5

Ranking Chart

Written Evaluation	
Supervisor Comments	Peter needs to develop a more conventional work ethic.

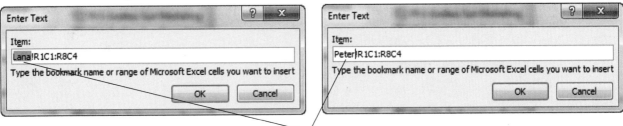

FIGURE E-11: Enter Text dialog box

Enter Text

Item:
Lana!R1C1:R8C4

Type the bookmark name or range of Microsoft Excel cells you want to insert

OK   Cancel

Enter Text

Item:
Peter!R1C1:R8C4

Type the bookmark name or range of Microsoft Excel cells you want to insert

OK   Cancel

Delete Lana and replace with Peter

Sales Report for Paradise Resorts

Paradise Resorts manages a chain of hotels on four Hawaiian islands: Oahu, Maui, Kauai, and Hawaii. As the sales manager for the chain, you want to attract more guests to the hotels in the spring months of April, May, and June in order to ensure that those months are profitable. You need to determine the number of rooms to rent during these spring months in order to show a profit. For this project, you need to **Summarize Sales**, **Calculate Projected Sales**, and **Create the Sales Report**. The completed sales report appears as shown in Figure E-17 on page 113.

Summarize Sales

You need to enter labels and values in an Excel worksheet and then calculate total sales.

Hint

The title is 26 pt and bold. The subtitle is 14 pt, bold, and italic.

Steps:

1. **Start a new workbook in Excel, enter and enhance the labels and values so that the worksheet appears as shown in Figure E-12, then save the workbook as** PR E-Paradise Resorts Sales Data **to the location where you save the files for this book**

2. **Click cell** B8, **enter the formula to multiply the** Average Cost per Room **by the** Total Number of Rooms Rented, **copy the formula through cell** E8, **then increase the column widths to fit content as needed**

   As you complete the required calculations, refer to Figure E-13 to verify your totals.

3. **Click cell** B13, **enter the formula to multiply the** Number of Rooms Available **by the** Operating Cost per Room, **then copy the formula through cell** E13

   Note that the value for the Operating Cost per Room is based on the cost over a three-month period.

4. **Click cell** B15, **enter the formula to add the** Total Operating Costs **to the** Advertising Costs, **then copy the formula through cell** E15

5. **Calculate the Net Revenue in cell** B17 **as the** Total Expenses **subtracted from the** Total Room Rental Revenue, **then copy the formula through cell** E17

   The hotels on Oahu and Maui lost money during the spring months of April, May, and June. Only the Kauai and Hawaii hotels made a profit.

6. **Select cells** B7:F8, **click the** Sum button **Σ** **in the Editing group, then widen** Column F **as needed to fit content**

7. **Select cells** B13:F17, **click** **Σ**, **then verify that $374,800.00 appears in cell F17 as shown in Figure E-13**

8. **Select cells** B7:E7, **click the** Data tab, **click** What-If Analysis **in the Data Tools group, click** Scenario Manager, **click** Add, **type** 2013 Rentals, **click** OK, **click** OK, **then click** Close

   You create a scenario to preserve the existing data because in the next lesson you will change the data in order to calculate projected sales.

9. **Save the workbook**

	A	B	C	D	E	F	G
	A18			f_x			

Paradise Resorts

Sales Summary for April, May, June, 2013

		Oahu	Maui	Kauai	Hawaii	Totals	
5	REVENUE						
6	Average Cost per Room	$ 180.00	$ 175.00	$ 190.00	$ 260.00		
7	Total Number of Rooms Rented	1400	2000	3500	2800		
8	Total Room Rental Revenue						
9							
10	EXPENSES						
11	Number of Rooms Available	40	50	75	60		
12	Operating Cost per Room	$ 7,000.00	$ 7,000.00	$ 7,000.00	$ 7,000.00		
13	Total Operating Costs						
14	Advertising Costs	$ 9,500.00	$ 11,200.00	$ 14,000.00	$ 10,500.00		
15	Total Expenses						
16							
17	NET REVENUE						
18							
19							

	A	B	C	D	E	F	G

Paradise Resorts

Sales Summary for April, May, June, 2013

		Oahu	Maui	Kauai	Hawaii	Totals	
5	REVENUE						
6	Average Cost per Room	$ 180.00	$ 175.00	$ 190.00	$ 260.00		
7	Total Number of Rooms Rented	1400	2000	3500	2800	9700	
8	Total Room Rental Revenue	$ 252,000.00	$350,000.00	$ 665,000.00	$ 728,000.00	$ 1,995,000.00	
9							
10	EXPENSES						
11	Number of Rooms Available	40	50	75	60		
12	Operating Cost per Room	$ 7,000.00	$ 7,000.00	$ 7,000.00	$ 7,000.00		
13	Total Operating Costs	$ 280,000.00	$350,000.00	$ 525,000.00	$ 420,000.00	$ 1,575,000.00	
14	Advertising Costs	$ 9,500.00	$ 11,200.00	$ 14,000.00	$ 10,500.00	$ 45,200.00	
15	Total Expenses	$ 289,500.00	$361,200.00	$ 539,000.00	$ 430,500.00	$ 1,620,200.00	
16							
17	NET REVENUE	$ (37,500.00)	$ (11,200.00)	$ 126,000.00	$ 297,500.00	$ 374,800.00	
18							
19							

Sales Report (continued)

Calculate Projected Sales

You use the Goal Seek feature to determine how many rooms you should rent at the Oahu and Maui hotels to increase the net revenue from these hotels next year, and then you create a bar chart.

Hint

You use Goal Seek to determine how many rooms you need to rent at the Oahu hotel to increase the net revenue to $100,000. The value needed, 2163.888889, appears in cell B7.

Hint

The net revenue in cell F17 of the 2013 Rentals sheet is again $374,800.00.

Steps:

1. Click cell B17 (the net revenue for the Oahu hotel), click the What-If Analysis button in the Data Tools group, click Goal Seek, click the To value: text box, type 100000 (five zeroes), press [Tab], type B7 as shown in Figure E-14, click OK, then click OK

2. Click cell C17, click What-If Analysis, click Goal Seek, enter 120000 as the To value and C7 as the cell to change, click OK, click OK, select cells B7 through F7, click the Home tab, click the Comma Style button 🔘 in the Number group, then click the Decrease Decimal button 🔘 twice

   You need to rent 2,164 rooms at the Oahu hotel to make a profit of $100,000, and you need to rent 2,750 rooms at the Maui hotel to make a profit of $120,000.

3. Click the Data tab, click What-If Analysis, click Scenario Manager, click Add, type Projected Rentals, enter B7:C7 as the changing cells, click OK, click OK, then click Close

4. Double-click the Sheet1 tab, type 2013 Rentals, click the Select All button 🔘 in the upper-left corner of the worksheet frame to select all the data, click the Home tab, click the Copy button 🔘 in the Clipboard group, click the Sheet2 tab, click the Paste button in the Clipboard group, double-click the Sheet2 tab, type Projected Rentals, then press [Enter]

5. Show the 2013 Rentals worksheet, click the Data tab, click What-If Analysis, click Scenario Manager, click 2013 Rentals, click Show, click Close, then click cell A1

6. Show the Projected Rentals worksheet, click cell A20, click the Insert tab, click Bar in the Charts group, click the upper-left selection (Clustered Bar), click Select Data in the Data group, click the Collapse button 🔘 next to "Chart data range", click the 2013 Rentals tab, select cells B4:E4, press and hold [Ctrl], select cells B8:E8, click the Expand button 🔘, then click OK

7. Move the chart down so that it starts at cell A20, resize it so that it extends to cell G40, click Select Data in the Data group, click Series 1 in the Legend Entries (Series) list box, click Edit, type 2013 Rentals as shown in Figure E-15, click OK, click Add in the Legend Entries (Series) list box, type Projected Rentals, click the Collapse button 🔘 next to "Series values" in the Edit Series dialog box, select cells B8:E8 on the Projected Rentals tab, click the Expand button 🔘, click OK, then click OK

8. Click the Chart Tools Layout tab, click the Chart Title button in the Labels group, click Above Chart, type Comparison of Current and Projected Room Rentals, press [Enter], click the Legend button in the Labels group, then click Show Legend at Bottom

9. Right-click the value axis (x-axis) in the bar chart, click Format Axis, click the Fixed option button next to "Maximum", click Number in the left pane to open the Number pane, select the contents of the Decimal places text box, type 0, click Close, save the workbook, then compare the bar chart to Figure E-16

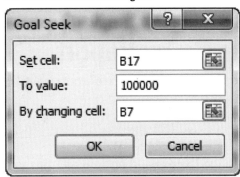

FIGURE E-14: Goal Seek dialog box

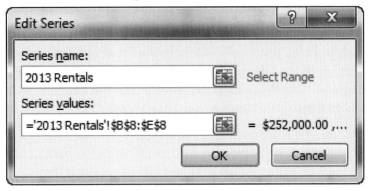

FIGURE E-15: Edit Series dialog box

FIGURE E-16: Bar chart resized and positioned

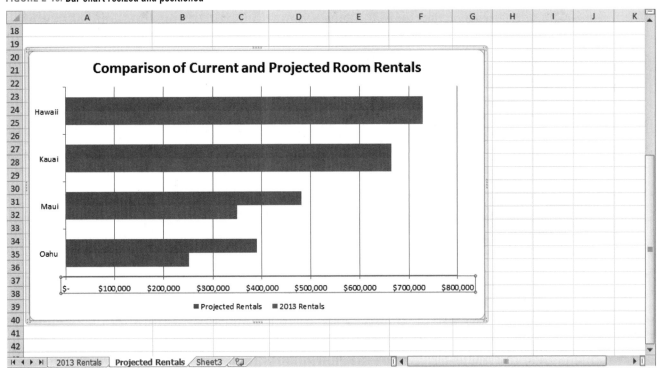

Sales Report (continued)

Create the Sales Report

You need to compile all the data from the Excel workbook in a report you create in Word. The completed report is shown in Figure E-17.

Trouble

To increase the After spacing to 12 pt for the Title style, right-click the Title style in the Style gallery, click Modify Style, click the Increase Paragraph Spacing button twice in the Modify Style dialog box, then click OK. Use a similar procedure to modify the Normal style.

Steps:

1. Start Word, change the top and bottom margins to .6", type Sales Report for Paradise Resorts, press [Enter], apply the Title style to the text, select the Fancy style set, modify the Title style so the After spacing is 12 pt, modify the Normal style so the font size is 12 pt, then save the document as PR E- Paradise Resorts Sales Report to the location where you save the files for this book

2. Click the Change Styles button, point to Colors, select the Metro color set, type and center the subtitle, then type paragraph one as shown in the completed sales report in Figure E-17

3. Switch to Excel, select cells A1:F17 in the Projected Rentals worksheet, click the Copy button 📋 in the Clipboard group, switch to Word, verify you are at the end of the paragraph you just typed, press [Enter], click the Paste list arrow, click Paste Special, click the Paste link option button, click Microsoft Excel Worksheet Object, then click OK

4. Right-click the copied worksheet object in Word, click Format Object, click the Size tab, set the Width of the object to 6", click OK, type the paragraph of text under the copied worksheet object as shown in Figure E-17, then press [Enter]

5. Double-click the copied worksheet object, click cell A2, select Summary in the formula bar, type Projections, select 2013, type 2014, then press [Enter]

Trouble

If the room rate was not updated, right-click the worksheet object, then click Update Link.

6. Scroll to the chart, click the chart, click the Copy button 📋, switch to Word, click below the last paragraph of text, click the Paste list arrow, click the Use Destination Theme & Link Data button 📋, set the Height of the chart to 3.1" and the Width to 6.1", switch to Excel, change the cost of the Kauai rooms (cell D6) to 220, return to Word, then verify that the Kauai room cost was updated to $220

   By selecting the Use Destination Theme & Link Data option, you ensure that the chart uses the color scheme and theme associated with the Word document, not the original Excel workbook.

7. Click in the text, click the Insert tab, click Shapes in the Illustrations group, select the Rounded Rectangular Callout shape in the Callouts section, draw a shape above the chart, click the More button ▾ in the Shapes Style gallery, click Subtle Effect - Green, Accent 1, type Increase to 2,750 rooms, then drag to resize the callout and position it to the right of Maui as shown in Figure E-17

   You will need to drag the yellow diamond handle on the callout shape to position the pointer correctly.

8. Click the border of the callout box, click the Home tab, click the Copy button 📋 in the Clipboard group, click the Paste button, then enter the required text and position the callout box next to Oahu as shown in Figure E-17

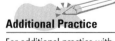

Additional Practice

For additional practice with the skills presented in this project, complete Independent Challenge 2.

9. Save and close the document, switch to Excel, add your name below the chart, save and close the workbook, then submit both files to your instructor

   If you wish to make changes to the Word document linked to the Excel workbook, open the Excel workbook first. Then, open the Word document and click Yes in response to the message that appears asking if you wish to maintain the link between the two files.

Sales Report for Paradise Resorts

Prepared by Your Name

In April, May, and June of 2013, both the Oahu and Maui resorts lost money. To increase revenue at the Oahu resort, we need to rent 2,164 rooms instead of the current 1,400 rooms. To increase revenue at the Maui resort, we need to rent 2,750 rooms instead of the current 2,000 rooms. By so doing, we will increase the Oahu resort revenue to $100,000 and the Maui resort revenue to $120,000.

Paradise Resorts
Sales Projections for April, May, June, 2014

	Oahu	Maui	Kauai	Hawaii	Totals
REVENUE					
Average Cost per Room	$ 180.00	$ 175.00	$ 220.00	$ 260.00	
Total Number of Rooms Rented	2,164	2,750	3,500	2,800	11,214
Total Room Rental Revenue	$ 389,500.00	$ 481,200.00	$ 770,000.00	$ 728,000.00	$ 2,368,700.00
EXPENSES					
Number of Rooms Available	40	50	75	60	
Operating Cost per Room	$ 7,000.00	$ 7,000.00	$ 7,000.00	$ 7,000.00	
Total Operating Costs	$ 280,000.00	$ 350,000.00	$ 525,000.00	$ 420,000.00	$ 1,575,000.00
Advertising Costs	$ 9,500.00	$ 11,200.00	$ 14,000.00	$ 10,500.00	$ 45,200.00
Total Expenses	$ 289,500.00	$ 361,200.00	$ 539,000.00	$ 430,500.00	$ 1,620,200.00
NET REVENUE	$ 100,000.00	$ 120,000.00	$ 231,000.00	$ 297,500.00	$ 748,500.00

The bar chart shown below compares the current room rentals in April, May, and June of 2013 with the projected room rentals in April, May, and June of 2014.

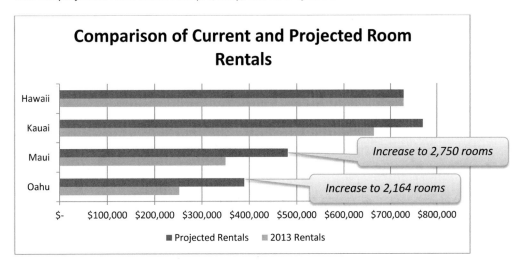

Marketing Update for Endless Sun Tours

Endless Sun Tours hosts four two-week cruises of the Mediterranean on small sailing ships. As the office manager, you've decided to create a one-page marketing update that describes the cruises offered by the company and summarizes current sales. You need to **Create the Update in Word** and then **Add Linked Data from Excel**. The completed document is shown in Figure E-20 on page 117.

Create the Update in Word

You need to enter the text for the marketing update, and then you enter data in Excel that relates to the sales of Endless Sun Tours.

Hint

If you completed Unit E Project 2, you can click Margins on the Page Layout tab, then select Last Custom Setting.

Trouble

If no link to a map appears, open your browser and use your favorite search engine to find an image of a map of the Mediterranean Sea.

Steps:

1. Start Word, change the top and bottom margins to .6", type and format the text as shown in Figure E-18, then save the document as PR E-Endless Sun Tours Marketing Update to the location where you save the files for this book

2. Click at the beginning of paragraph 1, click the Review tab, click the Research button in the Proofing group, type Mediterranean Map in the Search for text box, click the list arrow next to the text box immediately below the "Search for" text box, click All Research Sites, then click the Start searching button ➡ if the search does not start automatically

3. Scroll the search results and click a link that opens a map of the Mediterranean Sea
   Your browser opens and a map of the Mediterranean Sea appears.

4. When the browser window opens, scroll if needed to view the picture of the map, then return to Word

5. Click the Insert tab, click Screenshot, click Screen Clipping, then drag to select only the map of the Mediterranean Sea

6. Close the Research task pane, then set the height of the map picture at 1.7" (the width will adjust automatically)

7. With the map picture still selected, click Wrap Text in the Arrange group, click Square, click OK, drag the map picture to position it to the right of the first paragraph so that the top of the map picture is even with the first line of the paragraph, then save the document

8. Start Excel, apply the Composite theme, then enter and enhance the labels and values as shown in Figure E-19

9. Name the Sheet1 tab Sales, name the Sheet2 tab Chart, then save the workbook as PR E-Endless Sun Tours Marketing Data to the location where you save the files for this book

FIGURE E-18: **Text for marketing report**

Title style

Endless Sun Tours

Endless Sun Tours conducts tours in four categories each year to various destinations in the Mediterranean countries. These tours include Grecian Odyssey, Spanish Isles, Adriatic Dreaming, and the Eastern Mediterranean. All of Endless Sun's tours are two weeks in duration.

Since its incorporation in 2003, Endless Sun Tours has consistently sold virtually all of the Grecian Odyssey and Eastern Mediterranean tours. In most years, 80% of the Spanish Isles tours are sold. The Adriatic Dreaming tours were first offered in 2011 and are steadily gaining in popularity. Shown below is a breakdown of tour sales by category.

In 2013, Endless Sun Tours offered a total of xx tours and sold xx tours. The column chart shown below displays the number of tours sold in each category relative to the number of tours available. Grecian Odyssey tours rank the highest in terms of the number of tours sold relative to the tours available. Adriatic Dreaming tours rank the lowest.

You will replace the "xx" references with values later

FIGURE E-19: **Sales data in Excel**

	A	B	C	D
1	**2013 Sales by Category**			
2	**Tour Name**	**Tours Available**	**Tours Sold**	
3	Grecian Odyssey	50	48	
4	Spanish Isles	38	28	
5	Adriatic Dreaming	22	14	
6	Eastern Mediterranean	30	29	
7		140	119	
8				
9				

Bold, 18 pt, merged and centered across cells A1:C1, filled with Gold, Accent 3, Lighter 60%

Bold, centered, widen columns to fit content

Use AutoSum to calculate the totals in cells B7 and C7

Add Linked Data from Excel

You need to create a chart in Excel, and then copy the sales data and chart into Word as linked objects. The completed report is shown in Figure E-20.

Steps:

1. Select cells A2:C6 on the Sales tab, click the Insert tab, click Column, select the Clustered Column chart, click the Move Chart button in the Location group, click the Object in list arrow, click Chart, then click OK

2. Click the Chart Tools Layout tab, add a chart title above the chart containing the text Tours Sold Compared to Tours Available, show the legend at the bottom, size and position the chart so that it extends from cell A1 through cell J21, click the Sales tab, then save the workbook

3. Select cells A1:C7, click the Copy button 🖻, switch to Word, click after "category" at the end of the second paragraph, press [Enter], click the Paste list arrow, then click the Link & Keep Source Formatting button 📋

   The data is pasted into Word as a linked object that uses the formatting you applied in Excel.

Trouble

Update the column widths manually if they do not update automatically.

4. Click after category at the end of the second paragraph, press [Delete] to remove the extra blank line, switch to Excel, click the Bottom Border list arrow ⊞ ▾ in the Font group, click All Borders ⊞, switch back to Word, right-click the copied object, click Update Link, click the table move handle ⊞ at the upper-left corner of the copied object, then click the Center button ≡ in the Paragraph group

   The column widths are adjusted, the border lines are applied, and the table is centered on the page.

5. Switch back to Excel, click the Chart tab, click the chart, copy it, switch to Word, click after "lowest" at the end of the last paragraph, press [Enter], click the Paste list arrow, then click the Keep Source Formatting & Link Data button 📋

6. Set the height of the chart at 3.3" and the width at 5.5", center it, click after the chart, then press [Delete] as needed to remove the blank second page

7. Switch to Excel, show the Sales sheet, click cell B7, click 🖻, switch to Word, select the first xx in line 1 of paragraph 3, click the Paste list arrow, click Paste Special, click the Paste link option button, click Unformatted Text, click OK, then press [Spacebar] if you need to add a space between "140" and "tours"

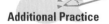

Trouble

Center the worksheet object if necessary.

8. Copy cell C7 from Excel and paste it as a link (Unformatted Text) over the second xx in paragraph 3, switch to Excel, change the number of available tours for Spanish Isles in cell B4 to 35, switch to Word, then if the data was not updated automatically, right-click the worksheet object, click Update Link, right-click 140 in paragraph 3, and click Update Link if the data did not update automatically

   In the chart, the green column representing the Spanish Isles is updated automatically.

Additional Practice

For additional practice with the skills presented in this project, complete Independent Challenge 3.

9. Double-click the footer area below the chart, type your name and right-align it, apply the Composite theme, adjust objects as needed so that all content fits on one page, save the document, switch to Excel, add your name to the Sales worksheet, save the workbook in Excel, submit both files to your instructor, then close both files

   If you wish to make changes to the Word document linked to the Excel workbook, open the Excel workbook first. Then, open the Word document and click Yes in response to the message that appears asking if you wish to maintain the link between the document and the workbook.

Endless Sun Tours

Endless Sun Tours conducts tours in four categories each year to various destinations in the Mediterranean countries. These tours include Grecian Odyssey, Spanish Isles, Adriatic Dreaming, and the Eastern Mediterranean. All of Endless Sun's tours are two weeks in duration.

Since its incorporation in 2003, Endless Sun Tours has consistently sold virtually all of the Grecian Odyssey and Eastern Mediterranean tours. In most years, 80% of the Spanish Isles tours are sold. The Adriatic Dreaming tours were first offered in 2011 and are steadily gaining in popularity. Shown below is a breakdown of tour sales by category.

2013 Sales by Category		
Tour Name	**Tours Available**	**Tours Sold**
Grecian Odyssey	50	48
Spanish Isles	35	28
Adriatic Dreaming	22	14
Eastern Mediterranean	30	29
	137	119

In 2013, Endless Sun Tours offered a total of 137 tours and sold 119 tours. The column chart shown below displays the number of tours sold in each category relative to the number of tours available. Grecian Odyssey tours rank the highest in terms of the number of tours sold relative to the tours available. Adriatic Dreaming tours rank the lowest.

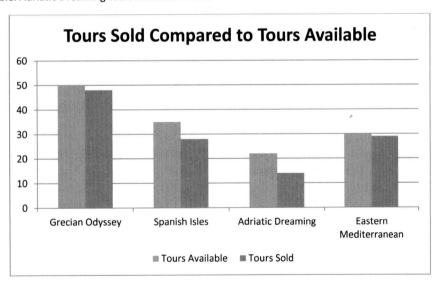

Your Name

Independent Challenge 1

Create a form in Word that you can use to record data related to a performance review for a position or situation of your choice. For example, you could create a form to review a course, a workshop, or an employee. Fill in the boxes below with the required information, then set up the form in Word. You need to insert content controls to contain information that will change each time you fill in the form for a different evaluation. You then need to enter data related to the evaluation in an Excel worksheet and finally copy the data and paste it as a link in Word. The completed document in Word should also include a linked chart created from the Excel data.

1. Determine the company name and the position or situation that requires a performance review form. You also need to determine at least five categories to review. For example, if you are creating a form to review a series of workshops, the categories could be Registration Procedure, Instructor, Course Materials, Learning Outcomes, and Facilities. In the box below, write the name of your company and the five categories that you will rank in the performance review:

Company name: _____

Categories to review:

1. _____

2. _____

3. _____

4. _____

5. _____

2. In the box below, identify information about one individual, course, or workshop that you plan to review. If you're reviewing a person, include the name, department, and position. If you're reviewing a course or workshop, include the title, subject, instructor name, date, and location.

Review subject:

_____

_____

_____

_____

3. In Word, set up a document that includes a title and a subtitle, then apply the Style Set of your choice and modify the Normal style (for example, change the font size or font style). Select the theme of your choice.

4. Create an attractively formatted table to contain the performance review form. Use the performance review you created for Unit E Project 1 as your guide.

5. Enter content controls where required in the table form. Use at least three types of content controls such as the Rich Text, Combo Box, and Date Picker content controls. Remember that you can use the Legacy Tools form controls when you want to specify exactly how a user should enter data in the cell. For example, if the form requires a course number, you can add a Text Form Field content control to specify that users enter only a 3-digit number for the course number. Type your name at the bottom of the page.

6. Save the form as **PR E-My Performance Review Form** to the location where you save the files for this book.

7. In Excel, provide an explanation of what this worksheet contains such as average student rankings, then enter labels for the categories that you plan to review (refer to Step 1).

8. Rename the worksheet tab with a meaningful name, such as the name of the individual or course being reviewed, and enter rankings for one individual or course/workshop you are evaluating. Set up the worksheet attractively.

Independent Challenge 1 (continued)

9. Create a chart that illustrates some aspect of the data. For example, you could create a column chart that shows a ranking for each category or you could create a bar chart that compares the rankings provided by two individuals. Format the chart attractively. Remember to specify the maximum value of the value axis.

10. Save the workbook as **PR E-My Performance Review Data** to the location where you save the files for this book.

11. In Word, enter appropriate information in the form fields related to the individual or course/workshop you are evaluating, then save the form as **PR E-My Performance Review 1** to the location where you save the files for this book.

12. In Word, copy data from the Excel worksheet and paste it as a linked Microsoft Excel Worksheet Object in an appropriate area of the form. Copy the chart and paste it as a link using the Use Destination Theme & Link Data option, resize the chart so the form fits on one page, then save the document.

13. In Excel, copy the worksheet (both the data and the chart) to a new worksheet, then replace the data with data related to a different individual, course, or workshop. Give the worksheet tab a meaningful name to reflect the worksheet content.

14. Modify the chart so that it references data in the second worksheet. Make sure the maximum value on the value axis scale is the same on both charts to ensure a meaningful comparison between the charted results.

15. In Word, save the document as **PR E-My Performance Review 2** to the location where you save the files for this book, change the form information to reflect who or what is being reviewed, open the Edit Links to Files dialog box, then change the link so that it refers to the data in the second Excel worksheet.

16. Click the chart, click the Chart Tools Design tab, click Select Data in the Data group, select the name currently entered in the Chart data range text box, type the correct reference, add your name to a worksheet, then close the Excel workbook.

17. Save the document, submit all files to your instructor, then exit Word and Excel.

Independent Challenge 2

In Excel, use the Goal Seek function to analyze a specific goal related to a company of your choice. In Word, create a sales report that includes data from Excel. For example, you could set a goal to increase your sales in two or three states or countries or increase the number of products of a certain type that you plan to sell.

1. In the box below, write the name of your company and a short description of your business goal. For example, you could name your company "Hollyhock Landscaping," and describe your goal as: To increase sales of perennials.

Company Name: _____

Description of Business Goal: _____

_____

_____

2. Set up a worksheet in Excel similar to the worksheet created for Paradise Resorts in Unit E Project 2. Note that you need to include two or three products or locations, the income generated from sales, and your various expenses. Apply the theme of your choice and name the worksheet **Current**.

3. Save the workbook as **PR E-My Sales Report Goals** to the location where you save the files for this book.

4. Create a current scenario of the data that you will use Goal Seek to change. For example, if you decide to increase the total number of bedding plants you sell in May, you need to create a current scenario of the sales data related to bedding plants.

Independent Challenge 2 (continued)

5. Use Goal Seek to change the value in one of the cells. Note that the cell you wish to change must not contain a formula; however, the cell must be referenced in a formula contained in another cell, such as a total. You use Goal Seek to specify a set value for the cell containing the formula. For example, you can ask Goal Seek to calculate how many bedding plants you need to sell in May if you want your net income in May to equal $30,000.

6. Create a scenario from the projected data generated by Goal Seek, name the scenario **Projected**, then show the current scenario.

7. Copy the sales data from the Current sheet into a new sheet called **Projected**, then show the Projected scenario.

8. In the Projected worksheet, create a bar chart (use the style of your choice) that compares the relevant values in the Current scenario in the Current worksheet with the new values generated by Goal Seek and shown as the Projected scenario in the Projected worksheet.

9. Format the bar chart attractively.

10. In Word, create a new document that includes the name of the company as a heading. Enter text that describes the company and summarizes the sales data.

11. Save the report as **PR E-My Sales Report** to the location where you save the files for this book.

12. Copy the data in the Projected worksheet, and paste it as a link into the Word report, using the Microsoft Excel Worksheet Object option in the Paste Special dialog box.

13. Copy the chart from the Projected worksheet, and paste it as a link into the Word report using the Keep Source Formatting and Link Data option. Enter a paragraph above the chart that summarizes the information in the chart.

14. Draw a callout to highlight each value in the chart that represents projected sales.

15. In Excel, change some of the data, then check that the data is updated correctly in the Word document.

16. Add your name to the worksheet, save and close the workbook, include your name in the sales report, submit a copy to your instructor, then save and close the document.

Independent Challenge 3

Create a one-page summary in Word that provides information about the sales and marketing efforts for a company of your choice. Use the marketing update you created for Endless Sun Tours in Unit E Project 3 as your model. The summary should include an appropriate screen clipping that you obtain by conducting a search of the Internet from the Research task pane.

1. In Excel, enter data related to your product line and create an appropriate chart in a second worksheet.

2. In Word, paste the data into the document as a linked object, then copy the chart and paste it as a link into the Word document using the Keep Source Formatting & Link Data paste option.

3. Copy additional links into the body of the report using the Unformatted Text option in the Paste Special dialog box.

4. Make changes to the data in Excel, then update the links in Word.

5. Add a screen clipping of a portion of an appropriate Web site, resize the screen clipping if necessary, modify the text wrapping, and position it attractively in the document.

6. Save the workbook as **PR E-My Update Data** to the location where you save the files for this book and the document as **PR E-My Update Report** to the same location. Select a different theme for the Word document and the Excel workbook so that when you use the "Use Source Formatting & Link Data" paste option, the formatting of the objects copied from the Excel workbook is retained.

7. Include your name on the Word document, save and close both files, then submit a copy of both files to your instructor.

Independent Challenge 4

Create an Excel worksheet with the projected income and expenses for Time Goes By, an online bookstore that specializes in historical books, maps, and periodicals. Then use the data in the worksheet to create a chart, which you link to a Projected Sales Summary in Word.

1. Open a blank workbook in Excel, then create the worksheet shown in Figure E-21. Note that the heading in cell A1 is formatted with the Heading 1 style. To save time, copy the values entered in column B across through column E.

FIGURE E-21

	A	B	C	D	E	F	G
1			Time Goes By				
2			Projected Income and Expenses				
3			September	October	November	December	Totals
4	Income						
5	Sales		32,000.00	32,000.00	32,000.00	32,000.00	
6	Less Returns (5%)						
7	Total Income						
8							
9	Expenses						
10	Salaries		$ 8,000.00	$ 8,000.00	$ 8,000.00	$ 8,000.00	
11	Rent		1,200.00	1,200.00	1,200.00	1,200.00	
12	Advertising		900.00	900.00	900.00	900.00	
13	Equipment Lease		800.00	800.00	800.00	800.00	
14	Operating Costs		700.00	700.00	700.00	700.00	
15	Cost of Sales (50%)						
16	Total Expenses						
17							
18	Total Profit						
19							
20							
21							

2. Save the workbook as **PR E-Time Goes By Sales Data** to the location where you save the files for this book.
3. Enter and copy the formulas required to calculate the cost of returns (sales multiplied by 5%), the total monthly income and the income for each of the four months, the Cost of Sales (sales multiplied by 50%), the total monthly expenses and the expenses for each of the four months, and the total monthly profit and the profit for each of the four months.
4. Format all totals with the Currency format, and verify that $11,200 appears in cell F18.
5. Create a pie chart that shows the breakdown of expenses by total amount for each expense category. You will need to use the [Ctrl] key to select cells A10:A15 and cells F10:F15 as the data range. Use the chart title **Breakdown of Expenses**, and show the labels as percentages.
6. Move the chart below row 18, then increase the chart size so the completed pie chart covers A20:F36.

Independent Challenge 4 (continued)

7. Switch to Word, then enter the text for the Sales Summary, as shown in Figure E-22. Note that you will replace each "XX" placeholder with a value that you paste as a link from the Excel worksheet. Apply the Slipstream theme, apply the Modern style set, then format the title with the Title style and the headings with the Heading 1 style.

FIGURE E-22

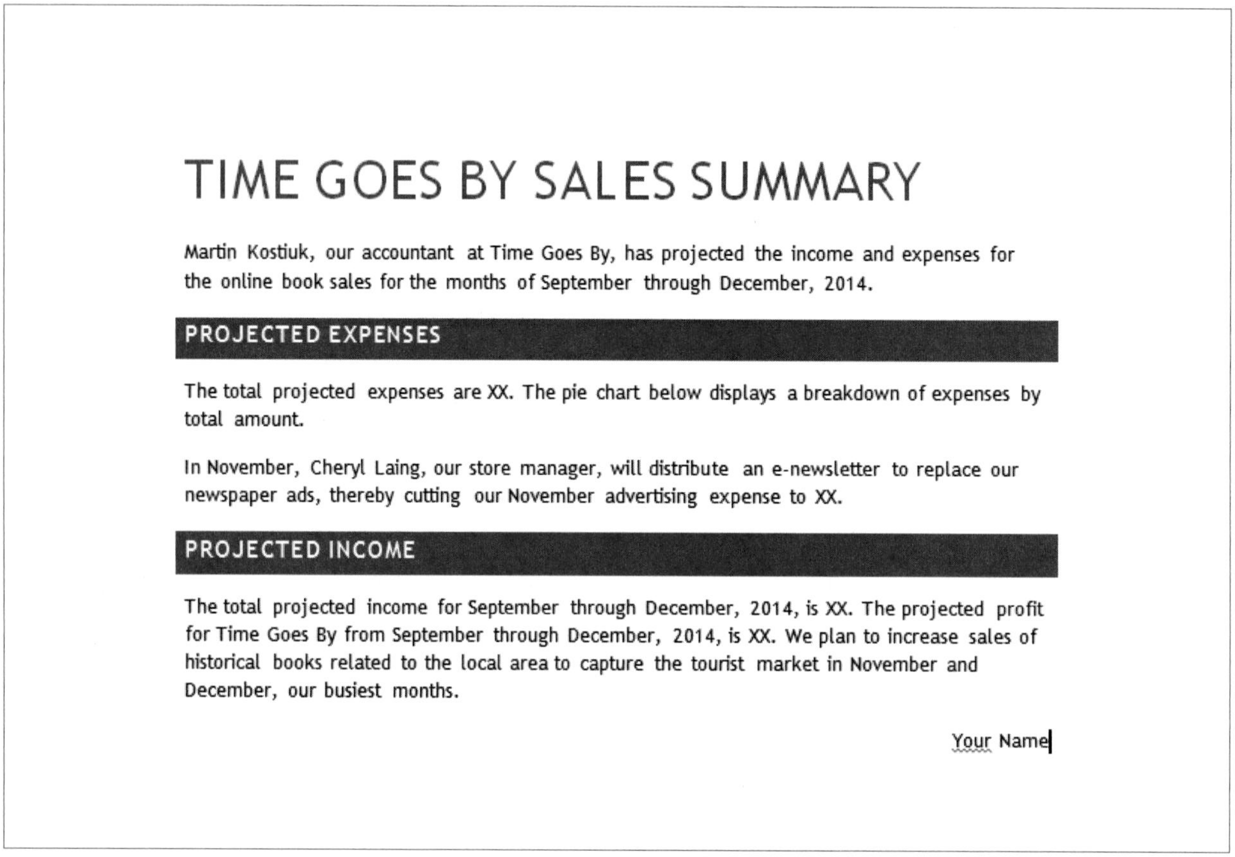

TIME GOES BY SALES SUMMARY

Martin Kostiuk, our accountant at Time Goes By, has projected the income and expenses for the online book sales for the months of September through December, 2014.

PROJECTED EXPENSES

The total projected expenses are XX. The pie chart below displays a breakdown of expenses by total amount.

In November, Cheryl Laing, our store manager, will distribute an e-newsletter to replace our newspaper ads, thereby cutting our November advertising expense to XX.

PROJECTED INCOME

The total projected income for September through December, 2014, is XX. The projected profit for Time Goes By from September through December, 2014, is XX. We plan to increase sales of historical books related to the local area to capture the tourist market in November and December, our busiest months.

Your Name

8. Save the document as **PR E-Time Goes By Projections** to the location where you save the files for this book.
9. In Excel, change the sales for November to $45,000 and the sales for December to $60,000.
10. Use Goal Seek to determine how much to spend on advertising in November to make a total profit in November of $9,000. (*Hint:* Set cell D18 to 9000 by changing cell D12.)
11. Copy the pie chart and paste it as a link using the Use Destination Theme & Link Data paste option.
12. Copy any totals required from Excel, and paste them as links into Word by replacing each "XX" placeholder with the corresponding total from Excel. Make sure you paste the totals as Unformatted Text from the Paste Special dialog box.
13. Switch to Excel, then increase the salaries expense for November and December to 15,000. Note the changes to the pie chart.

Independent Challenge 4 (continued)

14. Switch to Word, then update the links if necessary. Do not worry about removing extra spaces; they are inserted automatically each time you update data. The finished report is shown in Figure E-23.

15. Add your name to the Word document and the Excel workbook, submit the files to your instructor, then save and close both files.

FIGURE E-23

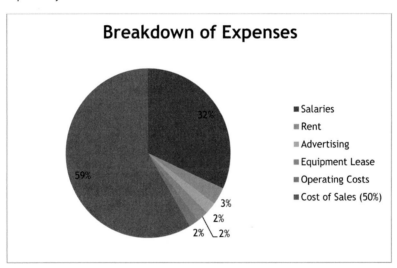

TIME GOES BY SALES SUMMARY

Martin Kostiuk, our accountant at Time Goes By, has projected the income and expenses for the online book sales for the months of September through December, 2014.

PROJECTED EXPENSES

The total projected expenses are $144,550.00 . The pie chart below displays a breakdown of expenses by total amount.

Breakdown of Expenses

- Salaries
- Rent
- Advertising
- Equipment Lease
- Operating Costs
- Cost of Sales (50%)

32%

59%

3%

2%

2% 2%

In November, Cheryl Laing, our store manager, will distribute an e-newsletter to replace our newspaper ads, thereby cutting our November advertising expense to 550.00 .

PROJECTED INCOME

The total projected income for September through December, 2014, is $160,550.00 . The projected profit for Time Goes By from September through December, 2014, is $16,000.00 . We plan to increase sales of historical books related to the local area to capture the tourist market in November and December, our busiest months.

Your Name

Visual Workshop

Create the worksheet shown in Figure E-24 in Excel, then save it as **PR E-Game Movers Sales Data** to the location where you save the files for this book. Apply the Austin theme. Calculate the total sales of each item by multiplying the Quantity by the Price, then calculate the total sales in cell E7. Create the text for the sales report in Word as shown in Figure E-25, using the Concourse theme and entering the values as links (Unformatted Text) copied from the Excel workbook. (*Note*: Your values will differ.) Save the document as **PR E-Game Movers Sales Report** to the location where you save the files for this book. In Excel, create a clustered cone chart that appears similar to the completed chart shown in Figure E-25. Copy the chart from Excel, and paste it into the Word document using the Keep Source Formatting & Link Data paste option. In Excel, change the unit price of Just for Kicks to $90, add your name to the worksheet, then save and close the workbook. Update the links in the sales report where needed, add your name under the chart, save the document, then submit both files to your instructor.

FIGURE E-24

	A	B	C	D	E
1	**Title**	**Category**	**Quantity**	**Price**	**Total**
2	Active Training Camp	Football	45	$ 75.00	
3	Just for Kicks	Soccer	75	$ 80.00	
4	Ultimate Basketball	Basketball	20	$ 50.00	
5	Icing	Hockey	25	$ 90.00	
6	Long and Lean	Fitness	59	$ 60.00	
7					
8					

FIGURE E-25

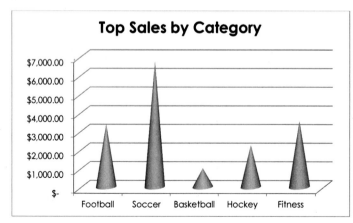

Game Movers Top Sellers

Sales of sports games have been brisk in 2013. Shown below are the unit sales of our top six sports titles. Our best–selling game is Just for Kicks in the Soccer category with sales in 2013 of 75 units for a total of $6,750.00.

The cone chart shown below compares the sales of each of the top selling sports games.

Top Sales by Category

Your Name

Access Projects

Files You Will Need:

PR F-1.jpg
PR F-2.jpg
PR F-3.jpg
PR F-4.jpg
PR F-5.jpg
PR F-6.jpg
PR F-7.accdb
PR F-8.docx
PR F-9.docx
PR F-10.accdb

You use a relational database program, such as Access 2010, to store information in related tables that you can use to perform queries and find specific data. For example, you can create a database containing the contact information and buying preferences of all your customers and then create a query to find all the customers who live in a certain area. You can then use this information to help develop a targeted marketing campaign. To create a database, you first identify categories—called fields—that describe and organize the contents of your database. Then you formulate queries or questions to retrieve the information you need. In this unit, you will use Microsoft Access to set up databases and then ask questions to find the information you need to perform specific tasks.

In This Unit You Will Create the Following:

Inventory Database

Author Database

Tour Database

Inventory for Global Artisan

Global Artisan distributes hand-crafted items to gift shops and specialty stores. You need to create an inventory database containing two tables: the Suppliers table and the Products table. For this project, you **Set Up the Tables**, **Create Forms**, **Create Queries**, and then **Format and Print an Order Report**.

Set Up the Tables

You need to set up the Global Artisan Suppliers table and the Global Artisan Products table.

Steps:

1. **Start Access, verify that Blank Database is selected, select the contents of the** File Name **text box,** type PR F-Global Artisan Inventory, **click the** Browse button , **navigate to the location where you save the files for this book, click** OK, **then click** Create

2. **Click the** View button **in the Views group,** type Global Artisan Suppliers **as the table name, then press** [Enter]

3. **Type** Supplier ID, **press** [↓], **type** Supplier Name, **press** [↓], **type** Email Address, **press** [Tab], **click the** Data Type list arrow, **click** Hyperlink, **click the** Close 'Global Artisan Suppliers' button ☒, **then click** Yes **to save the table**

4. **Click the** Create tab, **click** Table **in the Tables group, click the** View button, **type** Global Artisan Products **as the table name, press** [Enter], **type** Product ID, **press** [↓], **then enter the remaining field names as shown in Figure F-1**

5. **Click the** Region Data Type list arrow, **click** Open **if a warning appears, click the** "I will type in the values that I want." **option button, click** Next, **press** [Tab], **type** Africa, **press** [↓], **enter the remaining regions shown in Figure F-2, then click** Finish

6. **Click the** Category Data Type list arrow, **use the Lookup Wizard to enter the categories shown in Figure F-3, then click** Finish

   If you press [Enter] while typing values in the Lookup Wizard, click Back to return to the list of values.

7. **Click the** Supplier Name Data Type list arrow, **click** Lookup Wizard, **click** Next **to accept that you want the values to come from an existing table, click** Table: Global Artisan Suppliers, **click** Next, **click** Supplier Name **in the list of available fields, click the** Select Single Field button ⟩, **click** Next, **click** Next, **click** Finish, **then click** Yes

   You use the Lookup Wizard to identify the field in the Global Artisan Suppliers table that contains the names of the suppliers you want to include in the Global Artisan Products table. When you use the Lookup Wizard to create a relationship between two tables based on a common field, Access automatically uses the Primary Key field (Supplier ID) from the "one" table and changes the data type for the related field in the "many" table from Text to Number.

8. **Click the** Units in Stock Data Type list arrow, **click** Number, **change the data type for Unit Price to** Currency, **then close and save the table**

9. **Click the** Database Tools tab, **click** Relationships, **double-click the** line **between the two tables, click the** Enforce Referential Integrity check box **to select it, click** OK, **compare the Relationships window to Figure F-4, then close the Relationships window**

   You enforce referential integrity so that you can enter only the names of suppliers that are listed in the Global Artisan Suppliers table into the Global Artisan Products table.

Trouble

To see the list arrow, click the Region Data Type list box.

Trouble

If the Enforce Referential Integrity check box is grayed out, close the Edit Relationships dialog box and double-click the line again.

	Global Artisan Products		
	Field Name	Data Type	Description
🔑	Product ID	AutoNumber	
	Product Name	Text	
	Region	Text	
	Category	Text	
	Supplier Name	Text	
	Units in Stock	Text	
	Unit Price	Text ▼	

FIGURE F-2: Values for the Region field

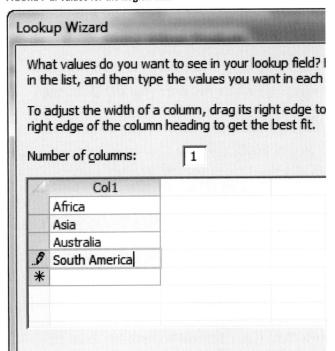

FIGURE F-3: Values for the Category field

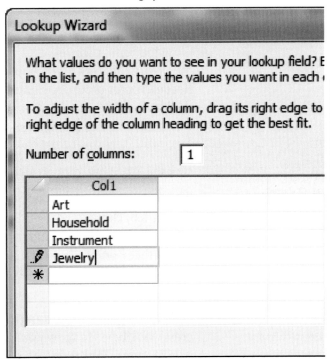

FIGURE F-4: One-to-many relationship

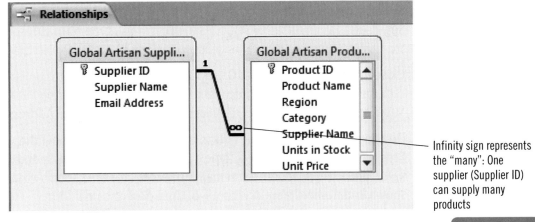

Access 2010

Inventory Database (continued)

Create Forms

You need to create forms into which you can enter the data for the Global Artisan Suppliers table and the Global Artisan Products table.

Hint

Move the pointer over each theme to read the ScreenTip. The themes are in alphabetical order.

Steps:

1. **Click** Global Artisan Suppliers **in the list of tables, click the** Create tab, **click** Form **in the Forms group, click the** Themes button **in the Themes group, then scroll to and click** Elemental

2. **Click the** View button **in the Views group, press** [Tab], **type** Outback Arts, **press** [Tab], **then type** sales@outbackarts.com

3. **Click the** Next record button ▶ **at the bottom of the form window, click in the** Supplier Name text box, **type** Out of Africa Crafts, **enter** sales@outofafricacrafts.com **as the Email Address, then go to the next record and create another form for** Rainforest Collective **with the address** sales@rainforestcollective.com

4. **Close the form, click** Yes, **click** OK, **click** Global Artisan Products **in the list of tables, click the** Create tab, **click** Form, **apply the** Elemental **theme, click the** Logo button **in the Header/Footer group, navigate to the location where you store your Data Files, then double-click** PR F-1.jpg

   The picture of the logo does not seem to appear in the logo area. You need to modify the picture size mode.

Trouble

If Size Mode does not appear in the list of options, click the All tab on the Property Sheet.

5. **Right-click the** logo, **click** Properties, **click** Clip **next to "Size Mode" in the Property Sheet, click the** list arrow, **click** Stretch, **then click the** Close button ✖

6. **Click the** ProductID label **(not the text box next to the label), click the** Form Layout Tools Format tab, **click the** Bold button **B** **in the Font group, double-click the** Format Painter button 🖌 **in the Font group, click each of the labels to apply bold, click** 🖌 **to turn off the Format Painter, then click** Supplier Name **and drag the yellow outline slightly to the right so the entire label is visible**

Hint

You can minimize typing time when you create lookup fields for as many of the fields as possible.

7. **Click the** Form Layout Tools Design tab, **click the** View button **in the Views group, press** [▼], **type** Opal Earrings **in the Product Name text box, press** [Tab], **type** au **to show australia, press** [Tab], **type** j **to show jewelry, press** [Tab], **type** o **to show outback Arts, press** [Tab], **type** 15, **press** [Tab], **type** 250, **press** [Enter], **click the** Previous record button ◀ **at the bottom of the form window to move back to record 1, then compare the form for record 1 to Figure F-5**

8. **Click the** Next record button ▶ **to start a new record, press** [Tab], **type** Lacquer Dinner Set, **press** [Tab], **type** as **to select Asia, press** [Tab], **type** h **for Household, then press** [Tab]

   You forgot to add the supplier for this product when you set up the suppliers table.

9. **Close the form, click** Yes, **click** OK, **double-click** Global Artisan Suppliers **in the list of forms, click the** New button **in the Records group, press** [Tab], **type** Asia Pacific Imports **for the Supplier Name and** sales@asiapacificimports.com **as the Email Address, then close the form**

10. **Double-click** Global Artisan Products **in the list of forms to show the Global Artisan Products form, go to record 2, type** a **for Asia Pacific Imports,** 9, **and** 220 **in the appropriate fields, press** [Enter], **enter the remaining records for the Global Artisans Products table as shown in datasheet view in Figure F-6, then close the final form**

Trouble

Check entries carefully to be sure AutoFill inserts the information you want. You may have to type more than one letter to see the correct entry.

FIGURE F-5: **Completed record for product 1**

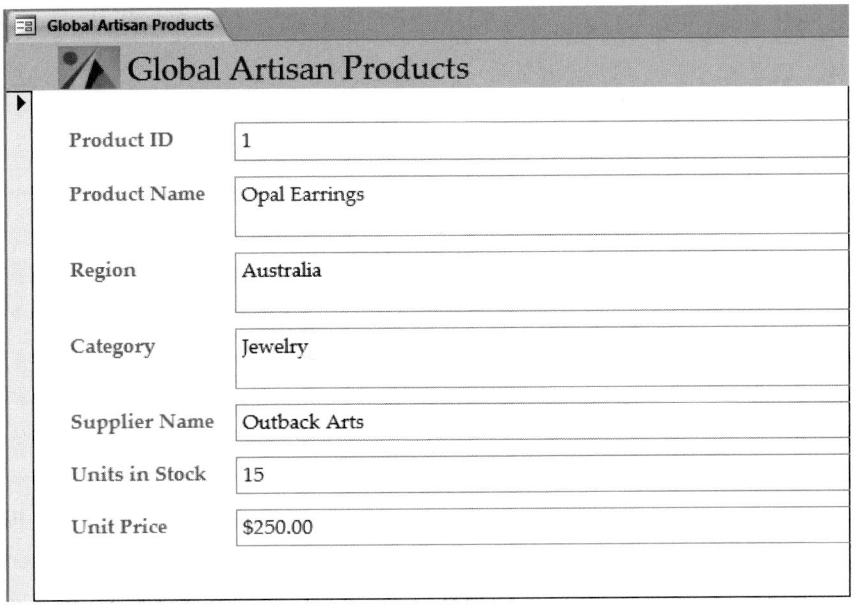

FIGURE F-6: **Datasheet for Global Artisan Products table**

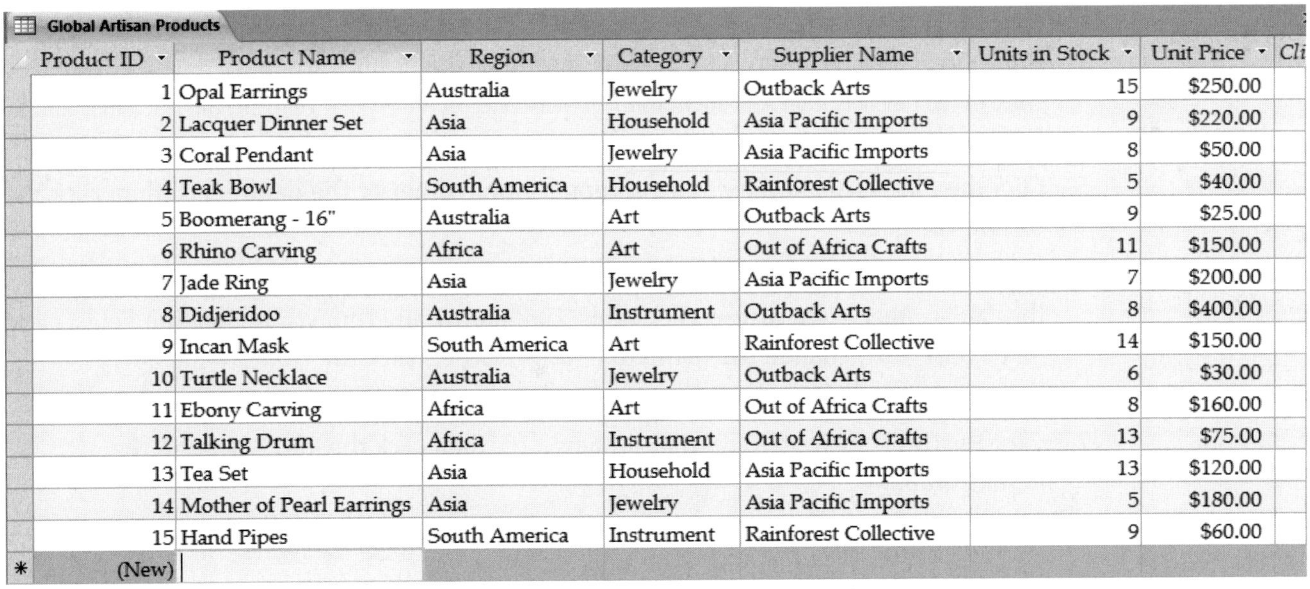

Product ID	Product Name	Region	Category	Supplier Name	Units in Stock	Unit Price	Cli
1	Opal Earrings	Australia	Jewelry	Outback Arts	15	$250.00	
2	Lacquer Dinner Set	Asia	Household	Asia Pacific Imports	9	$220.00	
3	Coral Pendant	Asia	Jewelry	Asia Pacific Imports	8	$50.00	
4	Teak Bowl	South America	Household	Rainforest Collective	5	$40.00	
5	Boomerang - 16"	Australia	Art	Outback Arts	9	$25.00	
6	Rhino Carving	Africa	Art	Out of Africa Crafts	11	$150.00	
7	Jade Ring	Asia	Jewelry	Asia Pacific Imports	7	$200.00	
8	Didjeridoo	Australia	Instrument	Outback Arts	8	$400.00	
9	Incan Mask	South America	Art	Rainforest Collective	14	$150.00	
10	Turtle Necklace	Australia	Jewelry	Outback Arts	6	$30.00	
11	Ebony Carving	Africa	Art	Out of Africa Crafts	8	$160.00	
12	Talking Drum	Africa	Instrument	Out of Africa Crafts	13	$75.00	
13	Tea Set	Asia	Household	Asia Pacific Imports	13	$120.00	
14	Mother of Pearl Earrings	Asia	Jewelry	Asia Pacific Imports	5	$180.00	
15	Hand Pipes	South America	Instrument	Rainforest Collective	9	$60.00	
(New)							

Create Queries

First, you view the records that relate to each of the four suppliers, and then you use the two tables that you've created to ask two questions, called queries. You create a query to find out how many products you have from Asia in the Jewelry category, and then you create a query to determine the number of products with fewer than 10 items in stock. Finally, you enter formulas in the Expression Builder to calculate how many units you need to order and the total cost.

Steps:

1. **Double-click** Global Artisan Suppliers **in the list of forms to open the form, then click the Next record button** ▶ **at the bottom of the form window to view the records from the Global Artisan Products table associated with each of the four suppliers**

   As a result of the one-to-many relationship you created between the Global Artisan Suppliers table and the Global Artisan Products table, you can create queries that list all the products purchased from a specific supplier.

2. **Close the Global Artisan Suppliers form, click the** Create tab, **click the** Query Wizard **button in the Queries group, then click** OK **to accept Simple Query Wizard**

Trouble

If Table: Global Artisan Suppliers appears in the list box, click the list arrow, then click Table: Global Artisan Products.

3. **Verify that Table: Global Artisan Products is selected in the Tables/Queries list box, click the** Select All Fields button ▶▶ **to select all the fields in the Available Fields list box, click** Next, **click** Next **to accept a Detail query, select the contents of the** text box, **type** Asia Jewelry **as the query name, click the** "Modify the query design." **option button, then click** Finish

4. **Click the** Region Criteria cell, **type** Asia, **click the** Category Criteria cell, **type** Jewelry **as shown in Figure F-7, then click the** Run button **in the Results group**

   Three of the products from Asia are from the Jewelry category—the Coral Pendant, the Jade Ring, and the Mother of Pearl Earrings.

5. **Click the** Close 'Asia Jewelry' button **(upper-right corner of the datasheet), then click** Yes **to save the query**

6. **Click the** Create tab, **click the** Query Wizard button **in the Queries group, click** OK, **click the** Tables/Queries list arrow, **click** Table: Global Artisan Products, **add all the fields, click** Next, **click** Next, **change the name to** Items to Order, **click the** "Modify the query design." **option button, then click** Finish

7. **Click the** [Units in Stock] Criteria cell, **type** <10, **then click the** Run button **in the Results group**

   A datasheet listing all the products with fewer than 10 units in stock appears. These are the items that you need to order.

8. **Click the** View button **in the Views group, click in the blank cell to the right of [Unit Price] (you may need to scroll right), click** Builder **in the Query Setup group, type the formula:** Units to Order: (10-[Units in Stock]) **as shown in Figure F-8, then click** OK

9. **Click in the blank cell to the right of "Units to Order", click** Builder **in the Query Setup group, type** Total: [Units to Order]*[Unit Price], **click** OK, **click the** Run button, **scroll right and adjust the column widths as needed, compare the query to Figure F-9, close and save the query, then close the Global Artisan Products table if it is still open**

FIGURE F-7: Selecting criteria

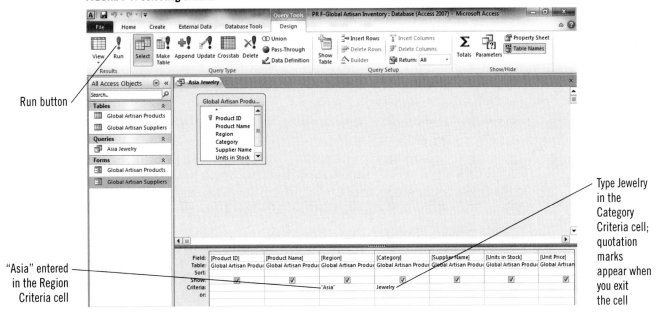

Run button

"Asia" entered in the Region Criteria cell

Type Jewelry in the Category Criteria cell; quotation marks appear when you exit the cell

FIGURE F-8: Formula in the Expression Builder

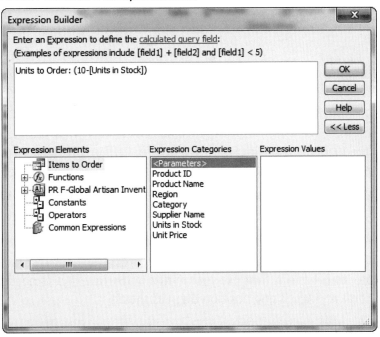

FIGURE F-9: Datasheet view of query results

Category	Supplier Name	Units in Stock	Unit Price	Units to Order	Total
Household	Asia Pacific Imports	9	$220.00	1	$220.00
Jewelry	Asia Pacific Imports	8	$50.00	2	$100.00
Household	Rainforest Collective	5	$40.00	5	$200.00
Art	Outback Arts	9	$25.00	1	$25.00
Jewelry	Asia Pacific Imports	7	$200.00	3	$600.00
Instrument	Outback Arts	8	$400.00	2	$800.00
Jewelry	Outback Arts	6	$30.00	4	$120.00
Art	Out of Africa Crafts	8	$160.00	2	$320.00
Jewelry	Asia Pacific Imports	5	$180.00	5	$900.00
Instrument	Rainforest Collective	9	$60.00	1	$60.00

Format and Print an Order Report

You add a field from the Suppliers table to the Items to Order query and then you format and print the Order report shown in Figure F-12.

Steps:

1. **Double-click** Items to Order **in the list of Queries, switch to** Design view, **click** Show Table **in the Query Setup group, click** Global Artisan Suppliers, **click** Add, **click** Close, **double-click** Supplier Name **in the Global Artisan Suppliers table, then scroll right to view Supplier Name if necessary**

Trouble

Make sure you sort by the Supplier Name field you inserted in Step 1.

2. **Click the** Supplier Name Sort cell list arrow, **click** Ascending, **then click the** Run button **in the Results group**

   The query results lists the 10 products to order and the names of the suppliers in alphabetical order.

3. **Close and save the Items to Order query table, click the** Create tab, **click the** Report Wizard button **in the Reports group, click** Product Name, **click the** Select Single Field button ▶ , **then select the** Region, Category, Units to Order, Total, **and** Global Artisan Suppliers:Supplier Name **fields**

4. **Click** Next, **click** by Global Artisan Suppliers, **click** Next, **click** Next, **click** Next **again (you don't need to sort), click the** Block option button, **click** Next, **change the title of the report to** Global Artisan Products to Order - Your Name, **then click** Finish

Hint

You can change your mind in the report formatting process and remove or add fields.

5. **Click the** Close Print Preview button **in the Close Preview group, click the** View list arrow **in the Views group, click** Layout View, **click** Region, **press** [Delete], **click** Asia **to select all the region fields, press** [Delete], **click the** date **below the last record, then press** [Delete]

6. **Double-click** [Global Artisan Suppliers.Supp], **delete all the text, type** Supplier, **click** Asia Pacific Imports, **then use your mouse to drag the right edge of the field to reduce its size as shown in Figure F-10**

7. **Refer to Figure F-11: Click** Product Name, **press the** left arrow key [◄] **to move the label closer to column 1, then use your mouse and arrow keys as needed to adjust the width of records and labels and position them as shown**

Trouble

The Alternate Row Color button is only active when all of the rows in the report are selected. Make sure you click a blank area between entries.

8. **Click** Global Artisan Products to Order - Your Name, **click the** Home tab, **reduce the font size to** 18 pt, **move the pointer below the text to show the** ↕, **click and drag to increase the height of the header area to approximately** 1", **click the** Report Layout Tools Design tab, **click the** Logo button **in the Header/Footer group, double-click** PR F-1.jpg, **click** Property Sheet **in the Tools group, select the contents of the** Width text box, **type** .8, **press** [Tab], **type** .7, **click** Zoom **next to "Size Mode", click the** list arrow, **click** Stretch, **click the** Property Sheet button, **then use the mouse to position the logo as shown in Figure F-12**

9. **Click a blank area between two entries (for example, between "Jewelry" and "5" in the first record) to select all of the rows, click the** Report Layout Tools Format tab, **click the** Alternate Row Color list arrow **in the Background group, then click** No Color

Additional Practice

For additional practice with the skills presented in this project, complete Independent Challenge 1.

10. **Click the** Report Layout Tools Design tab, **click the** View list arrow, **click** Print Preview, **compare the completed report to Figure F-12, close and save the report, submit a copy of the report to your instructor, then close the database**

FIGURE F-10: Resizing a report label

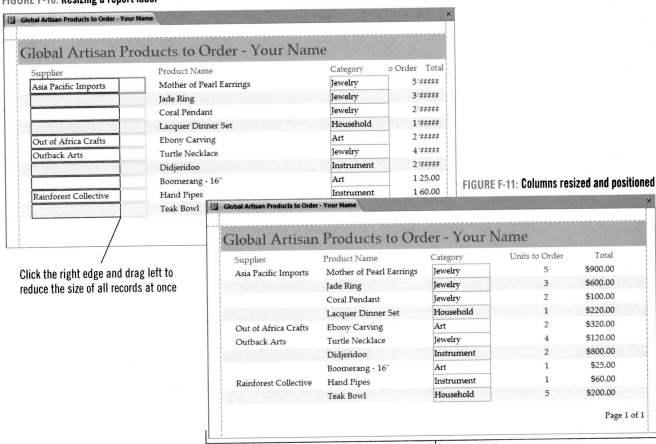

Click the right edge and drag left to
reduce the size of all records at once

FIGURE F-11: Columns resized and positioned

Adjust column widths and position
labels and records

FIGURE F-12: Completed report in Print Preview

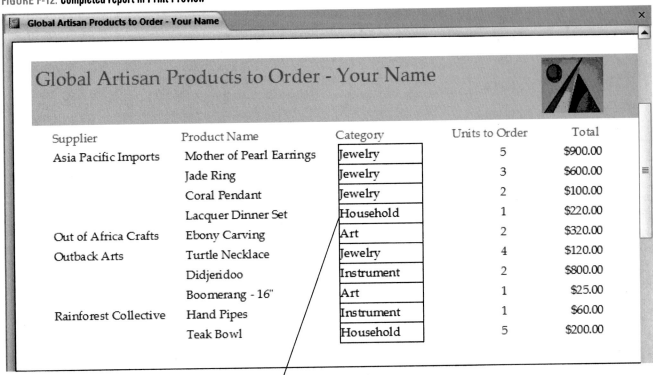

A border encloses lookup fields

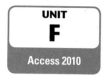

Author Database for Eaglecliff Books

Eaglecliff Books publishes nonfiction books that inspire people to action in the service of their communities. As the managing editor, you set up a database that you can use to identify the authors who have sold the most books, the titles that have earned revenues in excess of $50,000 during the last year, and the most popular topics purchased. For this project, you **Set Up the Tables, Enter Records and Create Queries,** and then **Create and Format a Report.** The completed report is shown in Figure F-20 on page 139.

Set Up the Tables

You set up the Authors table and the Books table.

Steps:

1. Start Access, then create a database called PR F-Eaglecliff Books and saved to the location where you save the files for this book

2. Click the View button in the Views group, type Eaglecliff Authors as the table name, press [Enter], enter the fields shown in Figure F-13, then close and save the table

3. Click the Create tab, click Table in the Tables group, click the View button, type Eaglecliff Books as the table name, then press [Enter]

4. Type the following fields: Book ID (to replace ID), Book Title, Author, Topic, Price, and Units Sold

Hint

By using the Lookup Wizard, a relationship between the Eaglecliff Authors table (the "one" table) and the Eaglecliff Books table (the "many" table) was created. One author can write many books.

5. Click the Author Data Type list arrow, click Lookup Wizard, click Open if prompted, click Next to accept that you want the values to come from an existing table, click Next to accept the Eaglecliff Authors table, click Last Name in the list of available fields, click the Select Single Field button [>], click Next, click Next, click Finish, then click Yes

   When you complete the Eaglecliff Books table, each author's last name will be available to you because you created a lookup table for the Author field that uses the Last Name field in the Eaglecliff Authors table.

6. Click the Topic Data Type list arrow, click Lookup Wizard, click the "I will type in the values that I want." option button, click Next, press [Tab], type Diversity, press [▼], enter the remaining categories as shown in Figure F-14, click Next, then click Finish

7. Apply the Currency data type to the Price field and the Number data type to the Units Sold field

Trouble

If the Enforce Referential Integrity check box is grayed out, close the Edit Relationships dialog box and double-click the line again.

8. Close and save the table, click the Database Tools tab, click Relationships in the Relationships group, double-click the line between the two tables, click the Enforce Referential Integrity check box to select it, click OK, then compare the Relationships window to Figure F-15

   Notice that the relationship is set up between the Author ID field in the Eaglecliff Authors table and the Author field in the Eaglecliff Books table. The Author ID field is used because each last name has a unique Author ID. When you selected the Last Name field in the Lookup Wizard, Access automatically created the relationship between the Author ID field (a unique number) in the Eaglecliff Authors table and the Author field in the Eaglecliff Books table.

9. Close and save if prompted the Relationships window

FIGURE F-13: Fields for the Eaglecliff Authors table

Field Name	Data Type	Description
Author ID	AutoNumber	
Last Name	Text	
First Name	Text	
Location	Text ▼	

FIGURE F-14: Values for the Topic field

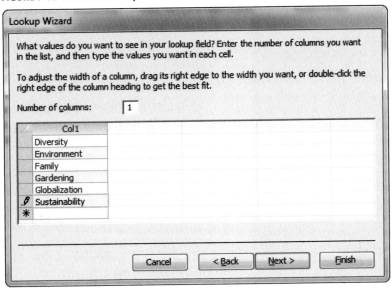

Lookup Wizard

What values do you want to see in your lookup field? Enter the number of columns you want in the list, and then type the values you want in each cell.

To adjust the width of a column, drag its right edge to the width you want, or double-click the right edge of the column heading to get the best fit.

Number of columns: 1

Col1
Diversity
Environment
Family
Gardening
Globalization
Sustainability

Cancel   < Back   Next >   Finish

FIGURE F-15: One-to-many relationship

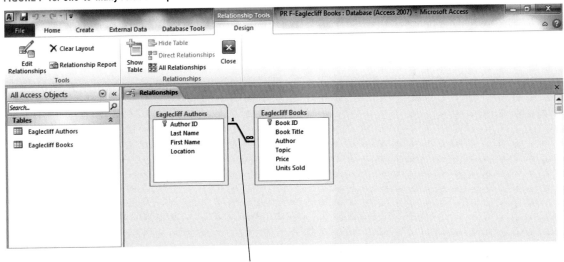

The one-to-many relationship: One author (Author ID) can write many books

Enter Records and Create Queries

Your market researchers have found that readers want more titles on the Globalization and Sustainability topics, so you decide to create a query that shows how many titles on these topics you have in stock. You then modify this query to list only those authors who sold more than $50,000 worth of books. Before you can create the query, you need to enter records for the Eaglecliff Authors and Eaglecliff Books tables.

Steps:

Hint

Remember that you can save time by typing only the first letter or two to show the required record for the Author and Topic fields.

1. **Open the** Eaglecliff Authors table, **enter the records shown in Figure F-16, adjust column widths as needed to fit content, then close and save the table**

2. **Open the** Eaglecliff Books table, **click the** Units Sold field, **click the** Table Tools Fields tab, **click the** Apply Comma Number Format button ⟨,⟩ **in the Formatting group, click the** Decrease Decimals button ⟨.00⟩ **two times, enter the records shown in Figure F-17 and adjust column widths as needed, then close and save the table if prompted**

3. **Click the** Create tab, **click the** Query Wizard button **in the Queries group, click** OK, **click the** Tables/Queries list arrow, **click** Table: Eaglecliff Authors, **then add only the** Location **field to the Selected Fields list box**

4. **Select** Table: Eaglecliff Books **in the Tables/Queries text box, add all the fields except the** Book ID **field to the Selected Fields list box, click** Next, **click** Next **again, change the name of the query to** Popular Topics, **click the** "Modify the query design." **option button, then click** Finish

5. **Click the** Topic Sort cell, **click the** Sort cell list arrow, **click** Ascending, **then click the** Run **button on the Standard toolbar**

   You can see at a glance that the two topics with the most available titles are Globalization and Sustainability.

6. **Switch to** Design view, **scroll to view the blank column to the right of Units Sold if it is not visible on the screen, then click in the blank cell**

7. **Click** Builder **in the Query Setup group, enter a formula that will designate "Total Sales" as the field name and multiply the Units Sold by the Price, then click** OK

   The required formula is Total Sales: [Units Sold]*[Price].

Trouble

If your query does not show eight results, recheck your Eaglecliff Books table to be sure the entries match Figure F-17. Remember, that for some AutoFill fields, you needed to type more than just the first letter.

8. **Click the** Topic Criteria cell, **type** Globalization, **click the** Total Sales Criteria cell, **type** >30000, **complete the criteria as shown in Figure F-18, then run the query**

   Eight books match the criteria.

9. **Close the Query Results window, then click** Yes **to save the modified query**

Access Projects

FIGURE F-16: Records for the Eaglecliff Authors table

Plus sign indicates that the table is related

	Author ID	Last Name	First Name	Location	Click to Add
⊞	1	Lalonde	Gabriel	Vancouver, BC	
⊞	2	Schwartz	Mike	Boston, MA	
⊞	3	Danson	Pierre	Miami, FL	
⊞	4	Torres	Maria	Madrid, Spain	
⊞	5	Quince	Elise	London, England	
⊞	6	Waters	Damien	Dublin, Ireland	
⊞	7	Washington	Darren	Los Angeles, CA	
⊞	8	Owen	Joanna	Chicago, IL	
✱	(New)				

FIGURE F-17: Records for the Eaglecliff Books table

Book ID	Book Title	Author	Topic	Price	Units Sold	Click to Add
1	Green Cars	Danson	Environment	$22.00	3,000	
2	Living Sustainably	Schwartz	Sustainability	$25.00	4,000	
3	Bringing Up Citizens	Quince	Family	$28.00	11,000	
4	The Conserving Way	Danson	Sustainability	$25.00	2,500	
5	Embracing Change	Waters	Globalization	$18.00	2,000	
6	Stretching Resources	Danson	Environment	$25.00	4,000	
7	Back to Villages	Washington	Globalization	$28.00	7,000	
8	Growing Organic	Lalonde	Gardening	$35.00	3,000	
9	Community Living	Danson	Sustainability	$28.00	2,000	
10	Thriving Together	Torres	Diversity	$18.00	1,000	
11	Our Planet's Way	Waters	Globalization	$24.00	6,000	
12	Celebration	Torres	Diversity	$18.00	3,000	
13	Sustain to Survive	Owen	Sustainability	$24.00	5,000	
14	Putting Peace First	Schwartz	Globalization	$30.00	7,000	
15	Landscaping with Vegetables	Lalonde	Gardening	$40.00	2,000	
✱	(New)					

FIGURE F-18: Selecting criteria

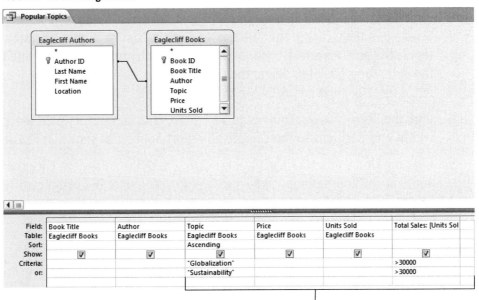

Criteria for Topic and Total Sales; do not type quotation marks, they are added automatically after exiting a cell

Access 2010

Create and Format a Report

You need to create a report and then format it to present to your colleagues at a meeting. Your finished report will look similar to the one shown in Figure F-20.

Steps:

1. Click Popular Topics in the list of queries, click the Create tab, click Report in the Reports group, click the Themes button in the Themes group, select the Aspect theme, click at the far left of the header area to select the entire header, click the Report Layout Tools Format tab, click the Shape Fill list arrow in the Control Formatting group, then click Dark Purple, Accent 5, Lighter 80%

2. Click the Report Layout Tools Design tab, click the Group & Sort button in the Grouping & Totals group, click Add a group at the bottom of the screen, then click Author as shown in Figure F-19

   The report records are grouped according to author so you can quickly see how many book titles belong to each author.

3. Scroll to and click the Total Sales label, click the Totals button in the Grouping & Totals group, then click Sum

   The total sales for each of the authors is calculated.

4. Right-click the first total (310000), click Properties, click the list box next to "Format", click the Format list arrow, click Currency, then close the Property Sheet

5. Drag the right edge of the selected box to the right to increase the width of all the boxes in the column and then down to increase the height of the total so the values and currency symbol are visible, scroll to the bottom of the report, change the format of the grand total (924500) to Currency, close the Property Sheet, then adjust the box height as needed to fit content

6. Press [Ctrl][A] to select all the fields and labels in the report, click the Home tab, click the Font Size list arrow (the text box is blank) in the Text Formatting group, then click 11

7. Scroll up, double-click in the title box and select Popular Topics, change the name of the report to Eaglecliff Books - Your Name, increase the font size of the title to 18 pt, click the date, press [Delete], delete the time, click File, click Save Object As, type Eaglecliff Books Popular Topics, click OK, then click the Home tab

8. Click the Report Layout Tools Page Setup tab, click Landscape, then modify the column widths and positions so the completed report appears as shown in Figure F-20

Additional Practice

For additional practice with the skills presented in this project, complete Independent Challenge 2.

9. Click the Home tab, click the View list arrow, click Print Preview, click the Zoom list arrow in the Zoom group, click Fit to Window, compare the completed report to Figure F-20, submit a copy of the report to your instructor, then close the database

FIGURE F-19: **Selecting a grouping field**

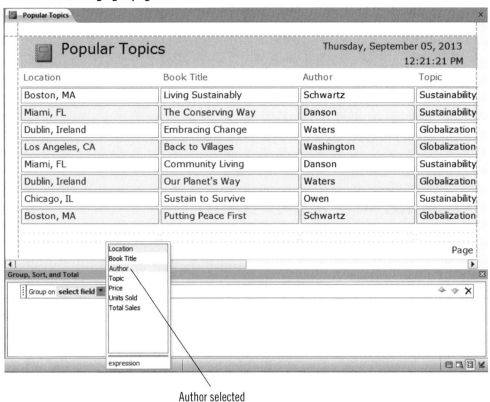

Author selected

FIGURE F-20: **Completed report in Print Preview**

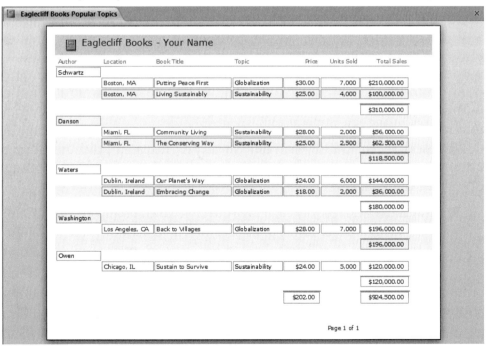

Tour Database for Winding Road Tours

Winding Road Tours conducts tours for small groups of 10 to 15 people to locations around North America. You create a database containing information about each tour and then relate this table to a list of tour participants that you import from another database. For this project, you **Create the Tours Table**, and then you **Import the Participants Table**. The completed report is shown in Figure F-26 on page 143.

Create the Tours Table

You need to create the Winding Road Tours database and then create the Tours table. The Tours table will include a field for attachments in the form of pictures. In Access 2010, you use the Attachment data type to attach files to a record.

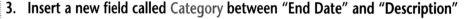

Steps:

1. **Start Access, then create a new database called** PR F-Winding Road Tours **and save it to the location where you save the files for this book**

2. **Switch to** Design view, **save the table as** Tours, **then enter the field names and assign data types as shown in Figure F-21**

   By default, a Text data type allows you to enter no more than 255 characters in a record. You select Memo as the data type for "Description" so that you have the option to enter more than 255 characters.

Hint

Right-click Description, then click Insert Rows.

3. **Insert a new field called** Category **between "End Date" and "Description"**

4. **Click the** Data Type list arrow **for Category, click** Lookup Wizard, **click** Open **if prompted, then follow the steps in the Lookup Wizard to create a lookup column consisting of three entries:** City, Cultural, **and** Outdoors

5. **Click** Date/Time **next to "Start Date", click in the cell next to "Format" in the Field Properties area below the fields list, then click the** list arrow **as shown in Figure F-22**

   You can modify a wide range of properties related to a field, including its format, rules for how an entry is validated, and even whether an entry is required.

6. **Click the** Long Date format, **click** No **next to "Required", click the** list arrow **and click** Yes, **then repeat the process to apply the Long Date format and the Required option to the End Date field**

7. **Switch to** Datasheet view **and save the table when prompted, press [Tab], type** Island Hopping **as the tour name, press [Tab] one time, click the** Date button 🔳 **to the right of the selected Start Date cell, select** July 12, 2013, **press [Tab], click** 🔳, **select** July 19, 2013, **press [Tab] select** Outdoors **as the category, press [Tab], type** Spectacular island jaunt, **then widen columns as needed to fit the content**

8. **Double-click the cell in the Attachments column for record 1 to show the Attachments dialog box, click** Add, **navigate to the location where you store your Data Files, double-click** PR F-2.jpg, **then click** OK

9. **Enter data for the remaining four records and add the required attachments as shown in Figure F-23, close the table, then answer** Yes **to save the table if prompted**

FIGURE F-21: Field list for Tours table

Field Name	Data Type
🔑 Tour ID	AutoNumber
Tour Name	Text
Start Date	Date/Time
End Date	Date/Time
Description	Memo
Picture	Attachment

— Date/Time data type selected

— Memo data type selected

— Attachment data type selected

FIGURE F-22: Changing the Date format

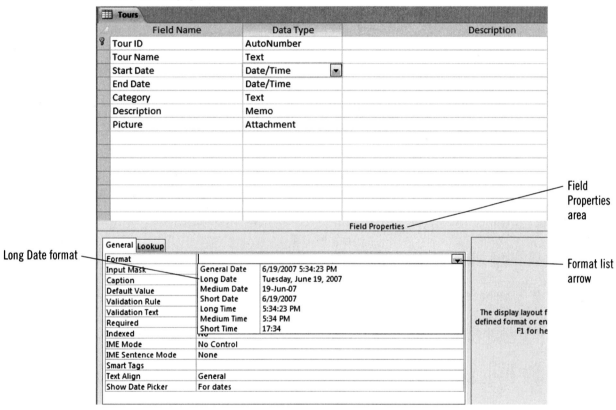

Long Date format

Field Properties area

Format list arrow

FIGURE F-23: Records for the Tours table

Tour ID	Tour Name	Start Date	End Date	Category	Description	📎	Click to
1	Island Hopping	Friday, July 12, 2013	Friday, July 19, 2013	Outdoors	Spectacular island jaunt	📎(1)	
2	Second City Architecture	Monday, July 22, 2013	Friday, July 26, 2013	Cultural	Chicago buildings	📎(1)	
3	San Antonio Relaxing	Monday, July 29, 2013	Friday, August 02, 2013	City	Heart of Texas tour	📎(1)	
4	Pacific Gardens	Friday, July 26, 2013	Friday, August 02, 2013	Outdoors	West coast garden tour	📎(1)	
5	Peak Experience	Monday, August 05, 2013	Friday, August 09, 2013	Outdoors	Hiking in the Cascades	📎(1)	
* (New)						📎(0)	

PR F-3.jpg   PR F-4.jpg   PR F-5.jpg   PR F-6.jpg

Import the Participants Table

You import the Participants table from another database, then create a relationship between the Tours table and the imported table. The relationship will be a one-to-many relationship because one tour can host many participants. The Tours table is the "one" table and the Participants table is the "many" table. Finally, you create two reports. One report shows all the tours and includes the picture of each tour, and the other report shows all the participants according to the tour they are taking.

Steps:

1. Click the External Data tab, click Access in the Import & Link group, click Browse, navigate to the location where you store your Data Files, double-click PR F-7.accdb, click OK, click Tour Participants in the list of tables, click OK, then click Close

2. Double-click Tour Participants to open it, scroll right to view the blank column, click Click to Add, click Lookup & Relationship, click Next to accept that the lookup field will come from an existing table, click Table: Tours, click Next, click Tour Name, then click the Select Single Field button ▶

3. Click Next, click Next, click Next, type Tour as the lookup field name, click Finish, then as shown in Figure F-24, select a tour for each of the participants, widening the column as needed to fit the content

4. Close and save the table, click the Database Tools tab, click Relationships in the Relationships group, double-click the line joining the two tables, click the Enforce Referential Integrity check box, click OK, then close the Relationships window

   By enforcing referential integrity, you ensure that a user can enter only the tour names in the Tour Participants table that exist in the Tours table.

5. Click Tours, click the Create tab, click the Report button in the Reports group, apply the Median theme, save the report as Winding Road Tour List, delete the date and time in the header, move the text box containing "Page 1 of 1" so that it appears to the left of the dotted line at the right side of the page, modify the report title and the column widths as shown in Figure F-25, then save and close the report

6. Click the Create tab, click the Query Wizard button in the Queries group, click OK, create a query that includes the Tour Name field from the Tours table and the Last Name, First Name (in that order) and Country/Region fields from the Tour Participants table, finish the query, then close the query

7. Click Tours Query in the list of Access objects, click the Report button in the Reports group, apply the Median theme, click the Group & Sort button in the Grouping & Totals group if it is not selected, click Add a group, click Tour Name, click Add a sort, then click Last Name

8. Click the Save button 🖫, type Tour Participants, then modify the report so that it appears as shown in Figure F-26 in Print Preview

9. Close the report, submit copies of both the reports you created to your instructor, then close the database

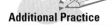

Additional Practice

For additional practice with the skills presented in this project, complete Independent Challenge 3.

FIGURE F-24: Matching tours with participants

Last Name	Address	City	State/Provir	ZIP/Postal C	Country/Reg	Tour
Andrews	1208 Balsam St	Vancouver	BC	V7H 1A7	Canada	Island Hopping
Henley	18 Peak Road	Littleton	CO	80122	United States	Second City Architecture
Wang	3809 Maple Str	Boston	MA	02111	United States	Island Hopping
Donwell	1200 Lake Stree	Cincinnati	OH	45206	United States	San Antonio Relaxing
Watson	230 Seaview Pl	Halifax	NS	B9A 1P3	Canada	Pacific Gardens
Grant	344 Cowan Roa	Green Bay	WI	54311	United States	Pacific Gardens
Steinberg	122 West 40th :	New York	NY	10010	United States	Island Hopping
Gresch	890 Glenaden [	Toronto	ON	M5W 1E6	Canada	Second City Architecture
Morales	67 Pacific Way	Santa Monica	CA	90405	United States	Second City Architecture
Singh	80 The Mews	London		SW1X 8PZ	United Kingdoı	San Antonio Relaxing
Martelli	Via Principe Ar	Roma		00187	Italy	Island Hopping
Jefferson	678 Rainier Roa	Seattle	WA	98110	United States	Peak Experience
Tamblyn	34 Atlantic Stre	Savannah	GA	31405	United States	Pacific Gardens
Bremmer	230 Sky Road	Sacramento	CA	94822	United States	Peak Experience
Villeneuve	450 Hyde Stree	Toronto	ON	M5E 3R5	Canada	Island Hopping

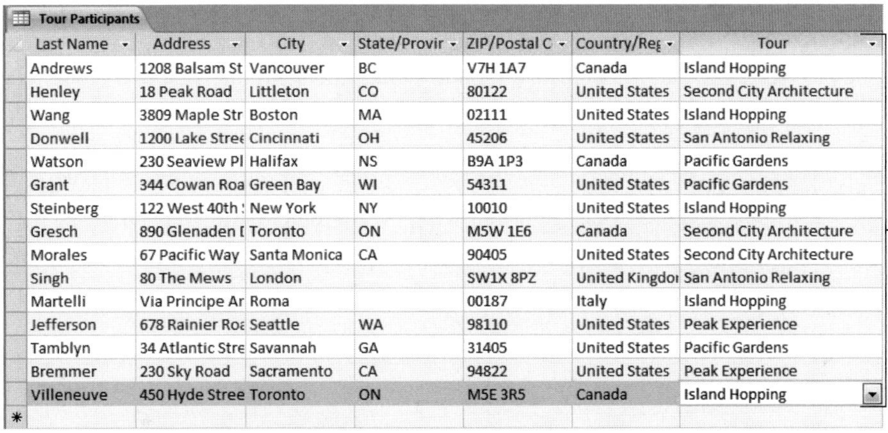

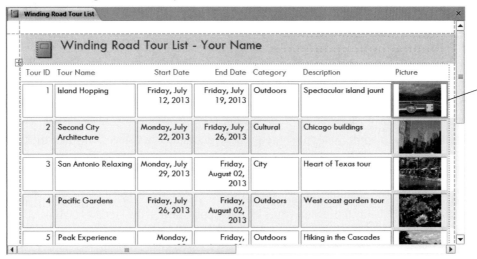

Type the first letter or two of each entry, then press the down arrow to quickly select the tour title and move to the next cell

FIGURE F-25: Winding Road Tour List report

Make sure the pictures do not extend beyond the dotted line

FIGURE F-26: Tour Participants report in Print Preview

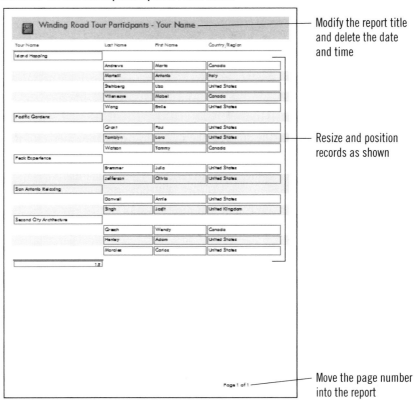

Modify the report title and delete the date and time

Resize and position records as shown

Move the page number into the report

Access 2010

Independent Challenge 1

Create a report based on tables that contain information about 20 to 30 products stocked by a company of your choice. Follow the steps provided to create the database, create a Products table and a Suppliers table that are related, make two queries, and then create a report.

1. Choose a name for your company and determine the type of products it sells. For example, you could call your company Par One and describe it as a retail operation that sells golf equipment and accessories, such as golf clubs, bags, shoes, umbrellas, and clothing. Write the name of your company and a brief description of the products it sells in the box below:

Company Name: _____

Description of Expansion Plans: _____

_____

_____

2. Start Access, then create a database called **PR F-My Inventory**, and save it to the location where you save the files for this book.
3. Create a Suppliers table similar to the table you created for Unit F Project 1 that includes a Supplier ID field, a Supplier field, and one or two additional fields such as an Email field or a Phone Number field.
4. Create a Products table similar to the table you created for Unit F Project 1. Include at least six fields, including the Supplier field and a Units in Stock field.
5. Identify fields that require a limited selection of responses. For example, a Category field for the Golf database could include the values "Shoes," "Accessories," "Clubs," "Clothing," and "Bags."
6. In the Products table, use the Lookup Wizard to create lookup values for the fields you identified, except for the values for the Supplier field.
7. Use the Lookup Wizard to identify the lookup values for the Supplier field in the Products table based on a field, such as Supplier Name, in the Suppliers table. When you identify the field in the Suppliers table (the "one" table) and make it available to the Products table (the "many" table), you create a relationship between the Suppliers and Products tables.
8. Open the Relationships window and enforce referential integrity so that you are not able to enter the name of any supplier not listed in the Suppliers table into the Products table.
9. Create a form for each table, and apply the AutoFormat of your choice.
10. Enter records for each table. You should enter a minimum of 15 records for the Products table and four records for the Suppliers table.
11. Determine one query you plan to make based on the Products and Suppliers tables. For example, you could ask which products are handled by a certain supplier, or which products are associated with a specific category, or which suppliers are located in a specific area.
12. Use the Query Wizard to create the query. Make sure you specify the criteria for the query in Design view and then rename the query to reflect the contents.
13. Use the Query Wizard to create a query called **Items to Order** that identifies the items you need to order so that stock levels do not fall below 10 for all items. Include appropriate criteria and formulas to calculate the total value of each item you need to order. For example, you need to set the criteria for Units in Stock to <10 and enter two formulas. One formula subtracts 10 from the Units in Stock field, and the other formula multiplies the result by the Unit Price to determine the total cost of the units you need to order.
14. Create a report that shows items you need to reorder based on the Items to Order query.
15. Group the report by Supplier. Apply the theme of your choice, and adjust column widths and heights and font sizes until you are pleased with the appearance of the report. Note that you can choose to format the report in Landscape orientation.
16. Remove the date and time from the report header.
17. Include an appropriate picture as a logo in the header, and apply the Stretch size option from the Properties sheet.
18. Be sure the report title includes your name, submit a copy of the report to your instructor, and then close the database.

Independent Challenge 2

Create a database that contains information related to a company such as a publisher, an art gallery, or a talent agency that deals with people and the products they create. For example, you could create a database for a recording company that includes two tables—one table lists the recordings and the other table lists the recording artists. One recording artist can create many recordings. Plan and then create the database as follows.

1. Start Access, then create a database called **PR F-My People List** and save it to the location where you save the files for this book.

2. Plan your database on paper by first listing all the fields you require. Here are some sample fields for an art gallery database, in no particular order: Artist Name, Painting Title, Artist Phone Number, Painting Medium, Painting Size, Painting Genre, and Painting Price.

3. Divide the field names into two tables and determine the relationship between the two tables. For example, the fields for an art gallery database could be arranged into an Artists table and a Paintings table as follows:
   Artists Table: Artist ID, Artist Name, Phone Number
   Paintings table: Painting ID, Painting Title, Medium, Size, Genre, Price, and Artist Name

4. Determine the relationship between the two tables. For example, the Artists and Paintings tables are related through the Artist Name field because one artist can create many paintings.

5. Determine which fields require a limited selection of responses. For example, the Genre field in the Paintings table for an art gallery database could include the values "Abstract," "Landscape," and "Photography."

6. Create the two tables in Access. Make sure you assign appropriate data types and that you use the Lookup Wizard to create lookup values for the fields you identified.

7. Use the Lookup Wizard to create a relationship between the two tables. For example, in an Art Gallery database, a relationship would be created between "Artist Name" in the Artists table (the "one" table) and "Artist Name" in the Paintings table (the "many" table). In this example, you only need to create the lookup values for the Artist Name field in the Artists table, and then use the Lookup Wizard to make that field available in the Paintings table.

8. Modify the relationship to enforce referential integrity so that you can enter only the names of artists included in the Artists table into the Paintings table.

9. Enter records for the two tables. You should enter a minimum of 15 records for the "many" table and four records for the "one" table.

10. Determine two queries that you could make based on the data in the two tables. If appropriate, you could include a formula in one of the queries. For example, if artists sold multiple copies of reproductions, you could include a formula that multiplied the Units Sold by the Unit Price to determine the total revenue.

11. Select one query to use as the basis for a report. For example, you could create a report that lists only painters who have sold more than $15,000 worth of paintings. Ensure the query you choose includes at least one formula.

12. Group the records in the report using one field (for example the "Artist Name" field), and sort the records in ascending order using another field (for example, "Painting Title").

13. Use the Total command to create a subtotal for each of the sort categories (for example, a subtotal of the value of all products sold by each artist). Also include the grand total. Format all totals with the Currency format.

14. Format the report attractively using the theme of your choice, include your name in the report title, submit a copy to your instructor, then close the database.

Independent Challenge 3

You need to create a database that contains information about dogs and their walkers. Follow the steps provided to create the database, create a Walkers table and a Dogs table, and then create a report. Note that the relationship is created on the basis that one walker can walk many dogs.

1. Start Access, then create a database called **PR F-My Dog Walking Service** and save it to the location where you save the files for this book.

Independent Challenge 3 (continued)

2. Create a table named **Walkers**, then add fields and specify data types as shown in Figure F-27.

FIGURE F-27

Field Name	Data Type
🔑 Walker ID	AutoNumber
First Name	Text
Last Name	Text
Email Address	Hyperlink
Cell Phone	Text
Resume	Attachment

(Table title: Walkers)

3. Click the Data Type for Cell Phone, click Input Mask in the Field Properties section, click the launcher at the far right of the Input Mask text box, click Open if prompted, click Yes, then click Finish. The Input Mask automatically inserts the brackets and the hyphen so you can enter just the numbers for the phone numbers.

4. Switch to **Datasheet view** and save the table, then add a Lookup & Relationship field called **Region** that contains four values of your choice. (*Hint*: To add a Lookup & Relationship field in Datasheet view, click Click to Add, then click Lookup & Relationship and complete the wizard.) The lookup values should list four regions (for example, "West Side," "City Center"). When you enter records for the Walkers table, you assign a region to each walker. Several walkers can work in the same region.

5. Move the Region field to the left of the Cell Phone field. (*Hint*: Click the field name ("Region"), then drag the selected column to the left of the Cell Phone field.)

6. Enter data for four records as shown in Figure F-28, selecting the Region of your choice and entering phone numbers using the area code of your choice. Add the **PR F-8.docx** attachment to the record for Rhonda Linz and the **PR F-9.docx** to the record for Yani Sharif. These documents are located in the location where you store your Data Files.

FIGURE F-28

Walker ID	First Name	Last Name	Email Address	Region	Cell Phone	📎	Click
1	Rhonda	Linz	rhonda@internetworld.com	Green Lake	(206) 555-6788	📎(1)	
2	Sofia	Keynes	sofia@internetworld.com	Ballard	(206) 555-7223	📎(0)	
3	Yani	Sharif	yani@internetworld.com	Green Lake	(206) 555-8811	📎(1)	
4	Gloria	Andrews	gloria@internetworld.com	Fremont	(206) 555-1990	📎(0)	
* (New)						📎(0)	

(Table title: Walkers)

7. Close and save the table.
8. Import the **PR F-10.accdb** database from the location where you store your Data Files, then select the Dogs table.
9. Open the Dogs table, then add the First Name field from the Walker table. (*Hint*: In the new field, select Lookup & Relationship, click Open if prompted, click Next, click Table: Walkers, click Next, add the First Name field, then complete the Wizard, typing **Walker** as the column name.)
10. Close and save the table, then modify the relationship so referential integrity is enforced.
11. Open the Dogs table again, then select a walker for each of the dogs.
12. Create a query called Dogs and Walkers that shows all the walkers and the dogs they walk, and includes the walker's last name, the region, the walker's résumé as an attachment if it is available, and the name and breed of the dog.
13. Create a report from the Dogs and Walkers query that is grouped by the Last Name and Region and that is sorted in alphabetical order by pet names.

Independent Challenge 3 (continued)

14. Apply the Theme of your choice, modify the column widths and row heights as needed to fit content, remove the date and time labels, include your name in the report title, move the page number label at the bottom of the page into the body of the report, and increase the height of the box containing "15" at the bottom of the report so that the number is visible.

15. In Report view, double-click the Word attachment for Rhonda Linz, click View in the Attachments dialog box, click Enable Editing, then save the document as **PR F-Walker Linz** to the location where you save the files for this book. Change the address and phone number for Rhonda to an address and phone number in your home town, then save and close the document and close the Attachments dialog box in Access.

16. From Report view, open and view the Word attachment for Yani Sharif, enable editing and save the document as **PR F-Walker Sharif** to the location where you save the files for this book, change the address and phone number, then save and close the document and exit the Attachments dialog box.

17. Close the report and open the Walkers table. Add the PR F-Walker Linz attachment to Rhonda's record and the PR F-Walker Sharif attachment to Yani's record. The two records will have two attachments each.

18. Submit a copy to of the report your instructor, then close the database.

Independent Challenge 4

You would like to investigate the possibility of studying in a foreign country for a summer, an academic term, or even a full year. To help you choose the best program, you will search the Web for information about programs for studying abroad, and then you will create an Access database that contains data related to at least three programs.

1. Start Access, then create a database called **PR F-Study Abroad Programs**, and save it in the location where you save the files for this book.

2. In Design view, enter field names and select data types as shown in Figure F-29. (*Note*: You select text for the Cost data type so you can enter N/A when you are not able to find cost information.)

FIGURE F-29

Study Programs	
Field Name	**Data Type**
Program ID	AutoNumber
Field of Study	Text
Country	Text
Location	Text
Description	Memo
Cost	Text
Web Address	Hyperlink

3. Save the table with the name **Study Programs**.

4. Open your Web browser and conduct a search for study abroad programs. Use keywords such as **study abroad**, **international study**, and **overseas study**. To narrow your search further, include the field of study and location that interests you. For example, you could search for "archaeology programs in Egypt." You could also explore study abroad Web sites such as www.studyabroad.com.

5. Identify a field of study and two or three countries that interest you. For example, you could decide to investigate art history study programs in Italy, France, and Spain, or natural history programs in Peru, Bolivia, and Ecuador.

6. Explore Web sites you've found to gather information about three programs. Copy and paste relevant information to the Study Programs table in the database. You can copy and edit text in the Description field because you chose the Memo data type, which allows you to enter unlimited text. You will need to follow several links to find the information required for each program. In some cases, you will not find all the information; for example, you may not be able to find cost information. You can enter N/A where applicable in the table.

7. For the Web Address field, enter the Web page address of the page that contains most of the information you've gathered about a particular program. To copy a Web address, click the Address box in your browser, press [Ctrl][C], return to Access, click the appropriate cell in the Web Address field, and then press [Ctrl][V]. The Web site address appears as a hyperlink because you selected the Hyperlink data type for the field.

8. When you have gathered information about at least three programs, create a report called **Study Programs** with the title **Study Programs - Your Name**. Apply the Theme of your choice, select the Landscape layout, and modify column widths as needed. Move the page number into the body of the report, and increase the size of the text box containing "3" (the number of Study Abroad programs listed) so the number is visible. Group the records according to Field of Study.

9. Submit a copy of the report to your instructor, then close the database.

Access Projects

Visual Workshop

Start Access, create a database called **PR F-Employee Travel Expenses**, create an **Employees** table and a **Trips** table. Use Figure F-30 and Figure F-31 to set up the tables and then use Figure F-32 to create the report. In the Trips table, create a lookup field called **Employee** that uses the Last Name of the Employees table, then in the Relationships window reinforce the referential integrity between the two tables. Create a query from the Trips table that includes a field called **Total Expenses** that multiplies the Daily Rate by the Days. The required formula is Total Expenses: [Daily Rate]*[Days]. Create the report from the query. Submit the report to your instructor, then close the database.

FIGURE F-30

Employees

	ID	First Name	Last Name	Click to Add
⊞	1	Gwen	Perry	
⊞	2	Martin	Harrison	
⊞	3	Sylvia	Weinstein	
⊞	4	Antonio	Parsons	
⊞	5	Maria	Gomez	
✱	(New)			

FIGURE F-31

Trips

	Trip ID	Destination	Trip Departure	Days	Daily Rate	Employee
	1	Amsterdam	Monday, July 22, 2013	5	$250.00	Perry
	2	Rome	Friday, July 26, 2013	10	$300.00	Harrison
	3	Singapore	Monday, July 29, 2013	10	$300.00	Weinstein
	4	Los Angeles	Friday, August 09, 2013	12	$300.00	Perry
	5	Mumbai	Monday, August 12, 2013	10	$300.00	Parsons
	6	Rome	Monday, September 02, 2013	8	$300.00	Perry
	7	Hong Kong	Monday, September 16, 2013	12	$350.00	Gomez
🖉	8	Tokyo	Monday, September 30, 2013	10	$400.00	Weinstein ▼
✱	(New)					

Trips table has five fields: **Trip ID, Destination, Trip Departure** (use the Date/Time data type and the Long Date format), **Days** (use the Number data type), and **Daily Rate** (use the Currency data type)

FIGURE F-32

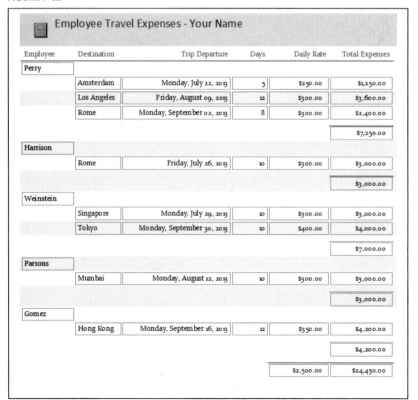

For the report shown in Figure F-32, the Flow Theme is used, the records are grouped by Employee and sorted by Trip Departure, the Totals command is used to calculate subtotals and totals, and the page number information is moved into the body of the report.

Integration Projects II

Files You Will Need:

PR G-1.docx
PR G-2.xlsx
PR G-3.docx
PR G-4.xlsx
PR G-5.docx

You can use Word, Access, and Excel in a variety of ways to perform business tasks quickly and easily. The key is to use each program in the Office suite efficiently. You often start by building an Access database that contains the names and addresses of customers and suppliers, information about inventory, and sales records. You can then use the database information in Word to produce form letters, labels, and other documents such as reports and proposals. You can also analyze database information in Excel so that you can then create charts and spreadsheets. In this unit, you will use Access, Word, and Excel to create a variety of common business documents.

In This Unit You Will Create the Following:

Job Search Package

Multipage Proposal

Collection Catalogue

UNIT
G

Integration 2010

Job Search Database for Marlene Daly

Marlene Daly is looking for a job in San Diego as an office manager or management trainee. To help coordinate her job search efforts, Marlene uses tools in Access, Word, and Excel. For this project, you need to **Create the Contacts Table**, **Create the Results Form**, **Create the Job Application Letter**, and then **Analyze the Job Search Results**. The form letter is shown in Figure G-9 on page 155.

Create the Contacts Table

First, you need to create the Job Search database, and then create a table to contain information about Marlene's job contacts. You design the Contacts table to include a lookup field.

Steps:

1. **Start Access, verify that Blank Database is selected, select the contents of the** File Name text box, **type** PR G-Marlene_Job Search Database, **click the** Browse button , **navigate to the location where you save the files for this book, click** OK, **then click** Create

2. **Click the** View button **in the Views group, type** Contacts **as the table name, then press** [Enter]

3. **Type** Job ID **to replace "ID", press** [↓] **to move the insertion point to the line below "Job ID", then enter the remaining fields as shown in Figure G-1**

4. **Click the** City/State field, **click the** Default Value text box **in the General tab of the Field Properties area, type** "San Diego, CA" **including the quotation marks, then press** [Enter]
   You make "San Diego, CA" the default value because every company Marlene has contacted is located in San Diego. As the default value, "San Diego, CA" will fill the City/State field automatically for each record.

5. **Click the** Position Data Type list arrow, **click** Lookup Wizard, **click** Open **if prompted, click the** "I will type in the values that I want." option button, **then click** Next

Trouble

If you press [Enter] instead of the down arrow, you go to the next screen; click Back to return to the list of values to finish entering them.

6. **Press** [Tab], **type** Junior Manager, **press** [↓], **type** Manager Trainee, **enter the remaining positions as shown in Figure G-2, then click** Finish

7. **Click the** View button, **then click** Yes

8. **Press** [Tab] **to move to the First Name field, type** Rachel, **press** [Tab], **type** Johansen, **press** [Tab], **type** 100 Pacific Drive, **press** [Tab] **two times ("San Diego, CA" will be entered automatically), type** 91912, **press** [Tab], **type** Energy Options, **press** [Tab], **type** m, **then press** [Tab] **to accept** Manager Trainee

9. **Enter the data for the remaining records in the Contacts table as shown in Figure G-3, adjust column widths as needed, then close and save the table**

FIGURE G-1: **Field Names for Contacts table**

Field Name	Data Type
🔑 Job ID	AutoNumber
First Name	Text
Last Name	Text
Address	Text
City/State	Text
Zip	Text
Company Name	Text
Position	Text

FIGURE G-2: **Lookup Wizard**

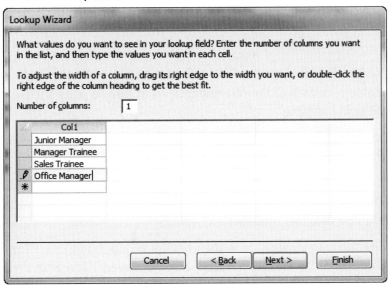

FIGURE G-3: **Records for the Contacts table**

Job ID	First Name	Last Name	Address	City/State	Zip	Company Name	Position
1	Rachel	Johansen	100 Pacific Drive	San Diego, CA	91912	Energy Options	Manager Trainee
2	Larry	Ng	24 Front Street	San Diego, CA	91915	Green Works	Sales Trainee
3	Cordelia	Morales	55 Palm Drive	San Diego, CA	91912	Datalink	Junior Manager
4	Stewart	Eliot	800 West Street	San Diego, CA	91910	Solar Utilities	Sales Trainee
5	Kate	Webb	150 Dade Road	San Diego, CA	91913	Pacific Solutions	Office Manager
6	Gerald	Zelnick	300 Lara Avenue	San Diego, CA	91910	Techno Works	Sales Trainee
7	Jasjit	Singh	160 Ocean Road	San Diego, CA	91916	Passage Insurance	Junior Manager
8	Elizabeth	Tilney	400 Byron Place	San Diego, CA	91912	Global Nutrition	Manager Trainee
9	Carlos	Ramirez	550 Johnson Road	San Diego, CA	91917	Alimeda Consultants	Office Manager
(New)				San Diego, CA			

Create the Results Form

You need to create a form that Marlene can use to track the results of her job search efforts. The form needs to include all the fields from the Contacts table along with a check box field and a Date/Time field.

Steps:

1. Double-click Contacts in the list of Access Objects, click the View button to open Design view, click the blank cell below "Position", type Response, press [Tab], click the Data Type list arrow, then click Yes/No

2. Press [Tab] twice, type Interview Date, press [Tab], type d to select the Date/Time data type, click the Format text box on the General tab in the Field Properties area, click the list arrow and select Medium Date, then close and save the Contacts table

3. Click the Create tab, click the Form Design button in the Forms group, click the Add Existing Fields button in the Tools group, click Show all tables in the Field List pane, then click the expand button ⊞ next to Contacts to show all the fields

   A blank grid appears. You use the grid and rulers to position the labels and text boxes representing the fields from the Contacts table.

Hint

The left box contains the label, and the right box will contain the data that varies from record to record.

4. Double-click Job ID in the Field List pane to place it in the grid, double-click First Name, double-click each of the remaining fields in turn to place them in the grid, then close the Field List pane

5. Place the pointer above and to the left of the Job ID label, then click and drag to select all the labels and text boxes as shown in Figure G-4

6. Drag to position the selected labels so the left edge of the labels lines up with 2 on the horizontal ruler bar and the top edge lines up with 1 on the vertical ruler bar as shown in Figure G-5, then deselect the labels

7. Click the Label button ⎡Aa⎤ in the Controls group, point just below 1 on the horizontal ruler bar, click and drag to create a box between 1 and 5 on the horizontal ruler that is approximately .5" in height, type Job Search Results, click a blank area of the grid, click the label text box you just created, click the Form Design Tools Format tab, click the Font Size list arrow in the Font group, click 24, then click the Center button ⎡≡⎤ in the Font group

Trouble

Skip the records not listed in Step 8.

8. Click the Home tab, click the View button, click the Response check box in Form 1 for Energy Options to select it, click the Interview Date text box, type June 1 as the interview date, click the Next record button ▶ on the Navigation bar to move to Form 2, then enter the responses and the dates for selected records as shown below:

Company Name	Response	Interview Date
Green Works	Yes	June 2
Solar Utilities	Yes	June 3
Global Nutrition	Yes	June 6
Alimeda Consultants	Yes	June 8

9. Click the Save button 🖫 on the Quick Access toolbar, type Job Search Results, click OK, click the View button, use the mouse to widen the Address, Company Name, and Position text boxes as shown in Figure G-6, then close and save the form if prompted

FIGURE G-4: Selecting the fields in the Form grid

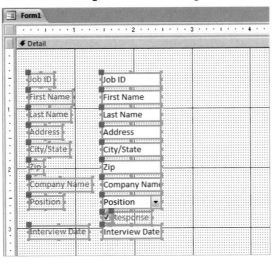

FIGURE G-5: Positioning fields on the design grid

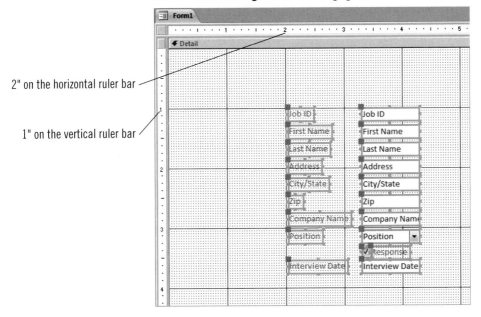

2" on the horizontal ruler bar

1" on the vertical ruler bar

FIGURE G-6: Completed form for Alimeda Consultants

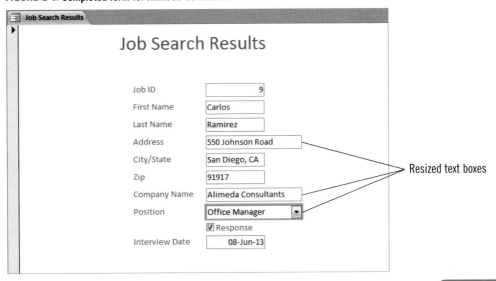

Resized text boxes

Integration Projects II

Create the Job Application Letter

You need to switch to Word and create the letter that Marlene plans to send to each job prospect. You then need to merge the letter with the Job Search database to produce individually addressed letters.

Steps:

Trouble

If you receive a warning that the database is open in exclusive mode, click OK, close the database, open it again, enable content if prompted, then repeat Step 2.

1. Start Word, open PR G-1.docx from the location where you store your Data Files, save the document as PR G-Marlene_Job Search Form Letter.docx to the location where you save the files for this book, then close the document and exit Word

2. In Access, click Contacts in the list of Access Objects, click the External Data tab, click the Word Merge button in the Export group, click Open if prompted, then click OK

3. Navigate to the location where you store your files for this book, click PR G-Marlene_Job Search Form Letter.docx, click Open, maximize the Word window, click Next: Write your letter in the Mail Merge task pane, replace Current Date in the letter with the current date, click below the date, click Address block in the Mail Merge task pane, then click OK

   When you run the mail merge, the address will be inserted in place of the field code.

4. Click after "Dear" in the letter, click Greeting line in the Mail Merge task pane, click OK, select [Position] in the first paragraph, click More items in the Mail Merge task pane, click Position in the Insert Merge Field dialog box, click Insert, click Close, press [Spacebar] if you need to create a space between <<Position>> and "with", select [Company Name], then replace it with Company Name from the Insert Merge Field dialog box

5. Follow Step 4 to replace [Company Name] and [Position] in the fourth paragraph with Company Name and Position from the Insert Merge Field dialog box, press [Ctrl][Home] to move to the top of the document, then click Next: Preview your letters in the Mail Merge task pane

   As you can see, the address and salutation appear incorrectly. Manager Trainee Rachel Johansen is the name, the city and state are missing, and the salutation includes "Dear" two times.

6. Click Previous: Write your letter in the Mail Merge task pane, select <<AddressBlock>> in the letter, press [Delete], click Address block in the Mail Merge task pane, click Match Fields in the Insert Address Block dialog box, make changes in the Match Fields dialog box as shown in Figure G-7, click OK, click OK, then press [Enter] if needed to create one blank line between the address block and the greeting line

7. Select and delete <<GreetingLine>>, click Greeting line in the Mail Merge task pane, make the change to the Greeting line dialog box as shown in Figure G-8, click OK, then press [Enter] if needed so a blank line appears between the greeting line and the first paragraph of the letter

8. Click Next: Preview your letters in the Mail Merge task pane, select the four lines of the address for Rachel Johansen, click the Page Layout tab, select 10 pt in the After box in the Paragraph group, type 0, press [Enter], press [→] to deselect the text, press [Enter] to create a blank line, then compare the address and salutation text to Figure G-9

9. Click Next: Complete the merge, click Edit individual letters, type 1 in the From box, type 2 in the To box, click OK, save the two merged letters as PR G-Marlene_Job Search Merged Letters to the location where you save the files for this book, close the document, then save and close the PR G-Marlene_Job Search Form Letter document and exit Word

FIGURE G-7: **Match Fields dialog box**

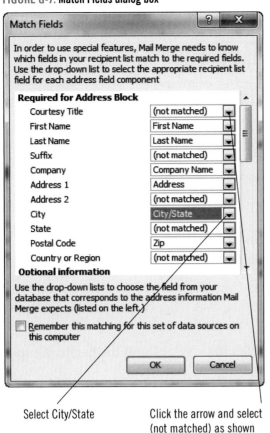

Select City/State

Click the arrow and select
(not matched) as shown

FIGURE G-8: **Insert Greeting Line dialog box**

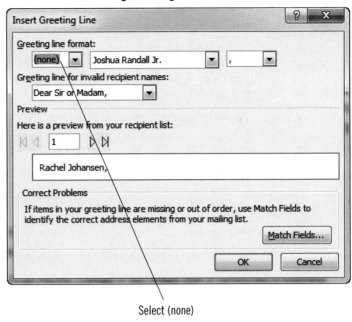

Select (none)

FIGURE G-9: **Completed letter for Rachel Johansen**

Analyze the Job Search Results

All of the companies that interviewed Marlene have offered her employment. Now she needs to decide which offer to accept. To help her make a wise decision, you create a query table in Access that lists only those companies that interviewed her. Then you add several new fields that Marlene can use to rank each company in terms of its location, pay, benefits, and opportunities for advancement according to the rating scale as follows: 3 = Poor, 6 = Good, 9 = Excellent. Once you have completed the table, you need to analyze the data in Excel and then create a chart to illustrate the overall ranking for each company.

Steps:

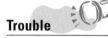
Trouble

Click Open if a warning box appears.

1. In Access, verify that Contacts is selected, click the Create tab, click the Query Wizard button in the Queries group, then click OK to accept Simple Query Wizard

2. Click Company Name, click the Select Single Field button ⟩, add the Position and Response fields to the Selected Fields list, click Next, click Next, change the query title to Positive Results, click the "Modify the query design." option button, then click Finish

3. Click the Response Criteria cell, type Yes, then click the Run button in the Results group

   All five of the companies that responded positively to Marlene's form letter appear.

4. Click the Select All button ◢ to select the entire query as shown in Figure G-10, click the Copy button in the Clipboard group, close the query datasheet, click Yes, click the Create tab, click Table in the Tables group, click the Home tab, click the Paste button in the Clipboard group, then click Yes

5. Click the View button, type Ratings, click OK, click the blank cell below "Response", then as shown in Figure G-11, type the field names Location, Pay, Benefits, and Advancement and change the data type to Number for all four fields

6. Click the View button, click Yes, enter the values as shown in Figure G-12, then close and save the table if prompted

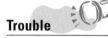
Trouble

Make sure you click the Excel button in the Export group, not in the Import group.

7. Click Ratings in the list of Access Objects, click the External Data tab, click Excel in the Export group, click Browse, navigate to the location where you save the files for this book, change the name of the file to PR G-Marlene_Job Search Ratings, click Save, click OK, then click Close

8. Start Excel, open PR G-Marlene_Job Search Ratings.xlsx from the location where you save the files for this book, select cells E2:I6, click the Sum button Σ in the Editing group, select cells B2:B6, press and hold [Ctrl], select cells I2:I6, click the Insert tab, click the Column button in the Charts group, then select the Clustered Column chart type (upper-left type)

   Each "Yes" response is entered as "TRUE" when the Access table is exported to Excel.

9. Click the More button ⊡ in the Chart Styles group, select Style 30 (purple), click the Chart Tools Layout tab, click Chart Title in the Labels group, click Above Chart, type Employer Ratings, press [Enter], click Legend in the Labels group, then click None

Additional Practice

For additional practice with the skills presented in this project, complete Independent Challenge 1.

10. Adjust column widths, size and position the chart as shown in Figure G-13, type your name below the chart, save the workbook, submit all files to your instructor, then close all files and exit all programs

    Marlene can see at a glance that the job offered by Solar Utilities most closely matches her employment criteria.

FIGURE G-10: Selecting the Positive Results query datasheet

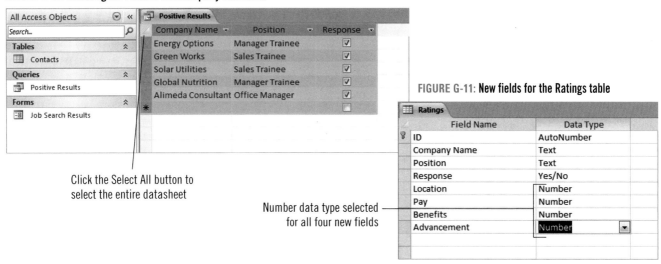

Click the Select All button to select the entire datasheet

FIGURE G-11: New fields for the Ratings table

Number data type selected for all four new fields

FIGURE G-12: Records for the Ratings table

ID	Company Na	Position	Response	Location	Pay	Benefits	Advancemer	Clic
1	Energy Options	Manager Traine	☑	3	3	6	3	
2	Green Works	Sales Trainee	☑	3	3	3	3	
3	Solar Utilities	Sales Trainee	☑	3	6	9	9	
4	Global Nutritio	Manager Traine	☑	6	3	3	3	
5	Alimeda Consu	Office Manage	☑	9	6	3	3	
(New)			☐					

FIGURE G-13: Completed Column chart in Excel

Proposal for Natura Beauty Products

You are the owner of Natura Beauty Products, a small business that sells organically made beauty products. To increase sales, you've decided to propose a partnership with Deep Bay Spa, a local health resort. To create the proposal, you need to **Import an Excel Workbook**, **Create the Proposal in Word**, and then **Add Excel and Access Objects to Word**. The three pages of the completed proposal are shown in Figure G-20 on page 163.

Import an Excel Workbook

You need to create an Access database containing a Product List table, add records for some of the company's products, and then import an Excel workbook that contains information about the aromatherapy products into the Product List table.

Hint

Make sure you change the data type for Price to Currency.

Steps:

1. **Start Access, then create a new database called** PR G-Natura Beauty Products.accdb **saved to the location where you save the files for this book**

2. **Click the** View button, **save the table as** Product List, **type** Product # **as the first Field Name, change the Data Type to** Number, **then enter the remaining fields as shown in Figure G-14**

3. **Click the** Category Data Type list arrow, **click** Lookup Wizard, **click** Open **if prompted, click the** "I will type in the values that I want." **option button, click** Next, **press** [Tab], **type** Bath, **press** [Tab], **type** Cleansing, **then click** Finish

4. **Click the** View button, **click** Yes, **enter the data as shown in Figure G-15, then close and save the table if prompted**

5. **Start Excel, open the file** PR G-2.xlsx **from the location where you store your Data Files, then save the file as** PR G-Natura Beauty Products_Aromatherapy.xlsx **to the location where you save the files for this book**

   The worksheet contains three columns. Before you can import this worksheet into the Access table, you need to ensure that both the Excel worksheet and the Access table contain the exact same column headings and data types.

6. **Select** column C, **click the** right mouse button, **click** Insert, **type** Category **in cell C1, click cell C2, type** Essential Oil, **then drag the fill handle to cell C32 to fill all the cells with the Essential Oil label**

7. **Save and close the workbook without exiting Excel, return to Access, click** Product List **in the list of Access Objects, click the** External Data tab, **click** Excel **in the Import & Link group, click the** Browse button, **navigate to the location where you save the files for this book, then double-click** PR G-Natura Beauty Products_Aromatherapy.xlsx

8. **Click the** "Append a copy of the records to the table:" **option button, click** OK, **click** Open **if prompted, click** Next, **click** Next, **click** Finish, **then click** Close

9. **Double-click** Product List **to open it, scroll down so you can see the records you originally entered in the Product List table at the bottom of the list along with some of the new records as shown in Figure G-16, then close the table**

FIGURE G-14: Fields for the Product List table

Field Name	Data Type	
Product #	Number	
Description	Text	
Category	Text	
Price	Currency	

FIGURE G-15: Records for the Product List table

Product #	Description	Category	Price	Click to Add
5777	Peppermint Spray	Bath	$5.00	
5778	Lemon Verbena Bath Oil	Bath	$5.50	
5779	Ylang Ylang Soap	Cleansing	$6.00	
5780	Raspberry Lemon Wash	Cleansing	$5.00	
5781	Papaya Oil	Bath	$6.00	
5782	Lavender Lime Wash	Cleansing	$5.00	
5783	Strawberry Soap	Cleansing	$6.00	

FIGURE G-16: Excel data imported into the Product List table

Product #	Description	Category	Price	Click to Add
3564	Juniper Berry	Essential Oil	$6.00	
3565	Key Lime	Essential Oil	$6.50	
3566	Lavender	Essential Oil	$6.00	
3567	Lemongrass	Essential Oil	$5.50	
3568	Lovage Leaf	Essential Oil	$5.00	
3569	Marjoram	Essential Oil	$5.00	
3570	Myrtle	Essential Oil	$7.00	
3571	Patchouli	Essential Oil	$6.50	
3572	Pine Needle	Essential Oil	$6.00	
3573	Ravensara	Essential Oil	$4.50	
3574	Rosemary	Essential Oil	$5.00	
3575	Rue	Essential Oil	$4.50	
3576	Sandalwood	Essential Oil	$7.00	
3577	Spearmint	Essential Oil	$5.00	
3578	Tea Tree	Essential Oil	$5.50	
3579	Thyme	Essential Oil	$5.50	
3580	Wintergreen	Essential Oil	$6.50	
5777	Peppermint Spray	Bath	$5.00	
5778	Lemon Verbena Bath Oil	Bath	$5.50	
5779	Ylang Ylang Soap	Cleansing	$6.00	
5780	Raspberry Lemon Wash	Cleansing	$5.00	
5781	Papaya Oil	Bath	$6.00	
5782	Lavender Lime Wash	Cleansing	$5.00	
5783	Strawberry Soap	Cleansing	$6.00	

Create the Proposal in Word

The proposal consists of three pages that will include objects copied from Excel and Access. First, you need to set up the document in Word and then you need to insert the text. You will insert the Excel and Access objects in the next lesson.

Steps:

1. Start Word, click the Page Layout tab, click the Margins button in the Page Setup group, click Custom Margins, change the Left margin to 2.5, click OK, then save the document as PR G-Natura Beauty Products Partnership Proposal.docx to the location where you save the files for this book

2. Click the Insert tab, click the Header button in the Header & Footer group, click Blank, click the Insert tab, click the WordArt button in the Text group, select the Fill – Red, Accent 2, Warm Matte Bevel style (fifth row, third column), then replace [Type Text] with Proposal

3. Select Proposal, click the Home tab, click the launcher in the Font group, change the Font Size to 80, click the Advanced tab, click the Spacing list arrow, click Expanded, select the contents of the By text box, type 5, press [Tab], compare the dialog box to Figure G-17, then click OK

4. Click the Drawing Tools Format tab, click Text Direction in the Text group, click Rotate all text 270°, click the View tab, click the One Page button in the Zoom group, then use the mouse and arrow keys to position the WordArt object as shown in Figure G-18

5. Switch back to 100% view, click the Header & Footer Tools Design tab, click the Go to Footer button in the Navigation group, type your name at the left margin, press [Tab] twice, click the Page Number button in the Header & Footer group, point to Current Position, then click Plain Number

   The page number does not appear because the Right tab marker is currently set at 6.5", which is beyond the current right margin.

6. Click the Home tab, click the launcher in the Paragraph group, click Tabs, click 6.5, click Clear, type 5, click Set, then click OK

   The page number appears at the right margin.

7. Double-click in the body of the report to exit the footer, press [Ctrl][Home], click the Insert tab, click the Object list arrow in the Text group, click Text from File, navigate to the location where you store your Data Files, then double-click PR G-3.docx

   The text required for the proposal is inserted into the document.

8. Scroll to the top of the document, select INTRODUCTION, click the Home tab, then click Heading 1 in the Styles gallery

9. Format all the headings in the document that are formatted in uppercase letters with the Heading 1 style, format all the headings in the document that are formatted in title case with the Heading 2 style, apply the Equity theme, then save the document

   Figure G-19 shows some of the formatted headings.

FIGURE G-17: Setting character spacing

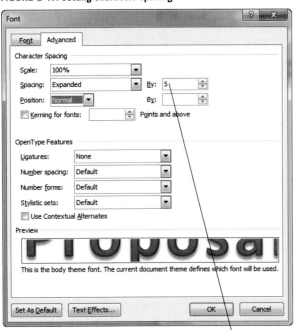

Enter "5" in the By text box

FIGURE G-18: Completed WordArt object in One Page view

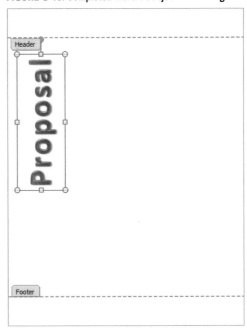

FIGURE G-19: Heading styles applied to selected text

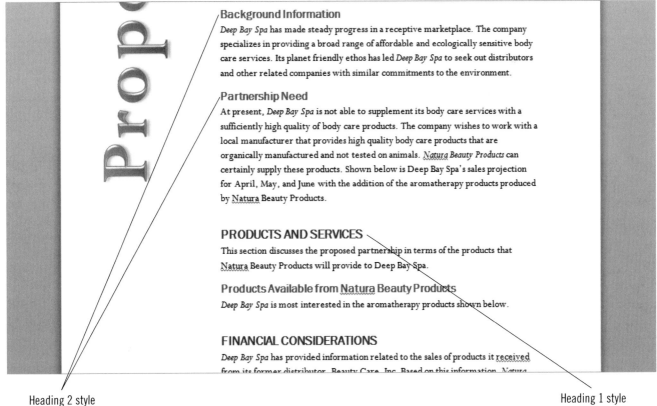

Heading 2 style

Heading 1 style

Add Excel and Access Objects to Word

You insert spreadsheet data, publish an Access query table in Word, and copy a chart from Excel.

Steps:

1. In Excel, open the file PR G-4.xlsx from the location where you store your Data Files and save it as PR G-Natura Beauty Products Partnership Data.xlsx, select cells A1:E14, click the Copy button in the Clipboard group, then switch to Word

2. Click at the end of the paragraph below the "Partnership Need" heading, press [Enter], click the Home tab, click the Paste list arrow in the Clipboard group, click Paste Special, click Microsoft Excel Worksheet Object, click OK, click the pasted object, then drag the lower-left corner up to resize the object so it fits at the bottom of page 1 as shown in Figure G-20

3. Switch to Access, click the Create tab, click the Query Wizard button in the Queries group, click OK, click Open if prompted, move all the records in the Product List table to the Selected Fields list box, click Next, click Next, then click Finish

4. Switch to Design view, type Essential Oil in the Criteria cell for Category, click the Run button in the Results group, then close and save the query

Hint

The .rtf extension in the filename stands for Rich Text Format.

5. Click Product List Query in the list of Access Objects, click the External Data tab, click the More button in the Export group, click Word, click the Browse button, navigate to the location where you save the files for this book, change the name of the file to PR G-Natura Beauty Products List Query, click Save, click the "Open the destination file after the export operation is complete." check box, then click OK

6. Select the table, click the Copy button in the Clipboard group, click the View tab, click the Switch Windows button in the Window group, click PR G-Natura Beauty Products Partnership Proposal.docx, scroll to the second page and click at the end of the paragraph below the "Products Available from Natura Beauty Products " heading, press [Enter], then click the Paste button

7. Select the table, click the Table Tools Design tab, click the More button ⊽ in the Table Styles group to show the Table Styles Gallery, select the Light Grid-Accent 1 style, click the Home tab, then click the Center button ≡ in the Paragraph group

8. Switch to Excel, click the Projected Revenue sheet tab, select cells A1:E3, click the Insert tab, click the Column button in the Charts group, click the Clustered Column chart style, click the Chart Tools Layout tab, click the Legend button in the Labels group, then click Show Legend at Bottom

9. Click the Home tab, click the Copy button , switch to the Proposal document in Word, click at the end of the paragraph below the "Projected Revenues" heading on page 3, press [Enter], click the Paste list arrow, then click the Keep Source Formatting & Embed Workbook button 📋

Additional Practice

For additional practice with the skills presented in this project, complete Independent Challenge 2.

10. Click the View tab, click the Zoom button in the Zoom group, click the Many Pages button and drag to select three pages, click OK, compare the completed proposal to Figure G-20, save the document, submit all files to your instructor, then close all files and exit all programs

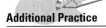

Proposal

INTRODUCTION

Natura Beauty Products has an opportunity to partner with *Deep Bay Spa*, a salon-style service that provides body care treatments. This proposal describes the partnership issues in terms of three factors: Partnership Requirements, Products and Services, and Financial Considerations.

PARTNERSHIP REQUIREMENTS

This section provides background information abo[ut]
how the partnership could benefit both companie[s]

Background Information

Deep Bay Spa has made steady progress in a recepti[on]
specializes in providing a broad range of affordabl[e]
care services. Its planet friendly ethos has led *Deep*
and other related companies with similar commit[ment]

Partnership Need

At present, *Deep Bay Spa* is not able to supplement
sufficiently high quality of body care products. Th[is]
local manufacturer that provides high quality body
organically manufactured and not tested on anima[ls]
certainly supply these products. Shown below is D[eep Bay Spa's]
for April, May, and June with the addition of the a[romatherapy products supplied]
by Natura Beauty Products.

Deep Bay S[pa]
Sales Projecti[ons]

	April	May
Revenue		
Aromatherapy Products	$ 40,000.00	$ 50,00[0.00]
Spa Treatments	$ 70,000.00	$ 100,00[0.00]
	$ 110,000.00	$ 150,00[0.00]

PRODUCTS AND SERVICES

This section discusses the proposed partnership in terms of the products that Natura Beauty Products will provide to Deep Bay Spa.

Products Available from Natura Beauty Products

Deep Bay Spa is most interested in the aromatherapy products shown below.

Product #	Description	Category	Price
3550	Angelica	Essential Oil	$7.50
3551	Bay	Essential Oil	$7.00
3552	Bergamot	Essential Oil	$5.50
3553	Birch Sweet	Essential Oil	$6.50
3554	Caraway	Essential Oil	$5.50
3555	Chamomile	Essential Oil	$6.00
3556	Clary Sage	Essential Oil	$6.00
3557	Cypress	Essential Oil	$5.50
3558	Eucalyptus	Essential Oil	$5.00
3559	Frankincense	Essential Oil	$5.50
3560	Geranium	Essential Oil	$6.00
3561	Ginger	Essential Oil	$5.50
3562	Hiba Wood	Essential Oil	$5.50
[35]63	Hyssop	Essential Oil	$5.50
[35]64	Juniper Berry	Essential Oil	$6.00
[35]65	Key Lime	Essential Oil	$6.50
[35]66	Lavender	Essential Oil	$6.00
[35]67	Lemongrass	Essential Oil	$5.50
[35]68	Lovage Leaf	Essential Oil	$5.00
[35]69	Marjoram	Essential Oil	$5.00
[35]70	Myrtle	Essential Oil	$7.00
[35]71	Patchouli	Essential Oil	$6.50
[35]72	Pine Needle	Essential Oil	$6.00
[35]73	Ravensara	Essential Oil	$4.50
[35]74	Rosemary	Essential Oil	$5.00
[35]75	Rue	Essential Oil	$4.50
[35]76	Sandalwood	Essential Oil	$7.00
[35]77	Spearmint	Essential Oil	$5.00
[35]78	Tea Tree	Essential Oil	$5.50
[35]79	Thyme	Essential Oil	$5.50
[35]80	Wintergreen	Essential Oil	$6.50

2

FINANCIAL CONSIDERATIONS

Deep Bay Spa has provided information related to the sales of products it received from its former distributor, Beauty Care, Inc. Based on this information, *Natura Beauty Products* could expect a minimum 20% increase in revenues on the sale of products used by *Deep Bay Spa*.

Projected Revenues

The chart illustrated below shows the revenues projected for each quarter in the first year of the proposed partnership with *Deep Bay Spa*.

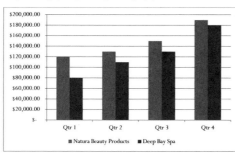

CONCLUSION

Natura Beauty Products has the opportunity to increase its market share by partnering with *Deep Bay Spa*. Both companies are seriously committed to the environment and to providing their customers with high-quality body care products and services. The market is growing daily as more and more consumers recognize the value of organic products that promote relaxation and well-being.

Your Name   3

Art Collection Catalogue for Horizons Art Gallery

As the office manager of the Horizons Art Gallery, you decide to create a database that lists the art pieces currently being shown at the gallery, produce identification labels to attach to each piece, and create a chart showing the breakdown of paintings by price category. For this project, you need to **Create the Database and Set Up the Merge**, and then you need to **Merge the Labels and Create a Chart**.

Create the Database and Set Up the Merge

You create the database by copying a table from Word. Then, you need to create a query and merge the data in the query with identification labels you create in Word.

Steps:

1. Create a new database called PR G-Horizons Collection.accdb, **and save it to the location where you save the files for this book**

2. **Start Word, open** PR G-5.docx **from the location where you store your Data Files, select the table, click the** Copy button  **in the Clipboard group, close the document, switch to Access, click the** Home tab, **click the** Paste button, **then click** Yes

3. **Switch to Design view, type** Art List **as the table name, click** OK, **change the Data Type for Cost to** Currency, **close and save the table, then click** Yes **in response to the warning**

4. **Click** Art List, **click the** Create tab, **click the** Query Wizard button, **click** OK, **click** Open **if prompted, select all the fields** *except* **the ID and Price Category fields, click** Next, **click** Next, **name the query** Identification Labels, **then click** Finish

5. **Switch to** Design view, **click the** Creation Date Sort cell, **click the** list arrow, **select** Ascending, **click the** Run button **in the Results group, then close and save the query**

Trouble

If you receive a warning that the database is open in exclusive mode, click OK, close the database, open it again, enable content if prompted, then repeat Step 6.

6. **Click** Identification Labels, **click the** External Data tab, **click** Word Merge **in the Export group, click** Open **if prompted, click the** "Create a new document and then link the data to it." **option button, then click** OK

7. **Maximize the Word window, click the** Labels option button **in the Mail Merge task pane, click** Next: Starting document, **click** Label options, **click the** Label vendors list arrow, **click** Avery US Letter **if it is not the selected vendor, scroll to and select** 5163 Shipping Labels **in the Product number list as shown in Figure G-21, click** OK, **then if the gridlines are not visible, click the** Table Tools Layout tab **and click the** View Gridlines button **in the Table Group**

   A sheet of labels formatted as a table opens in a new Word document.

Trouble

Switch to 100% view if the view is different than 100%.

8. **Click** Next: Select recipients **in the Mail Merge task pane, click** Next: Arrange your labels, **click** More items, **click** Insert, **click** Close, **then press** [Enter]

   The Artist field is inserted.

9. **Click the** Insert Merge Field button **in the Write & Insert Fields group, double-click** Painting Title, **then insert the remaining fields and arrange them as shown in Figure G-22**

10. **Save the document as** PR G-Horizons Identification Labels.docx **to the location where you save the files for this book**

FIGURE G-21: Selecting the label type

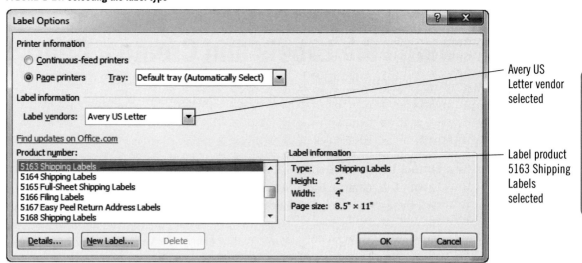

Avery US Letter vendor selected

Label product 5163 Shipping Labels selected

FIGURE G-22: Fields for the identification labels

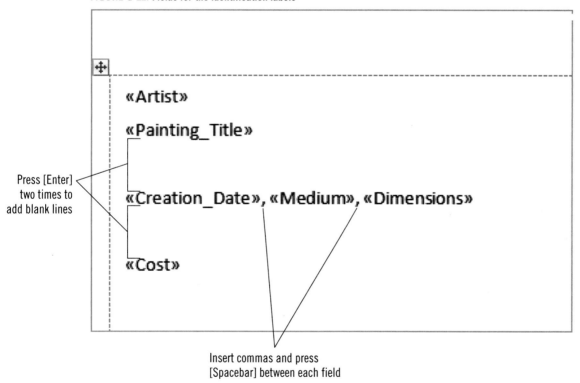

Press [Enter] two times to add blank lines

Insert commas and press [Spacebar] between each field

Merge the Labels and Create a Chart

You need to format the fields and run the merge. Then you need to analyze the Art List table in Excel so that you can create a separate chart that shows the breakdown of paintings by price category.

Steps:

1. **Format the field labels as shown in Figure G-23**, click the Artist field, **click the** Page Layout tab, **change the Spacing Before to** 12 pt, **click** Update all labels **in the Mail Merge task pane, then click** Next: Preview your labels **in the Mail Merge task pane**

   The cost for each painting is no longer formatted in Currency style. When you merge an Access database with a Word document, you need to use merge field codes to apply currency formatting to number amounts.

Trouble

You may need to press [Fn] on your keyboard when you are asked to press a function key, such as [F9]. For Step 2, you might need to press [Fn][Shift][F9].

2. **Click** Previous: Arrange your labels, **click the** Cost field **in the first label, press** [Shift][F9] **to display the merge field code, then type** \# $0 **as shown in Figure G-24**

3. **Click** Cost **in the merge field code, press** [F9] **to turn off the display of merge field codes, click** Update all labels, **click** Next: Preview your labels, **click** Next: Complete the merge, **close the Mail Merge task pane, compare the completed label sheet to Figure G-25, add your name after the cost field in the last label on the page, then save the file**

4. **Switch to Access, click** Art List, **click the** Excel button **in the Export group on the External Data tab, click** Browse, **navigate to the location where you save the files for this book, change the name to** PR G-Horizons Art List, **click** Save, **click** OK, **then click** Close

5. **Start Excel, open** PR G-Horizons Art List.xlsx, **widen columns to fit content, select cells** A1:H16, **click the** Sort & Filter button **in the Editing group, click** Custom Sort, **click the** Sort by list arrow, **click** Price Category, **then click** OK

6. **Click the** Data tab, **click** Subtotal **in the Outline group, click the** At each change in list arrow, **scroll to and click** Price Category, **click** OK, **then click cell** A1 **to deselect the table**

7. **Widen the Cost column, click the** Home tab, **click the** Find & Select button **in the Editing group, click** Replace, **type** Count, **press** [Tab], **click** Replace All, **click** OK, **then click** Close

8. **Select cells** G6:H6, **press and hold** [Ctrl], **select cells** G15:H15 **and cells** G19:H19, **click the** Insert tab, **click the** Other Charts button **in the Charts group, click the** Doughnut chart, **then drag the chart below the data**

Additional Practice

For additional practice with the skills presented in this project, complete Independent Challenge 3.

9. **Select** Layout 6, **format, size, and position the Doughnut chart as shown in Figure G-26, type your name below the chart, save the workbook, submit all files to your instructor, then close and save all files and exit all programs**

FIGURE G-23: Formatted fields

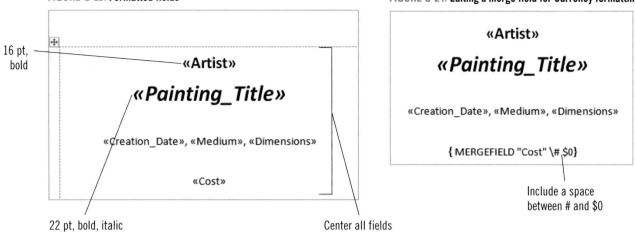

16 pt, bold → «Artist»

«Painting_Title»

«Creation_Date», «Medium», «Dimensions»

«Cost»

22 pt, bold, italic

Center all fields

FIGURE G-24: Editing a merge field for Currency formatting

«Artist»

«Painting_Title»

«Creation_Date», «Medium», «Dimensions»

{ MERGEFIELD "Cost" \# $0 }

Include a space between # and $0

FIGURE G-25: Completed label sheet

Takao Watanabe	Penelope Chow
Into the Wind	**Landlocked**
2009, Ink on paper, 26" x 30"	2009, Acrylic on canvas, 36" square
$1400	$1600
Liz Gibbons	Joz Garland
Ancestors	**Blue Swirl**
2010, Collage, 14" x 18"	2010, Oil on panel, 18" x 24"
$1000	$1500
Parminder Singh	Ron Bolton
Ulysses	**Ocean Currents**

FIGURE G-26: Completed Doughnut chart

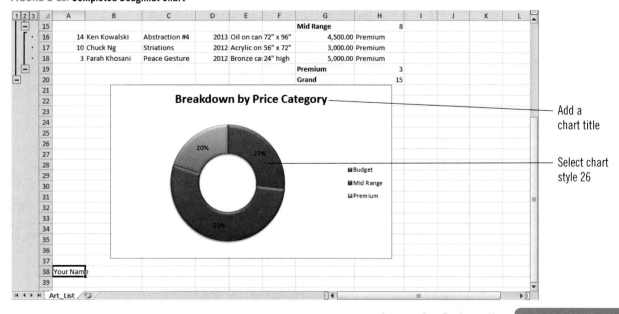

Add a chart title

Select chart style 26

Integration Projects II

Independent Challenge 1

Create a Job Search database similar to the database you created for Unit G Project 1 to track your own job search efforts. Even if you are not currently seeking employment, create a practice database and accompanying form letter for your dream job. You can then modify these files when you are ready to seek employment. Follow the steps provided to create the database, merge it with a form letter you create in Word, and then create a chart in Excel that graphically displays your hypothetical ratings of the companies that responded positively to your form letter.

1. Your first task is to determine the type of job position you are seeking and the type of company or organization you would like to work for. For example, you could seek a job as an office manager at a real estate or architectural company. In the box below, write the job positions you are seeking and the types of companies you would like to work for:

Job Positions: _____

Company Types: _____

_____

2. You need at least 10 employers for your job search database. Look through the employment advertisements in your local paper or online to find potential employers, or the names and addresses of at least 10 companies that you might like to work for. Try to include as many realistic records in your job search database as possible.
3. Create a database called **PR G-My Job Search Database.accdb** in the location where you save the files for this book.
4. Create a **Contacts** table that includes at least six fields. Make one field a lookup field.
5. Switch to Word and set up an application form letter, then save it as **PR G-My Job Application Letter.docx** to the location where you save the files for this book. Use the form letter you created in Unit G Project 1 to help you determine the information to include. Make sure you fully describe your qualifications and experience.
6. Close the Word document, then in Access merge the Contacts table with the form letter, insert fields where required, match fields where needed for the address, merge two of the letters, then save the merged letters as **PR G-My Job Application Letter_Merged** to the location where you save the files for this book.
7. Switch back to Access and create a custom form called **Job Search** that includes the fields from the Contacts table and two additional fields: a Yes/No field called "Response", and a text field for a date.
8. Use the form to enter positive responses for at least five of the employers.
9. Create a query that lists only the companies that responded positively to your form letter.
10. Copy the Company Name and Position records from the query to a new table called **My Job Ratings**, then enter your ratings for each company in terms of four criteria of your choice.
11. Export the My Job Ratings table to Excel, and change the name to **PR G-My Job Ratings**.
12. In Excel, create a column chart that shows the breakdown of companies according to your ratings. Remember that you will need to total the ratings for each company and then use the Chart Wizard to create a column chart that includes only the company names and the total ratings. Include a title on the column chart and remove the legend.
13. Type your name below the chart, save the workbook, submit all files to your instructor, then close all the files and applications.

Independent Challenge 2

Write a three-page proposal that discusses partnership opportunities between two companies of your choice. For example, you could write about the benefits of a partnership between a small computer store and a bookkeeping business. Follow the steps provided to create data in Excel, import it into an Access database, create a proposal in Word, and then add objects from Excel and Access.

1. Start Excel, then create a product list in Sheet1 that contains information about products you plan to mention in the proposal. Save the file as **PR G-My Partnership Data.xlsx** to the location where you save the files for this book.

Independent Challenge 2 (continued)

2. Start Access, create a new database called **PR G-My Partnership Database.accdb**, save it to the location where you save the files for this book, then import the Excel worksheet. Specify that row 1 includes the column headings.

3. Name the new table **My Products**.

4. Start Word, save the new document as **PR G-My Partnership Proposal.docx** to the location where you save the files for this book, then apply the theme of your choice.

5. Show the Header and Footer toolbar, then use WordArt to create an interesting background for your proposal similar to the background you created in Unit G Project 2.

6. Switch to the footer, enter your name at the left margin, then insert the page number at the right margin. (*Hint*: After you enter the page number, open the Paragraph dialog box, click Tabs, clear the tab set at 6.5", then set a tab at 5".)

7. Write approximately one page of text for the proposal. Make sure that you include text that introduces a table that you'll publish from Access, a worksheet that you'll copy from Excel, and a chart that you'll copy from Excel.

8. Include several headings and subheadings that you format with the Heading 1 or Heading 2 style.

9. Switch to the PR G-My Partnership Data.xlsx workbook, apply the same theme you applied to the proposal in Word, enter projected financial data regarding revenue and expenses in Sheet2, then enter projected quarterly data and create a chart in Sheet3. Add appropriate names to each of the three sheet tabs.

10. Copy the cells containing the financial data on Sheet2 and use Paste Special to paste them as a Microsoft Excel Worksheet Object into the proposal, then copy the chart to the proposal and use the Keep Source Formatting and Embed Workbook paste option.

11. From Access, publish the My Products table in Word and save it as **PR G-My Partnership Products.rtf**.

12. Copy the Word table to the proposal, then apply a Table style.

13. Add a title at the top of the first page, scroll through the document, add page breaks where appropriate, save the document, submit copies of all files to your instructor, then save and close all files and all programs.

Independent Challenge 3

Create a database that contains information about your personal collection of CDs, records, tapes, videos, photographs, or a collection of your choice. Use the database to create labels for items in your collection. Plan and create the database as follows.

1. In Word, create a table containing headings, such as genre, category, or type, that differentiate the records in your collection. If your table lists all of your DVDs, for example, you could include fields for Title, Genre, Date, and Price. Make sure your table includes one field that contains currency amounts (for example, the "Price" field).

2. Save the Word document as **PR G-My Collection Table.docx** to the location where you save the files for this book.

3. Create a database called **PR G-My Collection Database.accdb**, and save it to the location where you save the files for this book, copy the table from the Word document into the Access table, then save the table as **Collection List**.

4. Merge the table to a new document in Word, and then follow the steps in the Mail Merge task pane to select a label, insert fields, and then format and arrange the fields. Look through the list of labels available in the Label Options dialog box to find a label appropriate for the items in your collection.

5. Complete the merge. Edit the field that contains values that should be displayed in the Currency format. (*Hint*: To change the format for a merge field, click the field name, press [Shift][F9] to show the merge field code, type \# $0, click the field name again, press [F9] to preview the result, then update the labels. (*Note*: You can type \# $0.00 if you want the amount to show decimals as shown in Figure G-27.)

6. Add your name to the last label, then save the label sheet as **PR G-My Collection Labels.docx** to the location where you save the files for this book.

FIGURE G-27

«**Artist**»

«*Title*»

«**Music_Genre**»

{ MERGEFIELD "Price" \# $0.00}

Independent Challenge 3 (continued)

7. Switch back to Access and export the table to Excel as a workbook called **PR G-My Collection List.xlsx**, and save it to the location where you save the files for this book.

8. Open the workbook in Excel, sort one of the fields (for example, the category field) in ascending order, apply a Subtotals list that calculates the total number of items in each category, replace "Count" with nothing, then create a chart such as a pie chart or a doughnut chart that shows the breakdown of items by category. Apply a chart layout, add a title to the chart, then type your name below the chart. (*Hint:* Search for [space]Count so that Excel does not also remove the "count" in "Country.")

9. Submit all files to your instructor, save and close all open files, then exit all programs.

Independent Challenge 4

You work for Game Time, Inc., that creates imaginative computer games and sells them online. You've decided to analyze the types of customers who have purchased your games in the past month in terms of occupation and country. Follow the instructions to create a report similar to the one shown in Figure G-29.

1. Start Access, create a database called **PR G-Game Time Computers.accdb**, and save it to the location where you save the files for this book.

2. Create a table called **Customer List** as shown in Figure G-28. *Note:* The Occupation field is a lookup field (**Artist, Consultant, Lawyer, Manager, Teacher**), and the Country field is a lookup field (**Canada, India, Mexico, United States**).

FIGURE G-28

ID	Last Name	First Name	Occupation	Country	Product	Click to Add
1	Harris	Don	Manager	Canada	Pathways	
2	Dunst	Will	Lawyer	United States	Mars Voyager	
3	Singh	Parminder	Consultant	India	Grand Prix Racer	
4	Khosani	Parvin	Manager	Canada	Ancient Odyssey	
5	O'Rourke	Bridget	Teacher	United States	Music Quest	
6	Gonzales	Maria	Manager	Mexico	Pathways	
7	Rosas	Carla	Artist	Mexico	Planet Gazer	
8	Knutson	Sven	Lawyer	India	Mars Voyager	
9	Mumaba	Garth	Lawyer	United States	Ancient Odyssey	
10	Wong	Doris	Teacher	United States	Deep Space Diver	
11	Lapointe	Pierre	Manager	Canada	Music Quest	
12	Renfrew	Wade	Teacher	United States	Ancient Odyssey	
13	Malik	Mehdi	Teacher	India	Prehistory Journey	
14	Rao	Ajala	Teacher	India	Prehistory Journey	
15	Fuentes	Diego	Consultant	Mexico	Deep Space Diver	
*	(New)					

3. Export the Customer List table to an Excel workbook that you name **PR G-Game Time Analysis.xlsx** and save to the location where you save the files for this book. In Excel, create a column chart that shows the breakdown of customers by country. Sort the worksheet by country and use the Subtotal feature to count the number of records in each country before you create the column chart. In the Subtotal dialog box, select "Country" as the "At each change in selection" value. Also remove "Count" from the worksheet so that it does not appear in the chart labels. (*Hint:* Search for [space]Count so that Excel does not also remove the "count" in "Country.")

4. Format the chart so that it appears as shown in Figure G-29.

5. Start Word, enter the text shown in Figure G-29, apply the Modern style set and the Metro theme, change the top and bottom margins to .5", apply the Title style to the title, then save the document as **PR G-Game Time Report.docx**.

Independent Challenge 4 (continued)

6. Switch to Access, publish the table as an .rtf file called **PR G-Game Time Customer List.rtf** to the location where you save the files for this book, then delete the ID column, save the file, copy the table, switch to the PR G-Game Time Report document, then paste the table below the first paragraph of text in the Word document.

7. With the table selected, click the Table Tools Layout tab, click Sort, change the Sort by column to Country, click OK, then apply a table style of your choice and widen columns as needed to fit content.

8. Switch to Excel, copy the chart, then use the Use Destination Theme and Embed Workbook paste option to paste the column chart below the last paragraph in the Word document.

9. Adjust spacing and resize the chart so all content fits on page 1, type your name in the document footer, save the document, submit all files to your instructor, then close and save all files and programs.

FIGURE G-29

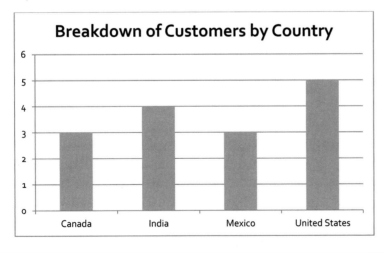

GAME TIME, INC.

Game Time, Inc., sells the majority of its computer games directly from its Web site. We have analyzed the types of customers who have purchased our computer games during one week in December 2013. The table shows the breakdown of these customers by Occupation and Country:

Last Name	First Name	Occupation	Country	Product
Harris	Don	Manager	Canada	Pathways
Khosani	Parvin	Manager	Canada	Ancient Odyssey
Lapointe	Pierre	Manager	Canada	Music Quest
Singh	Parminder	Consultant	India	Grand Prix Racer
Knutson	Sven	Lawyer	India	Mars Voyager
Malik	Mehdi	Teacher	India	Prehistory Journey
Rao	Ajala	Teacher	India	Prehistory Journey
Gonzales	Maria	Manager	Mexico	Pathways
Rosas	Carla	Artist	Mexico	Planet Gazer
Fuentes	Diego	Consultant	Mexico	Deep Space Diver
Dunst	Will	Lawyer	United States	Mars Voyager
O'Rourke	Bridget	Teacher	United States	Music Quest
Mumaba	Garth	Lawyer	United States	Ancient Odyssey
Wong	Doris	Teacher	United States	Deep Space Diver
Renfrew	Wade	Teacher	United States	Ancient Odyssey

As shown in the chart illustrated below, the majority of these customers live in India or the United States. A significant number of customers live in Canada and Mexico. To continue serving the Canadian and Mexican markets, Game Time plans to develop a marketing strategy in consultation with contacts in Toronto and Mexico City.

Visual Workshop

Start Word, create the table shown in Figure G-30, then save the file as **PR G-Garden Wizard Products.docx** to the location where you save the files for this book. Start Access, create a database called **PR G-Garden Wizard Database.accdb**, and save it to the location where you save the files for this book. Copy the table from the Word document to a new table in the Access database, then save the table as **Neighborhood Sales**. Add the **Design Services** field name and data as shown in Figure G-31, then select the Currency data type for the three fields as shown in Figure G-31. Export the table to an Excel file called **PR G-Garden Wizard Analysis.xlsx**, save it to the location where you save the files for this book, and then create a column clustered cone chart in Excel as shown in Figure G-32. Enter your name below the chart, save the Excel worksheet, submit all files to your instructor, then save and close all files and exit all programs.

FIGURE G-30

Neighborhood	Landscape Services	Garden Products
Arbor Lodge	45000	60000
South Tabor	55000	72000
Markham	58000	75000
Maplewood	33000	26000

FIGURE G-31

ID	Neighborhood	Landscape Services	Garden Products	Design Services
1	Arbor Lodge	$45,000.00	$60,000.00	$45,000.00
2	South Tabor	$55,000.00	$72,000.00	$30,000.00
3	Markham	$58,000.00	$75,000.00	$12,000.00
4	Maplewood	$33,000.00	$26,000.00	$18,000.00
*	(New)			

FIGURE G-32

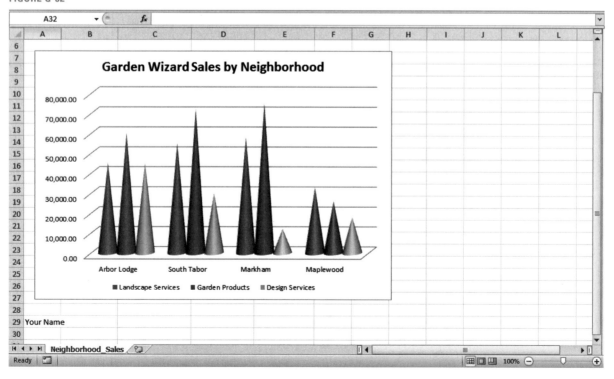

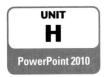

PowerPoint Projects

Files You Will Need:

PR H-1.jpg
PR H-2.jpg
PR H-3.jpg
PR H-4.jpg

You use PowerPoint to create attractively formatted presentations containing information that reinforces the content of an oral presentation. Suppose you have been asked to present to your coworkers what you learned at a recent seminar on project management. You could, of course, just talk to your audience and perhaps hand out a sheet or two of notes. But imagine how much more compelling your lecture would be if you accompanied it with colorful slides or overheads that provided your audience with a visual backup to your words. People learn best when they can see, hear, and then write down information. You supply the words, and PowerPoint supplies the visual information. You can also use the many graphics options in PowerPoint to help you create simple posters and flyers. In this unit, you will learn how to create and run PowerPoint presentations and how to create a one-page poster.

In This Unit You Will Create the Following:

Training Presentation

Poster

Lecture Presentation

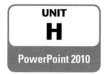

Training Presentation on Oral Presentation Skills

You have been asked to teach your coworkers how to give an oral presentation. To help emphasize the points you make, you will accompany your lecture with an on-screen presentation that you create in PowerPoint. For this project, you need to **Create the Presentation Outline**, **Customize a Theme**, **Modify Individual Slides**, and **Edit and Show the Presentation**.

Create the Presentation Outline

You need to enter the information you plan to display on the slides in the Oral Presentation Skills presentation.

Steps:

1. **Start PowerPoint, click the** Outline tab **in the pane that contains the Outline and Slides tabs, then click to the right of the slide icon in the Outline tab**

2. **Type** Oral Presentation Pointers, **then press** [Enter]

3. **Press** [Tab] **to indicate you want to type subtext on Slide 1, type your name, then save the presentation as** PR H-Oral Presentation Pointers **to the location where you save the files for this book**

   Slide 1 of the presentation appears as shown in Figure H-1. Notice how the text appears in the Outline tab and in the Slide pane.

4. **Click the** New Slide button **in the Slides group to start a new slide, type** Overview, **then press** [Enter]

   When you press [Enter] after typing a title, you start a new slide.

5. **Press** [Tab], **then type** Choose Your Topic

   When you press [Tab] after creating a new slide, you return to the previous slide (in this case, Slide 2). The text you typed appears as the first bulleted item on the slide titled "Overview."

6. **Press** [Enter], **type** Create Your Outline, **press** [Enter], **type** Prepare Your Slides, **press** [Enter], **type** Deliver Your Presentation, **then press** [Enter]

   When you press [Enter] after typing bulleted text, a new bullet appears.

7. **Click the** Decrease List Level button 🔲 **in the Paragraph group to start a new slide, type** Step 1: Choose Your Topic, **press** [Enter], **press** [Tab], **type** Persuade your audience to take a specific action or approve a specific request, **press** [Enter], **type** Sample Topics, **then press** [Enter]

8. **Press** [Tab], **enter the three items under Sample Topics as shown in Figure H-2, then click the** New Slide button **in the Slides group**

9. **Enter the information for Slides 4 through 7 as shown in Figure H-2**

   Remember to press [Tab] to move the insertion point to the right. You can press [Shift][Tab] to move the insertion point to the left. You can also click the Decrease List Level button 🔲 or the Increase List Level button 🔲 to change the outline level for the current line.

10. **Click the** Review tab, **click the** Spelling button **in the Proofing group, make any corrections required, press** [Ctrl][Home] **to move to the title slide, then save the presentation**

Hint

You can also press [Enter] and then [Shift][Tab] two times to return to the left margin and start a new slide.

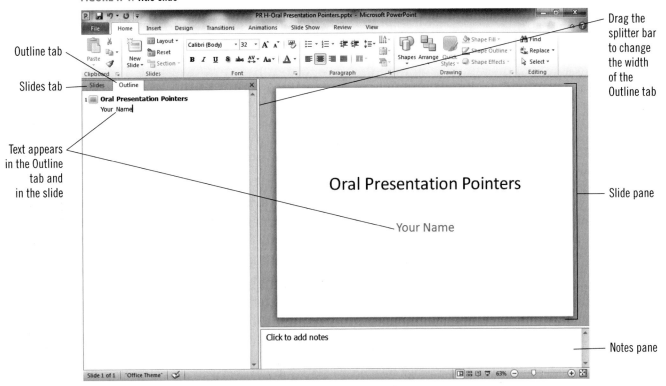

Outline tab

Slides tab

Text appears
in the Outline
tab and
in the slide

Drag the
splitter bar
to change
the width
of the
Outline tab

Oral Presentation Pointers

Your Name

Slide pane

Notes pane

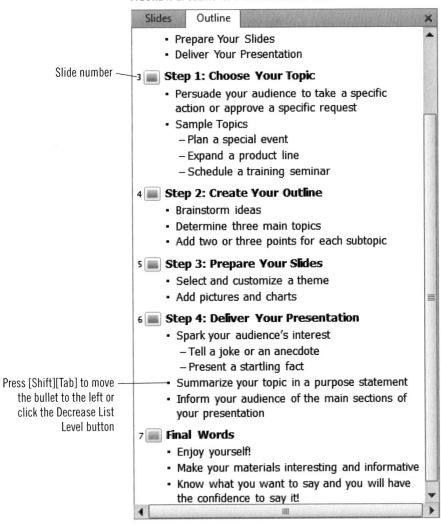

Slide number

Press [Shift][Tab] to move
the bullet to the left or
click the Decrease List
Level button

PowerPoint 2010

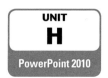
Customize a Theme

PowerPoint includes numerous built-in themes that you can use to format a presentation. You can change the color and font schemes and apply a new background style, and then you can work in Slide Master view to apply new formats to specific parts of each slide.

Hint

You can create hundreds of interesting presentation designs just by mixing and matching the various themes with new color schemes and font schemes.

Steps:

1. Click the Slides tab in the pane that contains the Outline and Slides tabs, click the Design tab, click the More button ⊡ in the Themes group, click Angles, click the Colors button in the Themes group, move the pointer over each color scheme to see how the colors of the objects on the title slide change, click Solstice, click the Fonts button in the Themes group, then click Opulent

2. Click the Background Styles button in the Background group, click Format Background, click the Color button, click Gold, Accent 2, Lighter 80%, select the contents of the Transparency text box (contains 0%), type 50, click Apply to All, then click Close

   The background color is slightly lighter. In addition to changing the background color, you can apply gradient fills, textures, and even patterns and pictures to further customize a presentation background.

3. Click the View tab, click Slide Master in the Master Views group, click the top slide master in the task pane, then click any word in the Click to Edit Master Title Style placeholder on the slide master as shown in Figure H-3

Trouble

If the text does not change, make sure you have clicked on a word, not a space.

4. Click the Home tab, click the Bold button **B** in the Font group, click any word in the phrase "Click to Edit Master text styles", increase the font size to 20 pt, then click the Bullets button ⋮☰ in the Paragraph group

   The formatting of the title text is changed on every slide in the entire presentation.

5. Click Second level, click the launcher ⌐ in the Paragraph group, change the Before text indentation to .5", click OK, click Third level, then repeat the process to change its Before text indentation to 1"

6. Click the large red shape at the bottom of the slide master, press [Delete], double-click the yellow shape that remains, click the Edit Shape button 🔣▾ in the Insert Shapes group, click Change Shape, then click the Right Triangle shape as shown in Figure H-4

   The yellow shape is changed into a triangle. You can modify the shapes that make up a presentation theme by modifying the fill color of shapes, removing shapes, and even drawing new shapes.

7. Click the Title Slide Layout (second slide in the task pane), click the large red triangle, press [Delete], click the Click to Edit Master Subtitle Style placeholder, press and hold the [Shift] key, then click the Click to Edit Master Title Style placeholder

8. Click Rotate in the Arrange group, click More Rotation Options, select the contents of the Rotation text box (currently filled with 319), type 0, click Close, then click away from the selected placeholders

9. As shown in Figure H-5, click and drag the Master Subtitle Style placeholder below and to the right of the Master Title Style placeholder and increase the width of the Master Title Style placeholder, click the View tab, click Normal in the Presentation Views group, then save the presentation

FIGURE H-3: Selecting the Master Title Style placeholder

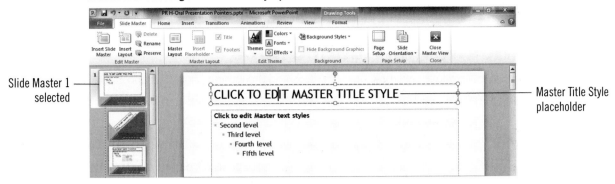

Slide Master 1 selected

Master Title Style placeholder

FIGURE H-4: Selecting the Right Triangle shape

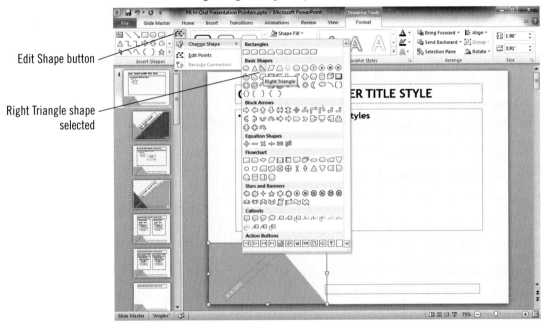

Edit Shape button

Right Triangle shape selected

FIGURE H-5: Positioning the Master Subtitle Style placeholder on the Title slide master

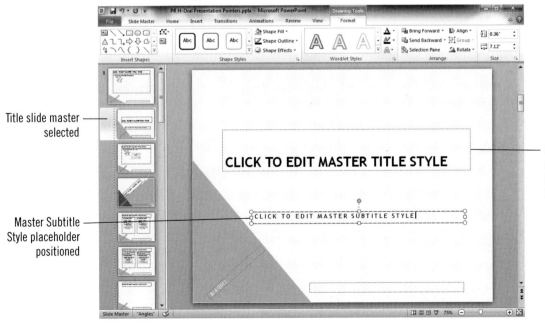

Title slide master selected

Master Subtitle Style placeholder positioned

Drag the right edge of the Master Title Style placeholder to increase its width

PowerPoint Projects

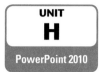
Modify Individual Slides

You need to add a clip art picture on Slide 2, and then insert a new slide and create a SmartArt graphic on the new slide.

Steps:

1. Click the Next Slide button ⬇ on the vertical scroll bar to display Slide 2, click the Insert tab, click the Clip Art button in the Images group, select the contents of the Search for text box, type checkmarks, click Go, click the picture of the check box (see Figure H-6), then close the Clip Art task pane

2. Use the mouse to drag the corner handles to increase the size of the clip art picture, then position the clip art picture as shown in Figure H-6

3. Click the Next Slide button ⬇ until Slide 6 appears (contains "Step 4: Deliver Your Presentation"), click the Home tab, click the New Slide button in the Slides group, click the Title placeholder, then type Four-Step Process

   The text is formatted in all capital letters because, as you type, the all caps setting is included in the format applied to text in the Title placeholder text box.

4. Click the Insert SmartArt Graphic button 🖼 in the body placeholder, click Cycle in the left pane, click Basic Radial (third row, second from left), then click OK

5. Click Text Pane in the Create Graphic group if the text pane is not open, type Great Presenting, press [↓], type Topic, then enter the labels for the remaining three circles as shown in Figure H-7

6. Click the More button ⏷ in the SmartArt Styles group, then select the Subtle Effect style

   Read the ScreenTips to find the Subtle Effect style.

7. Click the Change Colors button in the SmartArt Styles group, then click Colored Fill - Accent 2 (the second choice in the Accent 2, yellow group)

8. Click the gray border surrounding the SmartArt graphic, click the Home tab, then click the Bold button **B** in the Font group

9. Click the circle containing the "Great Presenting" text, press and hold [Shift], drag the upper-right sizing handle up and to the right to increase the size of the circle as shown in Figure H-8, click the SmartArt Tools Design tab, click Text Pane in the Create Graphic group to close the text pane, click away from the SmartArt graphic, then save the presentation

FIGURE H-6: Clip art picture

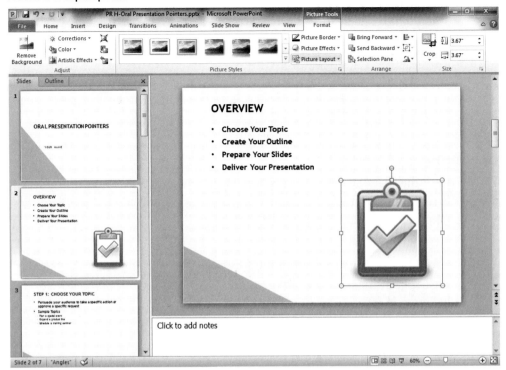

FIGURE H-7: Text typed in the SmartArt graphic

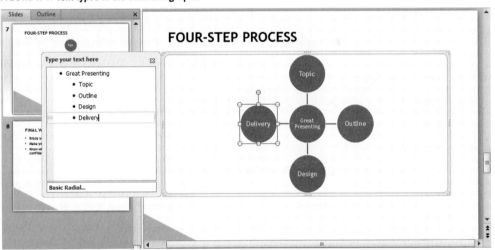

FIGURE H-8: Completed SmartArt graphic

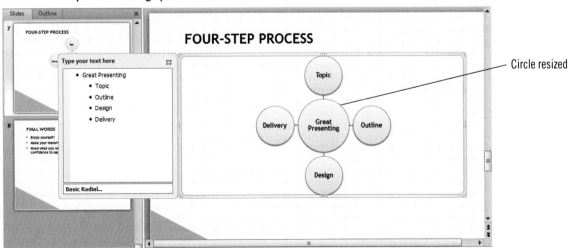

Circle resized

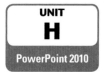
Edit and Show the Presentation

You need to select an animation scheme in Slide Sorter view, and then apply a custom animation scheme to the SmartArt graphic. Finally, you run the presentation in Slide Show view, and then print a copy of the presentation as a sheet of handouts with all eight slides on one page.

Steps:

1. **Click the** View tab, **click** Slide Sorter **in the Presentation Views group, verify that Slide 7 is selected, click the** Zoom button **in the Zoom group, click the** 66% option button, **click OK, then drag Slide 7 to the left of Slide 3**

   Slide 7 is now slide 3, as shown in Figure H-9.

2. **Click the** Transitions tab, **click the** More button ⏷ **in the Transition to This Slide group, click** Split **in the top row, click the** Effect Options button, **then click** Vertical In **as shown in Figure H-10**

   The animation effect previews on the selected slide.

3. **Click the** Apply To All button **in the Timing group**

4. **Verify that Slide 3 is still selected (it contains the SmartArt graphic), then click the** Normal button 🔳 **on the status bar at the bottom of the screen**

5. **Click the** SmartArt graphic **to select it (be careful not to select any one circle), click the** Animations tab, **click the** More button ⏷ **in the Animation group, move the pointer over each of the effects to see what happens to the SmartArt graphic, then click** Wheel **in the Entrance section**

6. **Click the** Effect Options button **in the Animation group, then click** One by One

   The animation effect is previewed on the slide. As you can see, each circle appears in turn, starting from the Great Presenting circle.

7. **Press [Ctrl][Home] to move to the first slide in the presentation, click the** Slide Show **tab, click the** From Beginning button **in the Start Slide Show group, then press [Spacebar] or click the** left mouse button **to move through the presentation**

   The animation scheme works nicely, and the custom animation effect on the SmartArt graphic adds interest.

8. **Click the** File tab, **click** Print, **click the** Full Page Slides list arrow, **then click** 9 Slides Vertical **in the Handouts area**

   A preview of how the eight slides will print is shown in Figure H-11.

Additional Practice

For additional practice with the skills presented in this project, complete Independent Challenge 1.

9. **Click the** Print button **if you wish to print the presentation; otherwise, save the presentation, submit a copy to your instructor, then close the presentation**

FIGURE H-9: **Slide 7 moved in Slide Sorter view**

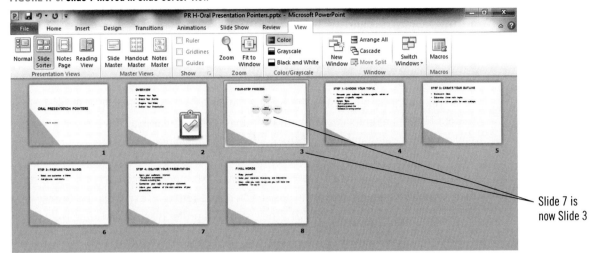

Slide 7 is now Slide 3

FIGURE H-10: **Vertical In effect selected**

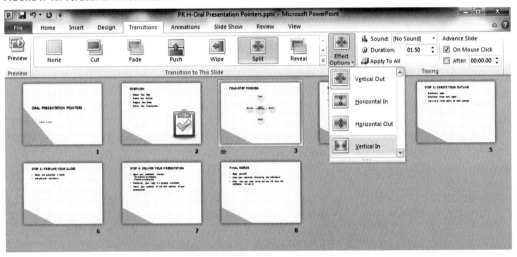

FIGURE H-11: **Selecting a format for handouts**

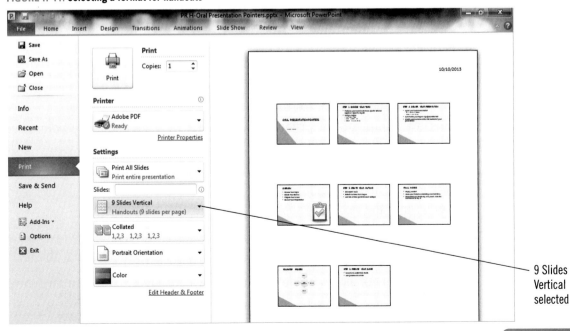

9 Slides Vertical selected

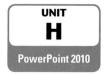
Poster for Seymour Nature Preserve

You are in charge of advertising the monthly information meetings held from May through August at Seymour Nature Preserve Area in North Vancouver, British Columbia. You have decided to create a poster to advertise the dates and times of these information meetings. The poster can be displayed on bulletin boards in libraries, community centers, and other neighborhood areas. In addition, the poster can be saved as a PDF (Portable Document Format) file and then distributed to members via e-mail or uploaded to the organization's Web site. To create the poster, you need to **Insert Text Objects**, **Create a Table**, and then **Add Graphics and Create the PDF**. The completed poster is shown in Figure H-20 on page 187.

Insert Text Objects

You need to start a new presentation, draw a shape, and then enter and format text.

Steps:

1. **Create a new presentation in PowerPoint, click** Layout **in the Slides group, click** Blank, **click the** View tab, **click the** Ruler check box **in the Show group if the ruler is not showing, then save the presentation as** PR H-Seymour Nature Preserve Poster **to the location where you save the files for this book**

2. **Click the** Insert tab, **click** Shapes, **click** Rounded Rectangle **in the Rectangles section (second from the left), draw a box approximately 8" wide (from 4 to 4 on the ruler bar) anywhere on the screen, then type** Information Meeting
   You do not need to worry about sizing the rectangle shape exactly at this point.

3. **Select the text, click the** Home tab, **click the** Font Size list arrow **in the Font group, click** 32, **then click the** Bold button **B** **in the Font group**

4. **Click the** Drawing Tools Format tab, **select the contents of the** Height text box **in the Size group, type** 1, **press** [Enter], **select the contents of the Width text box, type** 7.75, **press** [Enter], **then click an edge of the rectangle object and drag to position it as shown in Figure H-12**

5. **Click away from the text box, click the** Insert tab, **click** Text Box **in the Text group, click below the rounded rectangle, type** Location, **press** [Enter], **then type the** address text **shown in Figure H-13**
   You do not need to worry about positioning the text box exactly at this point.

Hint
You select the border so that any changes you make will be applied to all the text in the box.

6. **Select the word** Location, **change the font size to** 20 pt **and apply** bold, **select the** two address lines, **change the font size to** 16 pt, **click the** text box border, **then click the** Center button **≡** **in the Paragraph group to center all the text**

7. **Click at the end of the address line, press** [Enter] **two times, type** 2013 Meeting Times, **then format the text with** bold **and** 24 pt

8. **Add another text box near the bottom of the slide containing the text,** For more information, please call Your Name at (604) 555-3488., **then format the text with** 14 pt

Hint
You will align the boxes precisely in the next lesson.

9. **Drag the two text boxes to the positions shown in Figure H-14, then save the presentation**

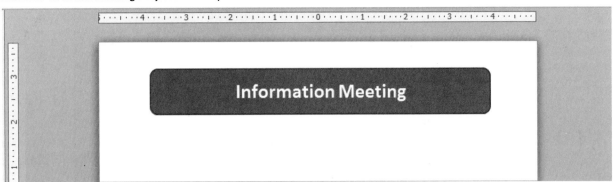

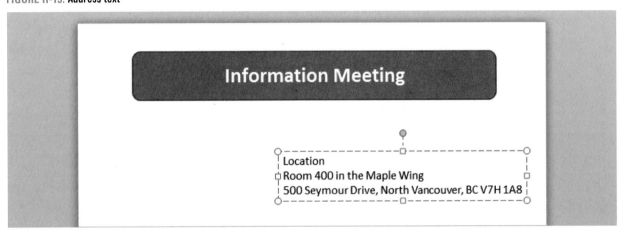

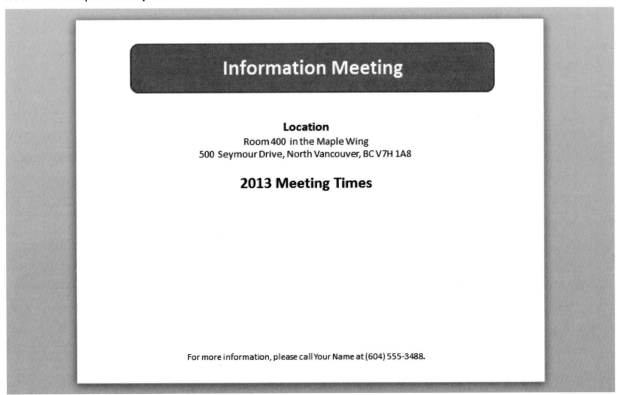

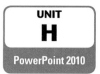

Create a Table

The poster includes a table that lists the meeting times for the months of April, May, and June. You need to create and then modify the table.

Steps:

1. Click the Insert tab, click the Table button in the Tables group, then drag to create a table consisting of two columns and four rows

2. Click the More button ⊡ in the Table Styles group, click Light Style 2 - Accent 3 (in the green column), then click the Banded Columns check box in the Table Style Options group to select it

3. Move the pointer over the top border to show the ⬚, click and drag to position the table below "2013 Meeting Times", click the first cell, then type the text for the table as shown in Figure H-15

4. Select the two cells in the top row, click the Home tab, click the Center button ≡ in the Paragraph group, select the three cells containing dates in column 1, apply bold, then deselect the cells

5. Move the pointer over the column divider between columns 1 and 2 to show ◄║►, double-click to autofit the text in column 1, move the pointer over the right border of column 2 to show ◄║►, then double-click to autofit the text in column 2

6. Click the table border, click the Table Tools Layout tab, select the contents of the Table Row Height text box in the Cell Size group, type .5, click the Center Vertically button ▤ in the Alignment group, then as shown in Figure H-16, position the table below "2013 Meeting Times"

7. Double-click the rounded rectangle, click the More button ⊡ in the Shape Styles group, select Intense Effect - Olive Green, Accent 3, then click away from the shape to deselect it

8. Click the Design tab, click Colors in the Themes group, click Create New Theme Colors, then type Poster for the custom color scheme name

9. Click the Accent 3 (green) color box, click More Colors, enter values for Red, Green, and Blue as shown in Figure H-17, click OK, click Save, then save the presentation

   The Poster color scheme is saved and available for use in other presentations. You can create your own color scheme from any of the existing color schemes.

FIGURE H-15: **Table text**

Information Meeting

Location
Room 400 in the Maple Wing
500 Seymour Drive, North Vancouver, BC V7H 1A8

2013 Meeting Times

Date	Time
Tuesday, April 16	7:30 p.m.
Tuesday, May 14	7:30 p.m.
Tuesday, June 11	8:00 p.m.

For more information, please call Your Name at (604) 555-3488.

FIGURE H-16: **Table sized and positioned**

Information Meeting

Location
Room 400 in the Maple Wing
500 Seymour Drive, North Vancouver, BC V7H 1A8

2013 Meeting Times

Date	Time
Tuesday, April 16	7:30 p.m.
Tuesday, May 14	7:30 p.m.
Tuesday, June 11	8:00 p.m.

For more information, please call Your Name at (604) 555-3488.

FIGURE H-17: **Creating a custom color**

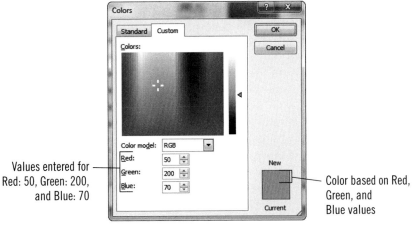

Values entered for Red: 50, Green: 200, and Blue: 70

Color based on Red, Green, and Blue values

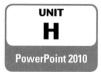

Poster (continued)

Add Graphics and Create the PDF

You need to create a WordArt object using the text "Seymour Nature Preserve" and then insert and manipulate a picture so the completed poster appears as shown in Figure H-20. Finally, you save the poster as a PDF file.

Steps:

1. Click the Insert tab, click the WordArt button in the Text group, click Fill - Green, Accent 3, Powder Bevel (fifth row, green selection), type Seymour Nature Preserve, then drag the WordArt object below the table (don't worry about precise positioning at this point)

2. Select the text, click the Home tab, reduce the font size to 36 pt, click the Drawing Tools Format tab, click the Text Effects button [A] in the WordArt Styles group, point to Bevel, click 3-D Options, then modify the settings in the 3-D Format pane in the Format Text Effects dialog box as shown in Figure H-18

3. Click Close, then position the WordArt object just above the information line

4. Click the Home tab, click Select in the Editing group, click Select All, click the Drawing Tools Format tab, click the Align button in the Arrange group, then click Align Center
   You use the Align function to precisely align objects in relation to each other.

5. Click a blank area of the slide to deselect the objects, click the Insert tab, click Picture in the Images group, navigate to the location where you store your Data Files, then double-click PR H-1.jpg

6. Click Remove Background in the Adjust group, click Keep Changes, click Color in the Adjust group, then click Green, Accent color 3 Light (bottom row)

7. Click the launcher [ ] in the Size group; click the Lock Aspect ratio check box to deselect it; as shown in Figure H-19, enter 3 in the Height box, enter 9.5 in the Width box, enter 275 in the Rotation box; then click Close

8. Move the graphic so that it appears along the left side of the slide as shown in the completed poster in Figure H-20, click the Home tab, click the Copy button [ ], click the Paste button, drag the copied graphic toward the right edge of the slide, click the Picture Tools Format tab, click the Rotate button [ ] in the Arrange group, click Flip Horizontal, then position the graphic as shown in Figure H-20

Additional Practice

For additional practice with the skills presented in this project, complete Independent Challenge 2.

9. Save the presentation, click the File tab, click Save & Send, click Create PDF/XPS Document, click the Create PDF/XPS button, verify the Save as type is set to PDF (*.pdf) in the Publish as PDF or XPS dialog box that opens, click Publish, submit the two files to your instructor, then close the files

FIGURE H-18: 3-D Format options

Click the list arrow and select the Cool Slant style

Change the Width to 20 pt

Change the Height to 6 pt

Click the list arrow and select the Freezing lighting style in the Cool section

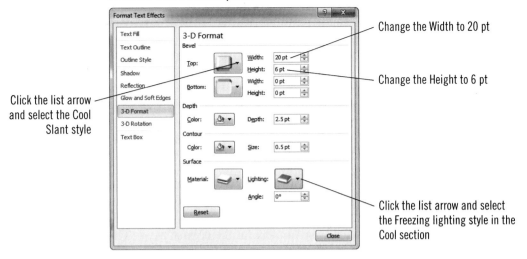

FIGURE H-19: Size options

Lock aspect ratio check box deselected

Height, Width, and Rotation options

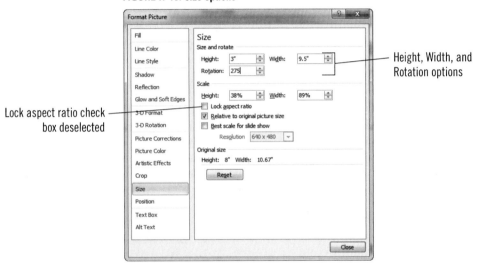

FIGURE H-20: Completed poster

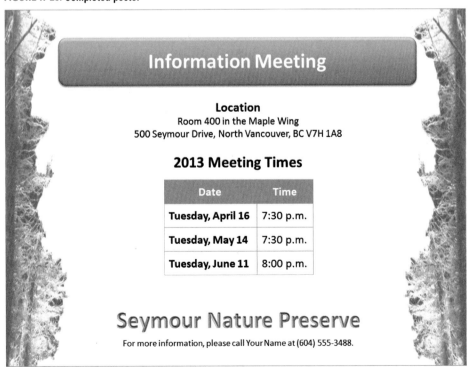

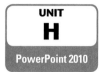
Lecture Presentation on Project Management

You need to give a presentation to your classmates on the basic concepts of project management. You will not have access to a projector, so you use PowerPoint to create transparencies that you can display on an overhead projector. You need to **Set Up the Presentation** and **Modify Graphics**. The completed presentation is shown in Slide Sorter view in Figure H-26 on page 191.

Set Up the Presentation

You need to enter and then edit text for the presentation in Outline view. Then you need to insert an organizational chart on Slide 6.

Steps:

1. **Create a new presentation in PowerPoint, click the** Design tab, **click** Page Setup **in the Page Setup group, click the** Slides sized for list arrow, **click** Letter Paper (8.5 × 11 in), **click the** Portrait option button **in the Slides section, then click** OK

2. **Click the** Outline tab **in the pane containing the Outline and Slides tab, enter the text for the seven slides shown in Figure H-21, check the spelling, then save the presentation as** PR H-Project Management Lecture **to the location where you save the files for this book**

3. **Click the** Design tab, **then select the** Module theme

4. **Move to** Slide 5, **click the** Insert SmartArt graphic button **in the object placeholder, click** Hierarchy **in the left pane, select** Organization Chart **(far-left selection in the top row), then click** OK

5. **Type** Project Manager, **click the border of the box immediately below and slightly left of the top box, press** [Delete] **to delete the box, type** Department Managers, **click the middle box, type** Vendors, **click the** right box, **then type** Customers

Trouble

Make sure you click the Add Shape list arrow and not the Add Shape button itself. Click Undo if you insert a text box below Department Managers.

6. **Click the** Project Manager box, **click the** Add Shape list arrow **in the Create Graphic group, click** Add Shape Below, **then type** Board of Directors
   The organization chart now contains a total of five boxes—one for the Project Manager and one each for the four stakeholders.

7. **Click the** More button **in the Layouts group, click** Horizontal Hierarchy **(right selection in the third row—use ScreenTips and refer to Figure H-22 as needed to find the layout), click the** More button **in the SmartArt Styles group, click** Cartoon **(third from the left) in the 3-D section, click the** Change Colors button **in the SmartArt Styles group, then click** Colorful Range - Accent Colors 2 to 3

8. **Click a blank area outside the slide, compare your slide to Figure H-22, then save the presentation**

FIGURE H-21: Outline for the Project Management lecture

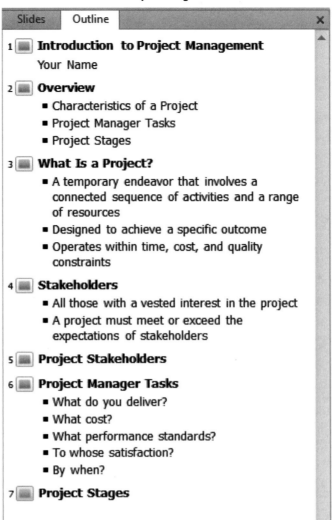

FIGURE H-22: Completed organization chart

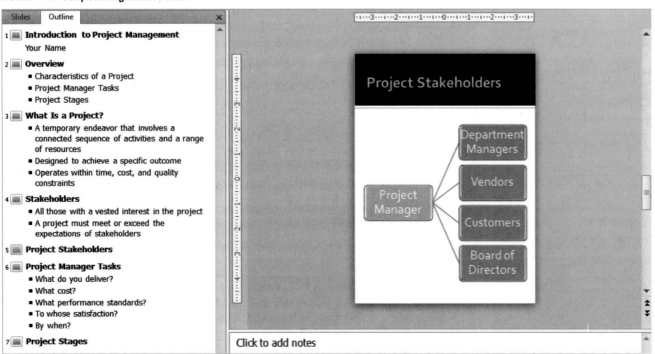

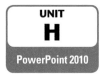

Modify Graphics

You need to insert a clip art picture and then modify it by removing an object in the picture that you do not want. You then need to create five aligned text boxes and draw arrows to connect them. The completed presentation in Slide Sorter view is shown in Figure H-26.

Trouble

You need to be connected to the Internet to find the clip art picture. Also verify that All media types is selected in the Clip Art task pane.

Steps:

1. Move to Slide 4, click the Insert tab, click Clip Art in the Images group, select the text in the Search for text box, type project, find and insert the picture shown in Figure H-23, then close the Clip Art task pane

   The picture you insert includes a light yellow background, which you will remove in a later step.

2. Move the picture to the lower-right area of the slide, click the Group button 🗗 in the Arrange group, click Ungroup, click Yes to convert it to a drawing object, then increase the zoom to 100%

Hint

Sometimes you need to ungroup a picture two or more times before you can select and delete specific objects.

3. Click away from the picture, right-click the picture, point to Group, click Ungroup, click away from the selected objects, click the top-left area of the yellow background, verify the yellow background shape is selected as shown in Figure H-23, then press [Delete]

   Most of the picture is deleted—which isn't quite what you had in mind.

4. Click the Undo button 🔄 on the Quick Access toolbar, be sure the image is still selected, right-click the top-left area of the yellow background, point to Group, click Ungroup, click away from the picture again, click just the yellow background again, then press [Delete]

   The yellow background object is removed from the picture.

5. Position the pointer above and to the left of the clip art picture, click and drag to select all the remaining objects that make up the picture, click the Drawing Tools Format tab, click Group in the Arrange group, then click Group

   The modified clip art object appears as shown in Figure H-24.

6. Move to Slide 7, click the View tab, click Fit to Window in the Zoom group, click the Home tab, click Layout in the Slides group, click the Title Only slide layout, draw a text box just below the slide title, type Initiating, fill the text box with Gold, Accent 1, Lighter 40%, select the text, change the font size to 28 pt, center the text, then apply bold

Trouble

The text box is selected when the border is a solid line.

7. Click outside the text box, click the text box border, click the Drawing Tools Format tab, set the width at 4", press [Ctrl][C], click [Ctrl][V] four times, drag the currently selected text box to about 1" from the bottom of the slide, press [Ctrl] and use the pointer to select all five text boxes, click the Align button in the Arrange group, click Distribute Vertically, click the Align button again, then click Align Center

8. Change the text in each of the four copied text boxes as shown in Figure H-25, draw a vertical arrow between the top two boxes (see Figure H-25), copy it and paste it three times, then position the arrows as shown in Figure H-25

Additional Practice

For additional practice with the skills presented in this project, complete Independent Challenge 3.

9. Switch to Slide Sorter view, click Slide 1, compare the completed presentation to Figure H-26, if you wish to print the presentation, print a copy of the presentation as Handouts – 9 Slides Vertical to a page, then save the presentation, submit a copy to your instructor, and close the presentation

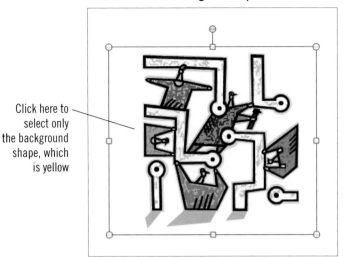

Click here to select only the background shape, which is yellow

FIGURE H-25: Text boxes and arrows on Slide 7

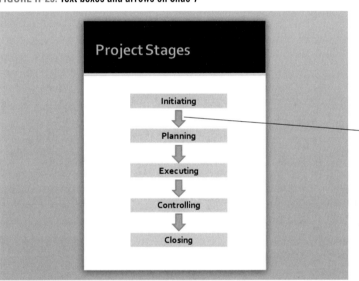

To draw the arrow, click the Insert tab, click Shapes in the Illustrations group, then click the Down Arrow shape in the Block Arrows section

FIGURE H-26: Completed presentation in Slide Sorter view

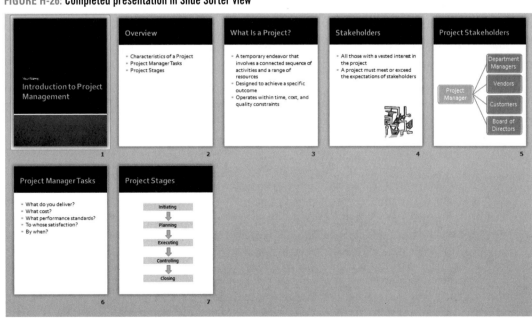

Independent Challenge 1

Create a six-slide presentation that you could use to help teach a specific concept or task. For example, your presentation could offer guidelines for purchasing a computer system, taking effective vacation photographs, or planning an event such as a wedding. Follow the steps provided to create the presentation in PowerPoint.

1. Your first task is to determine the subject of your presentation. Think about an activity or task that you know well and that you can present in short, easy-to-understand steps. To help get started, write the words "How to", followed by a verb and then the activity. For example, your presentation subject could be "How to Design an Organic Vegetable Garden" or "How to Plan a Cycling Trip." In the box below, write the subject of your presentation:

Presentation Subject: _____

_____

2. You need to determine three main topics that cover a specific activity related to your subject. For example, the three topics for a presentation titled "How to Find a Job" could be: 1. Personal Profile, 2. Employment Sources, and 3. Interview Techniques. You should present each of these topics on separate slides along with three or four bulleted points that describe each topic. Write the three topics of your presentation in the box below:

Topic 1: _____

Topic 2: _____

Topic 3: _____

3. Start PowerPoint and create an outline of your presentation. Save the presentation as **PR H-My How-To Presentation** to the location where you save the files for this book. Here's a suggested format:

Slide #	Slide Title	Text
1	Presentation Subject	Title: Presentation Topic; Subtitle: Your Name
2	Overview	List the three topics that you will cover in your presentation
3	Topic 1	List three or four bulleted points related to topic 1
4	Topic 2	List three or four bulleted points related to topic 2
5	Topic 3	List three or four bulleted points related to topic 3
6	Conclusion	Create a "motivational" slide to summarize your presentation

4. Apply the presentation theme of your choice, then customize it by selecting a new color scheme and font scheme.
5. Change the background style. For example, you could apply a texture fill or a gradient fill.
6. Switch to Slide Master view, and modify the appearance of the text in the placeholders. You may decide, for example, to change the font size and style of the text in the Master Title Style placeholder.
7. In Slide Master view, modify the appearance of one or more of the graphic objects included with the design. For example, you can fill an object with a different color and delete selected objects.
8. Exit Slide Master view, then add a clip art picture to at least one slide.
9. Insert an appropriate SmartArt graphic on one slide. Insert a new slide if necessary. Modify the SmartArt graphic attractively by applying a new style and color scheme.
10. Switch to Slide Sorter view, then add a transition effect to all the slides in the presentation.
11. In Normal view, add an animation effect to the SmartArt graphic, then edit the effect so that the various components that make up the graphic appear one by one.
12. Switch to Slide Show view and run the presentation. If you are able to print, print a copy of the presentation as handouts with six slides to a page. Save the presentation, submit a copy to your instructor, then close the presentation.

Independent Challenge 2

Create a poster that announces some kind of event, such as a concert series, sports tournament, or club meeting.

1. Determine the type of event you will announce. If you are involved in sports, you could create a poster to advertise an upcoming game or tournament. If you belong to a club, you could create a poster to advertise a special event such as a fund-raising bake sale.

2. Think of an interesting title for your event. For example, a poster that announces a celebrity golf tournament could be called "Stars on Par," while a poster that advertises running events for cash prizes could be called "Dash for Cash."

3. Determine the details that readers of your poster will need to know in order to participate in the event that you plan to advertise. You need to specify where the event will be held, when it will be held (date and time), and what activities will occur at the event. List yourself as the person readers should contact for more information.

4. On a blank piece of paper, create a rough draft of your poster. Determine where you will place the various blocks of text and one or two photographs or clip art images.

5. Create the poster on a blank PowerPoint slide. Create a custom color scheme called **Poster**. You can base the color scheme on any of the existing color schemes. Change at least one of the accent colors.

6. Include a table on your poster. Format the table attractively with one of the table styles.

7. Include at least one photograph to which you have removed the background and applied one or more effects such as an artistic effect, a color correction, or a color effect. Use the modified photograph as a design element in your poster.

8. Include a WordArt object to which you have applied and modified special effects such as a bevel or reflection. Experiment with the many ways in which you can modify the WordArt object.

9. Save the presentation as **PR H-My Poster** to the location where you save the files for this book, then save the presentation as a PDF file to the same location.

10. Submit a copy of both files to your instructor, then close the presentation.

Independent Challenge 3

1. Create a short presentation that presents information about an academic subject of your choice. Then format and print the presentation in Portrait orientation, which is appropriate for delivery as transparencies on an overhead projector. Think of courses you are currently taking or have taken in the past, and then prepare slides that could accompany a short lecture on an aspect of a course that interests you. For example, you could create a presentation that outlines the principal causes of the Great Depression, or presents major issues in Shakespeare's *Hamlet*, or provides an overview of genetics. In the box below, write the subject of your presentation:

Presentation Subject: _____

2. Determine the three main topics you will discuss in your presentation. For example, three topics for a presentation on major issues in Shakespeare's *Hamlet* could be "The Tragic Hero," "Dramatic Irony," and "Imagery." Write the three topics of your presentation in the box below:

Topic 1: _____

Topic 2: _____

Topic 3: _____

3. Start PowerPoint and create an outline of your presentation. Save the presentation as **PR H-My Lecture** to the location where you save the files for this book. Use the same format suggested for Unit H Independent Challenge 1 to organize your presentation subject along with its three main topics.

Independent Challenge 3 (continued)

4. Change the page orientation for the presentation to Portrait, and then apply a presentation theme and color scheme.

5. Switch to Slide Master view, and modify the appearance of the text in the placeholders and of the various elements that make up the slide design. For example, you can choose to delete some objects, change the fill colors of other objects, or add a new clip art picture.

6. Add a clip art image to the presentation, then modify the clip art image by removing selected objects or filling other objects with different colors.

7. On one slide, draw text boxes and shapes to show a process. For ideas, refer to the Lecture Presentation for Project Management you completed for Unit H Project 3.

8. Be sure your name is on the presentation, such as on the Title slide as a subtitle, save the presentation, submit a copy to your instructor, then close the presentation.

Independent Challenge 4

You have helped to organize a three-day convention for home-based business people in your area. A few months prior to the convention, you will hold a meeting for local business people to inform them about the conference and encourage them to participate. Follow the instructions provided to create and then modify the presentation that you plan to give at this meeting.

FIGURE H-27

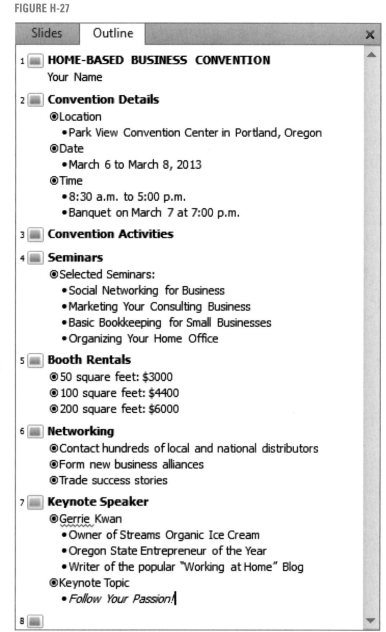

1. Create a new presentation in PowerPoint, show the Outline pane, then enter just the slide titles and text for the presentation as shown in Figure H-27.

2. Check the spelling, then save the presentation as **PR H-Home Based Business Presentation** to the location where you save the files for this book.

3. Apply the Technic slide design, change the color scheme to Slipstream, then apply Style 2 from the selection of Background Styles.

4. In Slide Master view, click the top slide master, then change the color of the far-right curved shape to Green, Accent 4, Darker 25%.

5. Apply bold to the Master Title Style placeholder, and change the color to Green, Accent 4, Darker 50%. (*Hint*: Be sure you click the text and not a space between words.)

6. Modify the Title Style slide master (second slide master in the task pane) as follows: change the color of the right curved shape to match the change you made to the top slide master, then change the color of the Title Style text to match the Master Title style on the top slide master in the task pane. (*Note*: The Title Style text on the Title Style slide master is formatted with a text effect that includes a text outline. Use the Drawing Tools Format tab to modify the fill color and to remove the text outline color.)

Independent Challenge 4 (continued)

7. Change the bullet color on the third slide master in the task pane for the First and Second level headings to Green, Accent 4, Darker 50%. *Hint*: Click the level to change, click the Home tab, click the Bullets list arrow, click Bullets and Numbering, click the Color button, then select the required color.

8. Exit Slide Master view, add the Pyramid List SmartArt graphic (in the List section) to Slide 3, select the Inset SmartArt style, select the color scheme of your choice, then add the text and a shape as seen on Slide 3 in Figure H-28.

FIGURE H-28

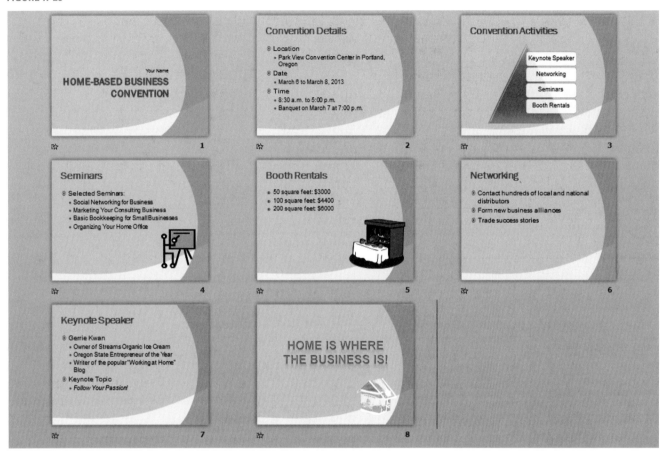

9. Add clip art pictures to some slides. Use the drawing tools to modify at least one of the clip art images after you have ungrouped it. For example, the clip art picture shown on Slide 4 in Figure H-28 was modified by removing a circle shape and then filling the flip chart shape. Use search keywords such as "seminar," "booth," "home," and "business" to find appropriate images. Note that the images you choose do not need to be the same as the images shown in Figure H-28. You can also choose to modify more than one clip art image.

10. Add a new slide at the end of the presentation, apply the Blank layout, then insert a WordArt object with the text **Home Is Where the Business Is!** using the style and settings of your choice.

11. Add an appropriate photograph of a house (use your own photograph or search the clip art task pane for a suitable photograph), then use the tools in the Adjust group on the Picture Tools Format tab to modify the photograph in a variety of ways. For example, you can remove the background, apply an artistic effect, and modify the color effects.

12. Add a transition effect to all slides and a custom animation scheme to the SmartArt graphic on Slide 3, then preview the presentation in Slide Show view.

13. Save the presentation, submit a copy to your instructor, then close the presentation.

Visual Workshop

As part of a presentation on Preserving the Rainforest that you are giving at a meeting of a local environmental group in Queensland, Australia, you need to create the two slides shown in Figures H-29 and H-30. Enter the title and subtitle text on Slide 1, use the Perspective presentation theme, the Austin color scheme, and Background Style 6 for the slide background, then work in Slide Master view to increase the Title Style text size to 54 pt on the Master title style slide (master slide 2 in the task pane) and apply bold. For Slide 2 of the presentation, change the layout to Blank, then create the Hexagon Cluster Picture SmartArt graphic shown in Figure H-30, using the data files PR H-2.jpg, PR H-3.jpg and PR-4.jpg. Select the Cartoon SmartArt style and the color scheme of your choice. Save the presentation as **PR H-Preserving the Rainforest** to the location where you save the files for this book, submit the file to your instructor, and then close the presentation.

FIGURE H-29

FIGURE H-30

Integration Projects III

Files You Will Need:

PR I-1.docx
PR I-2.accdb
PR I-3.pptx
PR I-4.docx
PR I-5.jpg
PR I-6.jpg
PR I-7.accdb

You can integrate Office applications to present information in a variety of ways. For example, you can compile source materials in Access and Excel, and then create a report in Word or a presentation in PowerPoint that includes objects from the source materials. You can create an outline in Word, and then export it to PowerPoint to create a presentation. Conversely, you can create a presentation in PowerPoint, and then export it to Word to create a report. You can also create links between objects from the various applications, and then you can update the links as new data becomes available. In this unit, you will integrate PowerPoint, Access, Excel, and Word to produce a report in Word and two presentations in PowerPoint.

In This Unit You Will Create the Following:

Status Report

Investor Orientation

Class Party Presentation

Status Report for Mount Grant Health Clinic

You've been asked to present a status report on the programs run by the Mount Grant Health Clinic to the clinic's Board of Directors. For this project, you need to **Format the Report in Word**, **Compile Source Materials**, **Add Excel and PowerPoint Objects**, and **Add a Report from Access**. The completed report is shown in Figure I-10 on page 205.

Format the Report in Word

You need to open and format a document containing the text for the report and placeholders that indicate the location of objects you plan to import from Excel, Access, and PowerPoint in later lessons.

Steps:

1. Start Word, open the file PR I-1.docx from the location where you store your Data Files, save the file as PR I-Mount Grant April Report, then scroll through the report to familiarize yourself with its contents and to view placeholders

2. Press [Ctrl][Home], press [Ctrl][Enter] to insert a page break, press [Ctrl][Home] again, then press [Enter] once

3. Click the Insert tab, click Object in the Text group, scroll the list of object types, click Microsoft PowerPoint Slide as shown in Figure I-1, then click OK

4. Click the title placeholder, type Mount Grant Health Clinic, click the subtitle placeholder, type April Status Report, press [Enter], then type your name

5. Click the Design tab, click the More button ⊡ in the Themes group, click Aspect, click outside the slide, click the Home tab, click the slide, click the Center button ☰ in the Paragraph group, click the Bottom Border list arrow ⊞ ▾, click Borders and Shading, click Box, change the border width to 3 pt, click OK, then click outside the slide
   The slide is centered and enclosed in a border as shown in Figure I-2.

Hint

The remaining document headings are Running Clinics, Lifestyle Seminars, Nutrition Workshops, and Summary.

6. Press [Ctrl][G], type 3, click Go To, click Close, select Introduction, click Heading 1 in the Styles gallery, then apply the Heading 1 style to the remaining document headings
   All the headings are formatted with the Heading 1 style.

7. Click Change Styles in the Styles group, point to Colors, then click Aspect

8. Scroll up to page 2, click below Table of Contents, click the References tab, click Table of Contents in the Table of Contents group, then click Insert Table of Contents

9. Click the Formats list arrow, select Formal as shown in Figure I-3, click OK, then save the document

FIGURE I-1: Selecting a PowerPoint Slide object

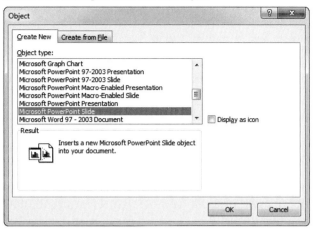

FIGURE I-2: Completed PowerPoint slide for the report title page

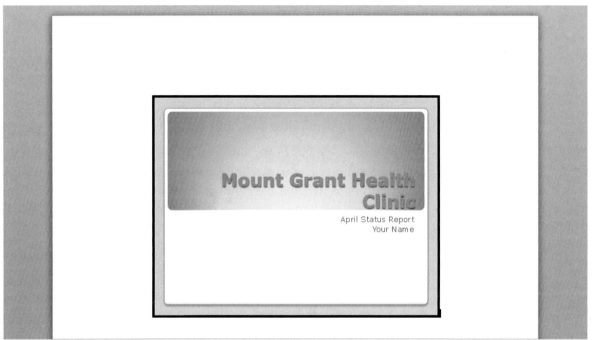

FIGURE I-3: Formal Table of Contents format selected

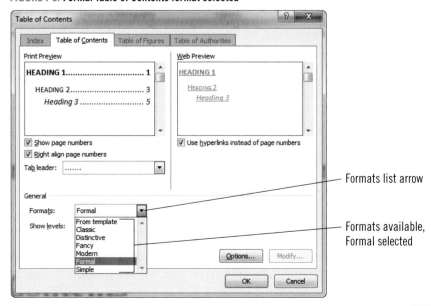

Compile Source Materials

You need to open a database that contains some of the data required for the report, and then you need to modify the format of selected fields. You also need to publish an Access table that you want to include in the Word report. Finally, you create two queries so you can use the results of the queries in the report.

Trouble

To save a database with a new name, click the File tab, click Save Database As, type the new filename, navigate to the location where you save the files for this book, then click Save. Click Enable Editing or Enable Content if prompted.

Hint

The table appears in Word as a document saved in Rich Text Format (.rtf).

Hint

To save time, you enter only the beginning of the criteria followed by the wildcard character to tell Access to list all records in the Program Area field that contain Life as the first four letters.

Steps:

1. **Start Access, open** PR I-2.accdb **from the location where you store your Data Files, save the database as** PR I-Mount Grant Health Clinic.accdb, **double-click** April Running Clinic, **click in the blank** Start Run Time cell **for Record 1, type** 14.55, **then press** [Tab]
    The number you entered is automatically rounded up to 15. You want to show decimals so you need to modify the format of the Number data type.

2. **Click the** View button, **click the** Number data type **next to "Start Run Time", click** Long Integer **next to "Field Size" in the Field Properties area, click the** list arrow, **click** Single, **click** Auto **next to "Decimal Places", click the** list arrow, **click** 2, **then repeat this procedure to change the format of the Number data type for the End Run Time field**

3. **Click the** View button, **click** Yes **to save the table, enter data for the Start Run Time and End Run Time fields as shown in Figure I-4, then close the table, saving it if prompted**

4. **Verify that "April Running Clinic" is selected, click the** External Data tab, **click the** More button **in the Export group, click** Word, **click** Browse, **navigate to the location where you save your files for this book, change the name of the file to** PR I-Mount Grant April Running Clinic, **click** Save, **click the** "Open the destination file after the export operation is complete." check box, **then click** OK

5. **Select the table, press** [Ctrl][C] **to copy it, switch to the report in Word, scroll to and select the placeholder text** [Running Times], **then press** [Ctrl][V] **to paste the table**

6. **Select the table again, click the** Table Tools Design tab, **click the** More button ▾ **in the Table Styles group, select** Light Grid - Accent 4 **(one of the green selections), click the** Header Row check box **to select it, click the** Banded Columns check box **to deselect it, press** [Ctrl][E] **to center the table, double-click any column divider to autofit the table contents, deselect the table, compare it to Figure I-5, then save the document**

7. **Switch to Access, click** Close, **click the** Create tab, **click** Query Wizard **in the Queries group, click** OK, **click** Open **if prompted, click the** Tables/Queries list arrow, **click** Table: Programs, **click the** Select All Fields button ▸▸, **click** Next, **click** Next, **enter** Lifestyle Seminars **as the title, click the** "Modify the query design." option button, **click** Finish, **click the** Program Area Criteria cell, **type** Life*, **click the** Run button **in the Results group, verify that three Lifestyle seminars are listed, then close and save the query**

8. **Click the** Create tab, **click the** Query Wizard button, **click** OK, **select the** Programs table, **select all the fields in the table** except **the ID field, click** Next, **click** Next, **name the query** April Programs, **then click** Finish

9. **Click the** Home tab, **click the** View button, **click the** blank field **to the right of the Fee field, type** Total: [Attendance]*[Fee], **click the** Date Criteria cell, **type** >31/03/2013, **click the** Run button, **compare the query to Figure I-6, then close and save the query**
    The query returns a list of all the programs run in April (that is, on any date following March 31, 2013) along with the total revenue generated from each program.

FIGURE I-4: **Data for the Start Run Time and End Run Time fields**

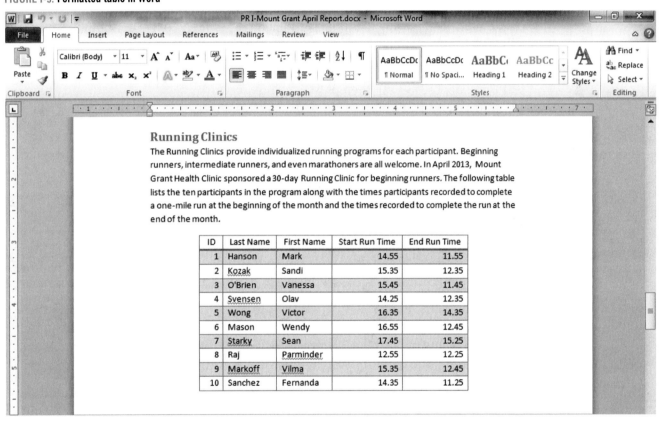

April Running Clinic

ID	Last Name	First Name	Start Run Time	End Run Time	Click to Add
1	Hanson	Mark	14.55	11.55	
2	Kozak	Sandi	15.35	12.35	
3	O'Brien	Vanessa	15.45	11.45	
4	Svensen	Olav	14.25	12.35	
5	Wong	Victor	16.35	14.35	
6	Mason	Wendy	16.55	12.45	
7	Starky	Sean	17.45	15.25	
8	Raj	Parminder	12.55	12.25	
9	Markoff	Vilma	15.35	12.45	
10	Sanchez	Fernanda	14.35	11.25	
*	(New)				

FIGURE I-5: **Formatted table in Word**

PR I-Mount Grant April Report.docx - Microsoft Word

Running Clinics

The Running Clinics provide individualized running programs for each participant. Beginning runners, intermediate runners, and even marathoners are all welcome. In April 2013, Mount Grant Health Clinic sponsored a 30-day Running Clinic for beginning runners. The following table lists the ten participants in the program along with the times participants recorded to complete a one-mile run at the beginning of the month and the times recorded to complete the run at the end of the month.

ID	Last Name	First Name	Start Run Time	End Run Time
1	Hanson	Mark	14.55	11.55
2	Kozak	Sandi	15.35	12.35
3	O'Brien	Vanessa	15.45	11.45
4	Svensen	Olav	14.25	12.35
5	Wong	Victor	16.35	14.35
6	Mason	Wendy	16.55	12.45
7	Starky	Sean	17.45	15.25
8	Raj	Parminder	12.55	12.25
9	Markoff	Vilma	15.35	12.45
10	Sanchez	Fernanda	14.35	11.25

FIGURE I-6: **April Programs query**

April Programs

Date	Program Area	Attendance	Fee	Total
4/1/2013	Running Clinic	12	$50.00	$600.00
4/4/2013	Lifestyle Seminar	20	$70.00	$1,400.00
4/10/2013	Running Clinic	25	$50.00	$1,250.00
4/20/2013	Nutrition Workshop	40	$40.00	$1,600.00
4/25/2013	Nutrition Workshop	38	$40.00	$1,520.00
*				

Add Excel and PowerPoint Objects

You need to analyze the Lifestyle Seminars query in Excel, calculate totals, and then copy selected cells to replace the [Attendance Figures] placeholder in the Word report. You then need to copy two PowerPoint slides from an existing presentation to replace the [PowerPoint Slides] placeholder in the Word report.

Steps:

1. Click Lifestyle Seminars in the list of Access objects, click the External Data tab, click Excel in the Export group, click Browse, then navigate to the location where you save your files for this book

2. Name the file PR I-Mount Grant Lifestyle Seminars, click Save, click OK, click Close, then start Excel and open PR I-Mount Grant Lifestyle Seminars.xlsx

3. Adjust column widths as needed, click cell F1, type Totals, press [Enter], type =D2*E2 in cell F2, press [Enter], copy the formula through cell F4, verify that cells F2:F4 are selected, then click the Accounting Number Format button $ in the Number group

4. Select cells B1:F4, press [Ctrl][C], switch to the report in Word, select the placeholder text [Attendance Figures], then press [Ctrl][V]

5. Select the table, double-click any column divider to autofit the text, click the Table Tools Design tab, apply the Light Grid - Accent 4 table style, press [Ctrl][E], click below the table, compare it to Figure I-7, then verify that the Nutrition Workshops heading and paragraph have moved to the next page

6. Start PowerPoint, open PR I-3.pptx from the location where you store your Data Files, then click the Slide Sorter button on the status bar to switch to Slide Sorter view

7. Verify that the title slide is selected, press [Ctrl][C], switch to the Word report, select [PowerPoint Slides] below the paragraph on Nutrition Workshops, press [Ctrl][V], switch to PowerPoint, click slide 3 (Basic Principles), press [Ctrl][C], switch to the Word report, press [Ctrl][V], then press [Enter]

8. Double-click the Basic Principles slide, select the contents of the Width text box in the Size group (contains 5"), type 2.8, press [Enter], click the Picture Border button in the Picture Styles group, point to Weight, then select 1½ pt

9. Repeat Step 8 to set the width of the first slide at 2.8" and change the weight of the border line to 1½ pt, click to the left of the two slides to select them, click Normal in the Styles Gallery in the Styles group, click below the slides, then save the document

The two slides appear side by side as shown in Figure I-8.

FIGURE I-7: **Excel data copied to Word and formatted**

Lifestyle Seminars

Debbie Jones presented three lifestyle seminars in March and April 2013. Each seminar provided advice to help participants initiate and maintain healthy eating and exercise patterns. Shown below are the attendance figures at the March and April lifestyle seminars.

Date	Program Area	Attendance	Fee	Totals
3/1/2013	Lifestyle Seminar	40	70.00	$ 2,800.00
3/15/2013	Lifestyle Seminar	15	70.00	$ 1,050.00
4/4/2013	Lifestyle Seminar	20	70.00	$ 1,400.00

FIGURE I-8: **Completed PowerPoint slides in Word**

Nutrition Workshops

Jasjit Singh facilitated two workshops on good nutrition to health practitioners in the Seattle area. Shown below are two slides from the presentation that Jasjit delivered at the workshop.

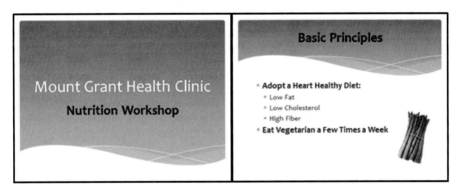

Add a Report from Access

You need to create a report from the April Programs query, then publish the report in Word and format it attractively. Finally, you need to update the table of contents in Word.

Steps:

1. Switch to Access, click April Programs, click the Create tab, click Report in the Reports group, click the Themes button in the Themes group, click Aspect, click the text box in the header that contains the date, press [Delete], click the text box in the header that contains the time, press [Delete], click the box containing $250.00, press [Delete], click the grey line remaining, then press [Delete]

Trouble

If clicking Properties closes the Property Sheet, right-click 6370, then click Properties again.

2. Click $600.00 in the Total column, click the Totals button in the Grouping & Totals group, click Sum, right-click 6370 at the bottom of the Total column, click Properties, click the blank cell next to "Format", click the list arrow, click Currency, close the Property Sheet, drag to increase the height and width of the total box as shown in Figure I-9, close and save the report, then name it Mount Grant April Programs

3. Click Mount Grant April Programs in the list of Access objects, click the External Data tab, click the More button in the Export group, click Word, click the Browse button and navigate to the location where you store the files for this book, change the filename to PR I-Mount Grant April Programs, click Save, click the "Open the destination file after the export operation is complete." check box, click OK, then click Open if prompted

   When the report is published in Word all the formatting applied to the report in Access is removed. You can convert the data into a table so that you can quickly apply formatting.

Trouble

Use the selection pointer 🔏 to click the margin to the left of the last line of text.

4. Scroll to the bottom of the document, click to the left of the last line of text (contains the page number), press [Ctrl][X] to delete a blank table row (the row will be very tall), click [Ctrl][A], click the Insert tab, click the Table button in the Tables group, click Convert Text to Table, then click OK to accept the number of columns entered (6)

   By default, Word enters a number of columns equal to the maximum number of tab characters in any one line of text. The first column in the table is blank.

5. Click to deselect the table, move the pointer over the top of column 1 to show ↓, click once to select all of column 1, press [Ctrl][X], select $6,370.00 at the bottom of the new column 1, press [Ctrl][X], click in the blank cell below $1,520.00, then press [Ctrl][V]

6. Select all the cells in row 1 of the table, click the Table Tools Layout tab, click Merge Cells, then center the heading in the row

7. Select the table, press [Ctrl][C], switch to the report in Word, select the text [Summary Report] at the end of the report, paste the table, select the table, apply the Light Grid - Accent 4 table style, center April Programs, then double-click column dividers as needed until none of the entries wraps to two lines

8. Scroll up to the table of contents, right-click the table of contents, click Update Field, click the Update entire table option button, then click OK

Additional Practice

For additional practice with the skills presented in this project, complete Independent Challenge 1.

9. Click the View tab, click the Zoom button in the Zoom group, click the Many Pages button, drag to select 2 × 2 Pages, click OK, compare the four pages of the report to Figure I-10, save the document, submit a copy of the report to your instructor, then save and close all open files and exit all applications

FIGURE I-9: **Row width and height adjusted**

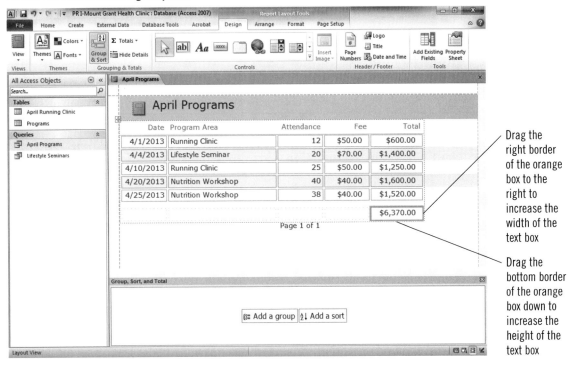

Drag the right border of the orange box to the right to increase the width of the text box

Drag the bottom border of the orange box down to increase the height of the text box

FIGURE I-10: **Completed report in Print Preview**

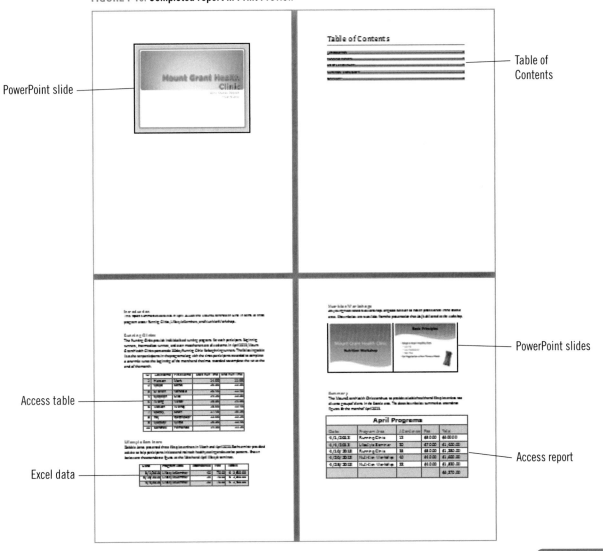

PowerPoint slide

Table of Contents

PowerPoint slides

Access table

Excel data

Access report

Investor Orientation for Otter Bay Estates

You work for the Sales Manager of Otter Bay Estates, a new resort development on one of the islands off the coast of Washington State. You need to prepare a presentation to welcome investors and provide them with important information about the resort. For this project, you need to **Create a Database**, **Create a Chart**, **Create the Presentation**, and **Update the Presentation**. The completed presentation appears in Figure I-21 on page 213.

Create a Database

You need to enter the data in an Access table and then copy the Access table to Excel and paste it as a link.

Steps:

1. **Start Access, then create an Access database called** PR I-Otter Bay Estates **and save it to the location where you save the files for this book**

2. **Switch to Design view, save the table as** Home Designs, **then enter the fields and data types shown in Figure I-11**

3. **Click the** Data Type list arrow **for Style, click** Lookup Wizard, **click** Open **if prompted, click the** "I will type in the values that I want." **option button, click** Next, **press** [Tab], **enter the values shown in Figure I-12, then click** Finish

4. **Create a lookup field for Location containing the values** Lake View, Forest View, **and** Ocean View

5. **Switch to Datasheet view (save the table), enter the records for the table as shown in Figure I-13, then close the table**

6. **Click the** Create tab, **click the** Query Wizard button **in the Queries group, click** OK, **add all the fields from the Home Designs table, name the query** Design Breakdown, **then show the query in Design view**

7. **Sort the** Style **and** Cost **fields in** Ascending **order, click the** Run button **in the Results group, close and save the query, click** Design Breakdown **in the list of Access objects, then click the** Copy button ▣ **in the Clipboard group**

8. **Start Excel, click the** Paste list arrow **in the Clipboard group, then click the** Paste Link button ▣

   The Currency format applied to the values in the Cost column is removed when you copy a table from Access and paste it into Excel as a link.

9. **Adjust the column widths, then save the workbook as** PR I-Otter Bay Estates Data **to the location where you save the files for this book**

FIGURE I-11: Fields for the Home Designs table

Home Designs	
Field Name	**Data Type**
Design ID (key)	AutoNumber
Style	Text
Bedrooms	Number
Location	Text
Cost	Currency
Quantity	Number
Sales	Number

FIGURE I-12: Values for the lookup field

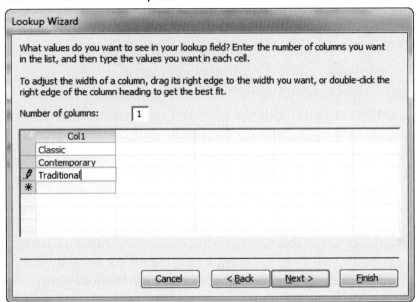

FIGURE I-13: Data for the Home Designs table

Design ID	Style	Bedrooms	Location	Cost	Quantity	Sales	Click to Add
1	Contemporary	3	Lake View	$400,000.00	8	5	
2	Traditional	4	Ocean View	$600,000.00	7	3	
3	Traditional	3	Lake View	$400,000.00	5	2	
4	Classic	4	Forest View	$350,000.00	8	3	
5	Contemporary	4	Forest View	$350,000.00	7	4	
6	Classic	3	Ocean View	$600,000.00	6	1	
7	Traditional	4	Lake View	$450,000.00	7	3	
8	Contemporary	3	Ocean View	$600,000.00	9	2	
9	Contemporary	4	Forest View	$350,000.00	4	1	
10	Classic	4	Forest View	$350,000.00	8	4	
*	(New)						

Create a Chart

You need to create a column chart to display information about the resort development. In a later lesson, you will copy the column chart and paste it as a link on a slide in the PowerPoint presentation.

Steps:

1. In Excel, click cell H1, type Total Worth, press [Enter], type =E2*F2, press [Enter], then copy the formula in cell H2 through cell H11

2. Click cell I1, type Total Sales, press [Enter], type =E2*G2, press [Enter], then copy the formula in cell I2 through cell I11

3. Click cell F12, click the Sum button **Σ** in the Editing group two times, then copy the formula through cell I12

4. Format cells E2:E11 and cells H2:I12 with the Accounting Number Format style

5. Click cell B14, then enter the labels and calculations shown in Figure I-14

    When you copy data from an Access database and paste it as a link into an Excel workbook, you cannot use tools such as the Subtotals function to calculate totals.

6. Select cells B14:D15, click the Insert tab, click Column in the Charts group, then click Clustered Column (the upper-left column style)

7. Move the chart below the data, click the Chart Tools Layout tab, click the Axes button in the Axes group, point to Primary Vertical Axis, click None, click the Legend button in the Labels group, click None, click the Data Labels button in the Labels group, then click Outside End

8. Right-click one of the data labels, click Format Data Labels, click Number in the left pane, click Number in the Category list, reduce the decimal places to 0, click Close, click the Home tab, then click the Bold button **B** in the Font group

9. Click below the chart, compare the completed chart to Figure I-15, then save the workbook

FIGURE I-14: Calculations of total worth

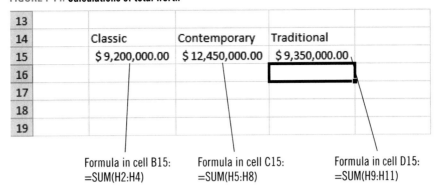

13			
14	Classic	Contemporary	Traditional
15	$9,200,000.00	$12,450,000.00	$9,350,000.00
16			
17			
18			
19			

Formula in cell B15:
=SUM(H2:H4)

Formula in cell C15:
=SUM(H5:H8)

Formula in cell D15:
=SUM(H9:H11)

FIGURE I-15: Completed column chart

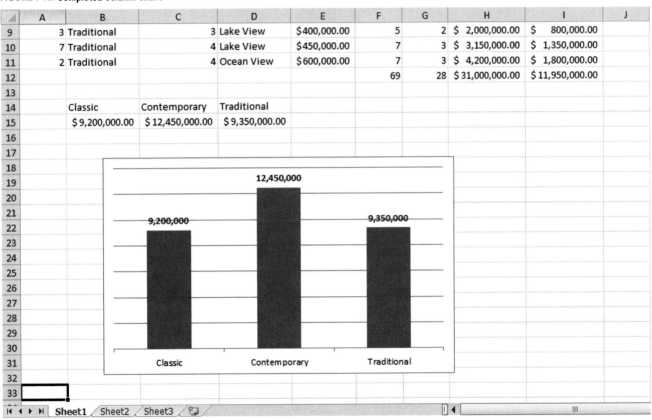

Create the Presentation

The text for the PowerPoint presentation is already stored in a Word document. You need to import the Word text into a new presentation and then modify the presentation design so that a picture appears on every slide in the presentation except the title slide.

Steps:

1. Start a blank presentation in PowerPoint, click the New Slide list arrow in the Slides group, click Slides from Outline, navigate to the location where you store your Data Files, select PR I-4.docx, click Insert, then save the presentation as PR I-Otter Bay Estates Investor Orientation to the location where you save the files for this book

2. Click Slide 1, press [Delete], click Layout in the Slides group, click Title Slide, click to the right of Investor Orientation on the slide, press [Enter], then type your name

3. Click the Design tab, apply the Slipstream presentation theme, switch to Slide Sorter view, click the Home tab, press [Ctrl][A] to select all the slides in the presentation, then click Reset in the Slides group

   When you insert an outline from Word into a PowerPoint presentation and then change the theme of the presentation, you need to reset all of the slides so that they use the formats of the new theme.

Hint

Click the border of the text box you want to move.

4. Click the View tab, click Slide Master in the Master Views group, click the slide next to 1 in the task pane, then as shown in Figure I-16, rearrange the placeholders for the Master title style and the Master text styles

5. Click the Insert tab, click Picture in the Images group, navigate to the location where you store your Data Files, double-click PR I-5.jpg, double-click the image to open the Picture Tools Format tab, select the contents of the Width text box in the Size group, type 2.5, press [Enter], position the picture as shown in Figure I-17, click the Slide Master tab, click the Close Master View button in the Close group, then return to Normal view

6. Move to Slide 4 in the presentation, switch to Excel, click the border of the column chart, press [Ctrl][C], switch to PowerPoint, click the Paste list arrow, then click the Use Destination Theme & Link Data button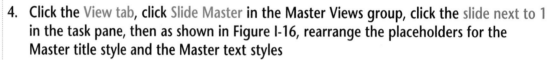

7. Click a blank area of the slide, click the Design tab, click the Hide Background Graphics check box in the Background group to select it, click Background Styles, then click Style 10

   The picture is removed only from Slide 4 and the background style is changed for all the slides in the presentation.

8. Click the chart to select it, click the gray border of the chart, click the Home tab, click the Increase Font Size button A˙ in the Font group until the font size is increased to 14 point, then apply bold

9. Right-click any column, click Format Data Series, click Fill in the left pane, click the Solid fill option button, click the Color list arrow, click Green, Accent 3, Darker 25%, click Close, size and position the chart on the slide as shown in Figure I-18, then save the presentation

FIGURE I-16: Rearranging the placeholders in the slide master

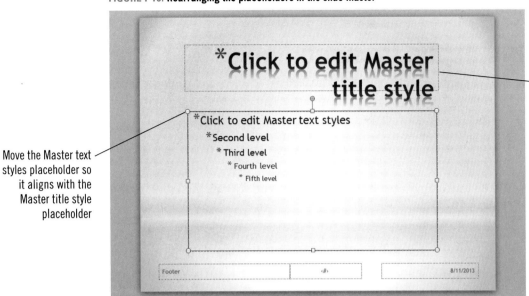

Move the Master title style placeholder toward the top of the slide

Move the Master text styles placeholder so it aligns with the Master title style placeholder

FIGURE I-17: Positioning the picture in the slide master

FIGURE I-18: Column chart sized and positioned

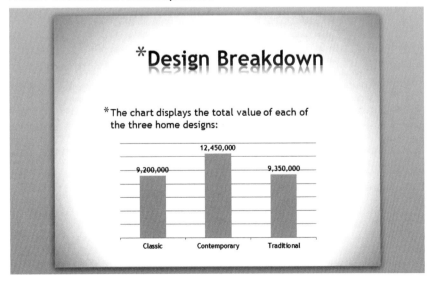

Investor Orientation (continued)

Update the Presentation

You need to summarize data in the Excel worksheet, copy it, and paste it as a link on Slide 5. Then, you need to change data in the Access database and update the links in Excel and PowerPoint. Finally, you break all the links so that you can easily move the files to different locations.

Steps:

Trouble

Make sure you enter formulas where indicated, *not* values, and that you apply the All Borders setting to cells I14:J17

1. Switch to Excel, click cell I14, then enter and format the labels and formulas as shown in Figure I-19

2. Select cells I14:J17, press [Ctrl][C], switch to PowerPoint, go to Slide 5, click the Paste list arrow in the Clipboard group, click Paste Special, click the Paste link option button, then click OK

Trouble

If the columns are not wide enough to fit the content, return to Excel, widen columns to fit the content, then return to PowerPoint and notice that the column widths are updated.

3. Apply the Title Only slide layout, size and position the object as shown in Figure I-20, then adjust the width of the Slides pane so that all five slides are visible in the Slides pane

4. Switch to a new document in Word, click the Insert tab, click Screenshot, click the window containing the PowerPoint presentation, type your name under the screenshot after it is inserted, then save the document as PR I-Otter Bay Estates Low Sale Prices to the location where you save the files for this book

5. Switch to Access, open the Home Designs table, increase the price of the homes in records 2 and 8 to $700,000, then close the table

Trouble

If the values in the Excel and/or PowerPoint files are not updated within a few seconds, click the File tab, click Edit Links to Files in the lower-right corner of Backstage view, click Update Values (Excel) or Update Now (PowerPoint), click Close, then click the Home tab

6. Switch to Excel, verify that the total in cells I12 and J17 is $12,450,000, switch to PowerPoint, then verify that the value for Total Sales has been updated to $12,450,000

7. Click the Slide Sorter button ⊞ on the status bar, then compare the completed presentation to Figure I-21

8. Click the File tab, click Edit Links to Files (lower-right corner in Backstage view), click the top link, click Break Link, click the new top link, click Break Link, then click Close

Additional Practice

For additional practice with the skills presented in this project, complete Independent Challenge 2.

9. Switch to Excel, click the File tab, click Edit Links to Files, click Break Link, click Break Links, click Close, save the workbook and submit a copy to your instructor, then save and close all open files

FIGURE I-19: **Total Quantity and Sales values**

Enclose all cells with a border line

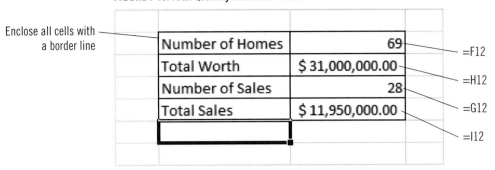

Number of Homes	69	=F12
Total Worth	$ 31,000,000.00	=H12
Number of Sales	28	=G12
Total Sales	$ 11,950,000.00	=I12

FIGURE I-20: **Excel object sized and positioned**

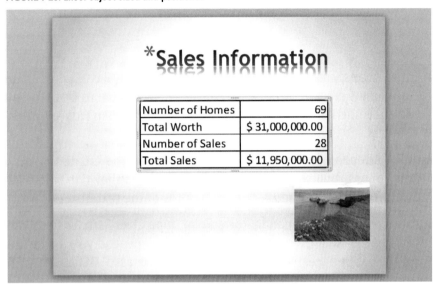

FIGURE I-21: **Completed presentation in Slide Sorter view**

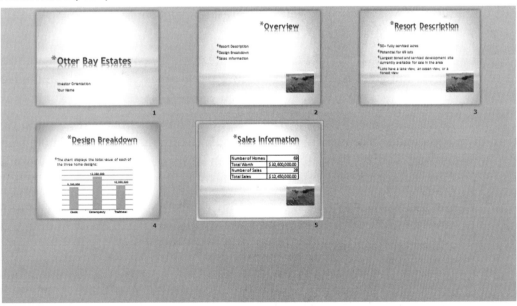

Maintaining links

If you choose to maintain the links between files, you need to keep the files all together in the same location to avoid receiving error messages when you open the files and re-establish the links. To re-establish links, you should start with the program that does not contain links and then open the remaining files in the order in which they are linked. For this presentation, you would open the Access database first, followed by the Excel workbook, and finally the PowerPoint presentation if you had maintained the links in each of the files.

Class Party Presentation

You are organizing a class party to celebrate graduation from the business diploma program at Markham Community College outside Denver. You need to create a presentation to inform classmates about the party and a database to keep track of the students who plan to attend. For this project, you need to **Create a Form** and **Create the Presentation**. The completed presentation appears in Figure I-28 on page 217.

Create a Form

You need to create a table in Access, and then create a form to enter information about students who plan to attend the party. The form includes the title slide from the presentation.

Steps:

Trouble

Reduce the width of the All Access Objects task pane as needed to view the right border of the text boxes.

1. Start Access, create an Access database called PR I-Class Party Data and save it to the location where you save the files for this book, switch to Design view, save the table as Attendees, enter the fields and data types as shown in Figure I-22, then close and save the table

2. Click Attendees in the list of Access objects, click the Create tab, click the Form button in the Forms group, apply the Verve theme, then as shown in Figure I-23, increase the widths of the labels and reduce the widths of the text boxes

3. Start a new presentation in PowerPoint, type Class Party as the slide title, enter Business Diploma Program, Markham Community College, and your name on three separate lines in the Subtitle area, then save the presentation as PR I-Class Party Presentation to the location where you save the files for this book

4. Click the Insert tab, click the Picture button in the Images group, navigate to the location where you store your Data Files, then double-click PR I-6.jpg

5. Click the Color button in the Adjust group, click the Washout option in the top row of the Recolor section, right-click the picture, click Save as Picture, navigate to the location where you save the files for this book, type PR I-Class Party Picture as the filename, then click Save

6. Delete the picture, click the Design tab, click the Background Styles button in the Background group, click Format Background, click the Picture or texture fill option button, click File, navigate to the location where you store your files, click PR I-Class Party Picture.jpg, click Insert, click Apply to All, then click Close

Trouble

The picture is inserted on top of the left side of the form. You will size and position the form in the next step.

7. Switch to Slide Sorter view, press [Ctrl][C], switch to Access, click the View list arrow in the Views group, click Design View, click the blank area to the right of the text boxes to position the insertion point in the Detail area, then press [Ctrl][V]

8. Right-click the picture, click Properties, find the Size Mode row, click Clip to display a list arrow, click the list arrow, click Stretch, close the Property Sheet, move and resize the picture as shown in Figure I-24, then close and save the form with the name Attendees
   You change the Size mode of the picture to Stretch so that the picture retains all its content when you resize it. When Clip is selected, the picture is cropped if you resize it.

9. Double-click Attendees to open the form in Form view, use the form to enter data for the five attendees listed in Figure I-25, then close the form

FIGURE I-22: Fields for the Attendees table

Field Name	Data Type
ID	AutoNumber
First Name	Text
Last Name	Text
Contact Date	Date/Time
Attending	Yes/No
Contribution	Text

FIGURE I-23: Resizing form components

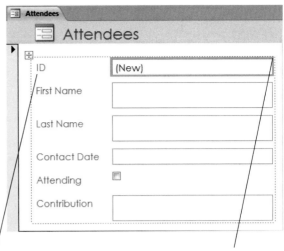

Click ID to display an orange box, then drag the right border of the orange box to the right to increase the width of all labels

Drag the right border of the orange box to the left to reduce the width of all the text boxes

FIGURE I-24: Completed form in Design view

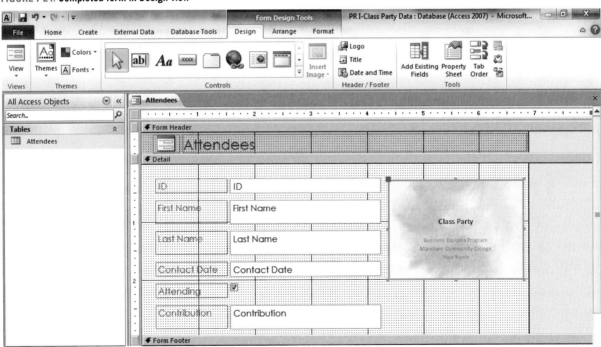

FIGURE I-25: List of attendees

ID	First Name	Last Name	Contact D	Attending	Contribution
1	Marta	Dhont	6/10/2013	☑	Appetizers
2	Maria	Fernandez	6/12/2013	☑	Fruit Plate
3	Jolene	Marches	6/12/2013	☐	
4	Olivia	Martelli	6/13/2013	☑	Chips and Salsa
5	Adam	Simpson	6/14/2013	☑	Vegetable Platter
*	(New)			☐	

Integration Projects III

Class Party Presentation (continued)

Create the Presentation

You need to complete the presentation, enter some of the data in Excel and Word, then copy the data to the presentation.

Steps:

1. Switch to PowerPoint, click the Normal button  on the status bar, click the Outline tab on the Navigation pane, click after your name in the Outline tab, press [Enter], press [Shift][Tab] to start a new slide, then enter the outline as shown in Figure I-26

2. Start Excel, enter and format the data shown in Figure I-27 in cells A1 through B5, then save the workbook as PR I-Class Party Expenses to the location where you save the files for this book

   This data will be used in a chart that you create in PowerPoint.

3. Switch to PowerPoint, go to Slide 4, apply the Title Only slide layout, click the Insert tab, click the Chart button in the Illustrations group, click Pie, then click OK

4. Click cell A1 in the Excel worksheet, move the pointer over the Excel program icon ⊠ on the taskbar, click the PR I-Class Party Expenses.xlsx window, select cells A1:B5, press [Ctrl][C], move the pointer over ⊠ on the taskbar, click the Chart in Microsoft PowerPoint window, press [Ctrl][V], widen columns as needed in the Excel worksheet, close the worksheet, then exit Excel, saving the workbook if prompted

   The chart is updated with the data you copied from the Class Party Expenses workbook.

5. Click the chart, click the Chart Tools Design tab, click the More button ⊡ in the Chart Styles group, click Style 26, click the Chart Tools Layout tab, click Legend in the Labels group, click Show Legend at Bottom, click Data Labels, then click Outside End

6. Start Word, type Date:, press [Tab], type June 30, press [Enter], type Time:, press [Tab], type 7 p.m. to ??, press [Enter], type Place:, press [Tab], type Rocky Mountain Hotel, then save the document as PR I-Class Party Details to the location where you save the files for this book

7. Press [Ctrl][A] to select all the text, press [Ctrl][C], switch to PowerPoint, view Slide 3: Party Details, apply the Title Only slide layout, click below the title, press [Ctrl][V], click the border of the copied object, then increase the font size to 40

8. Click the Drawing Tools Format tab, click the More button ⊡ in the Shape Styles group, select Subtle Effect - Red, Accent 2, apply bold to Date:, Time:, and Place:, size and position the object attractively on the slide as shown in the completed presentation in Figure I-28, then save the presentation

9. Go to Slide 5, apply the Blank slide layout, insert a WordArt object using the Fill - Red, Accent 2, Warm Matte Bevel effect and the text Let's Celebrate!, insert the balloon picture shown in Figure I-28 (search for balloons, parties, photographs in the clip art task pane and note that the picture you insert will include a white background and the balloons are yellow, lavender, and blue), click Color in the Adjust group, click Set Transparent Color, click a white area of the picture, then size and position the WordArt object and the picture as shown in Figure I-28

Additional Practice

For additional practice with the skills presented in this project, complete Independent Challenge 3.

10. View the presentation in Slide Sorter view, compare the completed presentation to Figure I-28, save the presentation and submit a copy to your instructor, then save and close all open files

FIGURE I-26: Outline for the Class Party Presentation

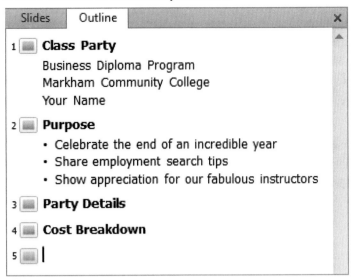

FIGURE I-27: Data for party costs entered in Excel

	A	B	C
1	Item	Cost	
2	Entertainment	$2,000.00	
3	Decorations	$ 400.00	
4	Gifts	$ 300.00	
5	Transportation	$ 200.00	
6			
7			

FIGURE I-28: Completed presentation in Slide Sorter view

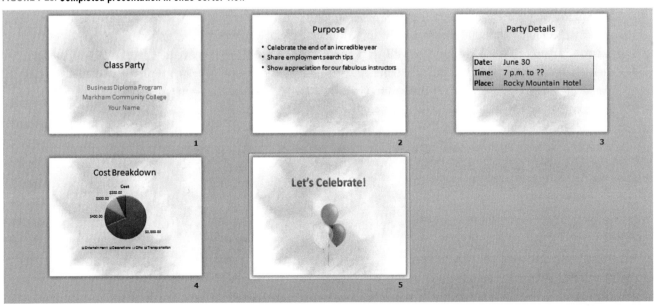

Independent Challenge 1

Create a multiple-page report in Word that includes objects from Excel, PowerPoint, and Access. Base the report on a business-oriented subject. For example, you could write a status report that describes activities over the past six months related to a company or organization of your choice, or you could write a report that proposes a change to a specific policy, such as the employee dress code or the establishment of an employee recognition program. Follow the steps provided to create the report in Word and then to include objects from the other applications.

1. Determine the name of your company or organization and the type of activities it has engaged in over the past six months. For example, you could call your organization Cypress Film Society and describe activities such as screenings, lectures, and film exchanges. Write the name and a brief description of the activities in the box below:

   Company Name: _____

   Description of Activities: _____

2. Start Word, then type text for the report. Include placeholders for objects that you will insert from other applications. Your report should include space for a worksheet or chart from Excel, a slide or two from PowerPoint, and a report from Access. You also need to include a table of contents.

3. Include your name and the page number in a footer.

4. Format headings with heading styles and generate a table of contents above the first page of the report text. Apply a new color scheme.

5. Save the report as **PR I-My Integrated Report.docx** to the location where you save the files for this book, switch to Excel, then create a worksheet containing data appropriate to a section of your report. Use data that you can also include in a chart.

6. Save the Excel workbook as **PR I-My Integrated Report Data.xlsx** to the location where you save the files for this book.

7. Copy the Excel worksheet and/or chart to the appropriate location(s) in your Word report. Format the worksheet with the table design of your choice and/or the chart with the style and formatting of your choice. Use the paste option that will apply the formatting of the destination file to the copied object.

8. Create a PowerPoint slide as an embedded object somewhere in the report. You can choose to include the slide as your title page or insert it in another location. Enter appropriate text and apply the presentation theme that corresponds to the color scheme you selected for the Word report. Apply a border to the slide object.

9. Start Access, create a database called **PR I-My Integrated Report Database.accdb** and save it to the location where you save the files for this book, create a table called **My Report Data** that contains data relevant to your report, then create a query called **My Report Data Query** and a report called **My Report** that highlights some aspect of the data. Refer to the database you created in Unit I Project 1 for ideas.

10. Adjust the column widths in the report, then apply the same theme you used in the Word report.

11. Export the report to Word in a file called **PR I-My Integrated Report.rtf**, remove the report title, the date and the time at the top of the page, and the page number at the bottom of the page, convert the text to a table, remove any blank columns and rows and adjust the location of the data where needed, then copy the table to an appropriate location in the report.

12. Format the table with a table style.

13. Update the table of contents, save the report, submit a copy to your instructor, then save and close all open documents and applications.

Independent Challenge 2

Create an on-screen presentation of six to eight slides that highlights sales information and recommends marketing strategies for a company or organization of your choice. For example, you could create a presentation for an online grocer that presents the revenues from the 10 best-selling products and recommends a marketing plan for the products that generated the most revenue. For ideas, check the business section of your local newspaper and browse the Web. Follow the steps provided to create a table in Access, charts in Excel, an outline for the presentation in Word, and the presentation in PowerPoint. Data in the Access table should be linked to the Excel worksheet and to the Excel objects copied into PowerPoint.

1. Determine the name of your company or organization and the type of products or services that it sells. For example, you could call your company Online Feast and describe it as an online grocer that delivers organic fruits and vegetables and health food products to households in the Boston area. Write the name and a brief description of your company in the box below:

   Company Name: _____

   Description: _____

2. Start Access, create a database called **PR I-My Sales Presentation Database.accdb** and save it to the location where you save the files for this book, then create a table consisting of at least four fields and 10 records. Call the table **Sales**. Include fields in the table that you can use in charts. For example, a table for the Online Feast presentation could include the following fields: Product, Category (e.g., Fruit, Vegetable, Dairy), Number of Sales, and Sale Price. Include at least one Lookup field in your table.

3. Create a query called **My Sales Query** that sorts the data by category. Copy the query and paste it as a link into a new workbook in Excel. Calculate total sales for each product category.

4. Create two charts that illustrate sales information about your company. For example, you could create a pie chart that shows the breakdown of product sales by category and a column chart that compares products by total sales. Save the workbook as **PR I-My Sales Presentation Data.xlsx** to the location where you save the files for this book.

5. Switch to Word, create an outline for the presentation, then save the document as **PR I-My Sales Presentation Outline.docx** to the location where you save the files for this book. Following are some ideas to help you get started:

Slide #	Slide Title	Text
1	Company Name	Sales Presentation
		Your Name
2	Goal	Describe your company's goals
3	Product Categories	Describe a chart that illustrates the breakdown of sales by category
4	Product Sales or Location	Describe a chart that shows the breakdown of sales by location or overall sales, depending on the type of chart you have created
5	Marketing Plan	Include two or three points to describe your marketing plan
6	[Motivational Slogan]	Create an interesting motivational slide to conclude your presentation

6. Add additional topics to your outline, if you wish. Remember to format all the headings with the Heading 1 style and all the bulleted items with the Heading 2 style. If you work in Outline view, the text is automatically formatted with the appropriate headings.

7. Save the outline in Word, then close Word.

8. Create a new presentation in PowerPoint, then create slides from the Word outline. Save the presentation in PowerPoint as **PR I-My Sales Presentation.pptx** to the location where you save the files for this book.

9. Remove the blank slide, apply the presentation design of your choice, and change the color scheme and background style. Apply the Title Slide layout to the title slide, then in Slide Sorter view, select all the slides and reset the layout.

Independent Challenge 2 (continued)

10. Switch to Slide Master view, then modify the slide master applied to the title slide and the slide master applied to all the remaining slides in the presentation in some way (for example, rearrange the placeholders or remove a portion of one of the graphics).

11. Add a clip art image to the slide master so the image appears on every slide in the presentation except the title slide.

12. In Normal view, paste the charts from Excel as links using the Use Destination Theme & Link Data paste option to the appropriate slides. Modify the charts as needed so that they are easy to read.

13. Start a new document in Word, then take a screen shot of each of the two slides containing charts copied from Excel. Adjust the sizes of the two screen shots so they fit on one page, then save the Word document as **PR I-My Sales Presentation Original Data** to the location where you save the files for this book.

14. Change some of the values in the Access table, then update the charts and/or other data in PowerPoint. (*Note*: If the data is not updated immediately in either or both applications, click the File tab, click Edit Links to Files, select each link in turn, then click Update Now or Update Values, depending on the application.)

15. Break the links between the Excel workbook and the Access database, then break the links between the PowerPoint presentation and the Excel workbook.

16. Save the presentation and submit a copy to your instructor, then save and close all open files.

Independent Challenge 3

Create a presentation that proposes a special event, entertainment, or party to a group of your choice. For example, you can create your own class party presentation similar to the presentation you created for Unit I Project 3. Alternatively, you can create a presentation that proposes a class reunion, a company picnic, or a weekend seminar.

1. Create an outline in PowerPoint that includes slide titles with the following information:
   a. Type of party or event
   b. Purpose of the party or event
   c. Location, time, and cost
   d. Chart showing the cost breakdown
   e. Motivational closing slide

2. Use as many slides as you wish. For ideas, refer to the presentation you created for Unit I Project 3. Save the presentation as **PR I-My Party Presentation.pptx** to the location where you save the files for this book.

3. Format the presentation attractively. Insert a picture and adjust the coloring so text will appear clearly when the picture appears as a background, then save the picture as a .jpg file called **PR I-My Party Presentation Picture** to the location where you save the files for this book.

4. Modify the background of the presentation so that the picture will appear as the background on every slide in the presentation.

5. In Access, create a database called **PR I-My Party Database.accdb** and save it to the location where you save the files for this book. Create a table to keep track of attendees (include at leave five appropriate fields), then create an attractive form for entering the data. In the form, modify the column widths and include a copy of the title slide of the presentation. Remember that you need to paste the title slide into Form Design view and then modify the properties.

6. Use the form to enter data for five attendees.

7. Enter the event details in Word, save the document as **PR I-My Party Details.docx** to the location where you save the files for this book, copy and paste the text into PowerPoint, then format the text to make it clear and easy to read. For example, you will need to increase the font size, and then you may want to format the text box with one of the preset shape styles.

8. Create a worksheet in Excel that shows the cost breakdown for the party, create a pie chart in PowerPoint, then copy the data from Excel and paste it into the worksheet for the chart. Format the chart attractively. Save the worksheet as **PR I-My Party Costs.xlsx** to the location where you save the files for this book.

9. Include a graphic and WordArt object on the final slide in the presentation.

10. Save the presentation and submit a copy to your instructor, then save and close all open files.

Independent Challenge 4

You need to create a presentation to welcome volunteers to Alder Cove Community Center and provide them with information about the center. Follow the instructions provided to create and then modify the presentation.

1. Start a new document in Word, save it as **PR I-Alder Cove Presentation Outline** to the location where you save the files for this book, switch to Outline view, then create the outline shown in Figure I-29.

FIGURE I-29

- **Alder Cove Community Center**
  - Volunteer Orientation
  - Your Name
- **Overview**
  - Center Growth
  - Current Programs
  - Volunteer Programs
- **Center Growth**
  - Established in 1985 by the Alder Cove Town Council
- **Volunteer Positions**
  - Assisting Instructors
  - Assisting Front Desk Staff
  - Assisting Facility Maintenance Staff
- **Volunteer Needs for Programs**
  - Volunteers Needed in Five Program Categories
- **Volunteer Expectations**
  - Arrive on time
  - Be courteous and helpful to facility visitors and staff
  - Verify instructions with your supervisor
  - Provide sufficient notice of absences

2. Save and close the document, create a new presentation in PowerPoint, then save it as **PR I-Alder Cove Volunteer Orientation.pptx** to the location where you save the files for this book.
3. Insert slides from the Word outline, delete the blank slide, apply the Title Slide layout to slide 1, apply the Grid presentation design, then in Slide Sorter view, select all the slides and reset the formatting.
4. Select the Perspective color scheme, switch to Slide Master view, click the top slide in the task pane, then fill the orange rectangle with Orange, Background 2, Lighter 80%.
5. Open the Insert Clip Art task pane, search for **community**, insert the picture shown in the completed presentation in Figure I-31 (or a similar picture), then size and position the picture in the lower-right corner of the slide master. Refer to Figure I-31 as you work.
6. Close Slide Master view, open a blank worksheet in Excel, save it as **PR I-Alder Cove Growth Data.xlsx** to the location where you save the files for this book, then enter the data shown below:

1985	1990	1995	2000	2005	2010	2015
5	15	35	75	100	150	180

7. Select the cells containing the data, then create a column chart.
8. Click the Select Data button in the Data group, click Edit under Horizontal (Category) Axis Labels, select cells A1:G1, click OK, click Series 1 under Legend Entries (Series), click Remove, then click OK.

Independent Challenge 4 (continued)

9. Click the Chart Tools Layout tab, click Axis Titles, click Primary Vertical Axis Title, click Rotated Title, change the name to **Number of Volunteers**, then delete the legend on the right side of the chart.

10. Copy the chart, go to Slide 3 in PowerPoint, paste the chart using the Use Destination Theme & Embed Workbook option, click one of the dates (e.g., 2000), increase the font size to 18 pt, increase the font size of the y-axis labels to 18 pt, then increase the font size of the y-axis title to 18 pt.

11. Refer to Figure I-31: Size and position the chart, click the Insert tab, click Shapes, select the Oval Callout shape, enter the text **Projected Growth**, and size and position the callout, then apply the shape style Subtle Effect - Indigo, Accent 5.

12. Start Access, open PR I-7.accdb from the location where you store your Data Files, then save the database as **PR I-Alder Cove Programs.accdb** to the location where you save the files for this book.

13. Click the Programs table, click the Create tab, click Report, click the Group & Sort button in the Grouping & Totals group if it is not active, click Add a group, then click Program Category.

14. Click the ID label and press [Delete], click any of the ID records and press [Delete], click any number in the Volunteers list, click Totals in the Grouping & Totals group, click Sum, click Hide Details, then click the Group & Sort button to deselect it.

15. Refer to Figure I-30: Delete the text boxes containing the date and time, delete the total number of courses (25), delete the Course label, adjust the width of the Volunteers column so it appears closer to the Program Category column, and increase the height of the boxes containing values.

FIGURE I-30

Programs	
Program Category	Volunteers
Aquatics	
	7
Arts and Crafts	
	8
Fitness	
	5
Seniors	
	4
Sports	
	10
	34

Page 1 of 1

Independent Challenge 4 (continued)

16. Switch to PowerPoint, go to Slide 5, click the Insert tab, click Screenshot, click Screen Clipping, drag to select only the portion of the report shown in Figure I-31, then size and position it as shown.

17. View the presentation in Slide Sorter view, then compare it to the completed presentation shown in Figure I-31.

18. Save the presentation, submit a copy to your instructor, close it, then save and close all open files.

FIGURE I-31

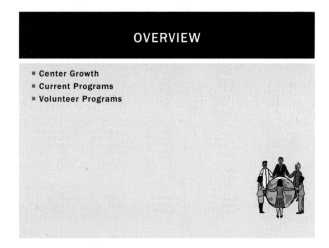

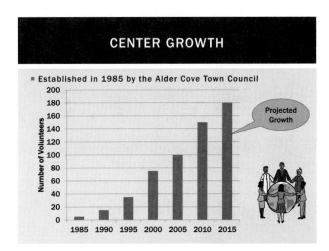

Integration Projects III

Integration 223

Integration 2010

Visual Workshop

You've been asked to create a presentation on cultural tours of Europe. Create the Tours table, as shown in Figure I-32, in an Access database called **PR I-Cultural Tours.accdb** and saved to the location where you save the files for this book. Create a query called **Tours Query** that sorts the records in ascending order by Theme. Copy the query table and paste it as a link into a new Excel workbook. Find the total revenue for each tour (Participants*Price), format the currency amounts with the Euro format, then create a pie chart that shows the percent of total revenue generated by each tour theme. (*Note*: At this point, your values will differ from Figure I-33.) Copy the pie chart and paste it as a link using the Use Destination Theme and Link Data paste option in a new PowerPoint slide. Add a title to the slide, apply the Module theme, and format the slide and pie chart as shown in Figure I-33. Create a document in Word, take a screen clipping that includes only the slide, apply a border to the screen clipping in Word, then save the Word document as **PR I-Cultural Tours Original Tour Totals.docx**. Switch to Access, then change the number of participants in the Taste of Italy tour to **75** and close the table. Verify that the pie chart is updated in Excel, save the Excel workbook as **PR I-Cultural Tours Data.xlsx**, verify that the slide is updated in PowerPoint, then save the PowerPoint presentation as **PR I-Cultural Tours Presentation.pptx**. Break the links to all the files, add your name to the presentation footer, save the presentation and submit the file to your instructor, then save all open files and exit all applications.

FIGURE I-32

Tour ID ▾	Tour ▾	Theme ▾	Country ▾	Participants ▾	Price ▾	Click to Add ▾
1	Ancient Greece	History	Greece	40	€3,200.00	
2	Magical Granada	Culinary	Spain	30	€3,500.00	
3	A Taste of Italy	Culinary	Italy	35	€4,200.00	
4	Medieval Tuscany	History	Italy	70	€3,800.00	
5	Cezanne's World	Art	France	25	€3,500.00	
6	Mozart Madness	Music	Austria	35	€4,000.00	
7	Renaissance Florence	Art	Italy	20	€3,300.00	
8	Dutch Masters	Art	Netherlands	15	€3,700.00	
9	In the Steps of the Oracle	History	Greece	20	€3,300.00	
10	Basque Country	History	Spain	35	€2,900.00	
*	(New)					

FIGURE I-33

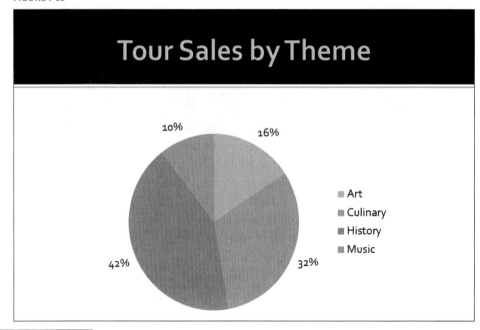

Index